The Animal Rights Debate

Critical Perspectives on Animals

THEORY, CULTURE, SCIENCE, AND LAW

Critical Perspectives on Animals
Series Editors: Gary L. Francione and Gary Steiner

The emerging interdisciplinary field of animal studies seeks to shed light on the nature of animal experience and the moral status of animals in ways that overcome the limitations of traditional approaches to animals. Recent work on animals has been characterized by an increasing recognition of the importance of crossing disciplinary boundaries and exploring the affinities as well as the differences among the approaches of fields such as philosophy, law, sociology, political theory, ethology, and literary studies to questions pertaining to animals. This recognition has brought with it an openness to a rethinking of the very terms of critical inquiry and of traditional assumptions about human being and its relationship to the animal world. The books published in this series seek to contribute to contemporary reflections on the basic terms and methods of critical inquiry, to do so by focusing on fundamental questions arising out of the relationships and confrontations between humans and nonhuman animals, and ultimately to enrich our appreciation of the nature and ethical significance of nonhuman animals by providing a forum for the interdisciplinary exploration of questions and problems that have traditionally been confined within narrowly circumscribed disciplinary boundaries.

The Animal Rights Debate

Abolition or Regulation?

Gary L. Francione
and Robert Garner

Columbia
University
Press
New York

Columbia University Press

Publishers Since 1893

New York   Chichester, West Sussex

Copyright © 2010 Gary L. Francione and Robert Garner

Library of Congress Cataloging-in-Publication Data

Francione, Gary L. (Gary Lawrence), 1954–

The animal rights debate : abolition of regulation? / Gary L. Francione and
Robert Garner

p. cm.—(Critical perspectives on animals)

Inclues bibliographical references and index.

ISBN 978-0-231-14954-9 (cloth : alk. paper) — ISBN 978-0-231-14955-6 (pbk. : alk.
paper) — ISBN 978-0-231-52669-2 (e-book)

1. Animal rights. 2. Animal welfare. I. Garner, Robert, 1960– II. Title. III. Series.

HV4708.F727   2010

179'.3—dc22   210010202

Columbia University Press books are printed on permanent
and durable acid-free paper.

This book is printed on paper with recycled content.

Printed in the United States of America

c 10 9 8 7 6 5 4 3 2

p 10 9 8 7 6 5 4 3 2

References to Internet Web sites (URLs) were accurate at the time of writing.
Neither the author nor Columbia University Press is responsible for URLs that
may have expired or changed since the manuscript was prepared.

For Anna, in gratitude for her love and inspiration, and
for Simon, a blind dog who was slated to be killed at a local
shelter and whom we adopted. He was a brave boy,
a great privilege to have as a member of our family,
and an absolute joy to love.

To Filza—Thank you for your patience and love.

Contents

Introduction

What This Book Is and Is Not About

This book does not involve a debate about whether humans should regard nonhuman animals as members of the moral community deserving of at least some legal protection or, instead, as mere *things* to which humans do not have *any* direct moral obligations. On this point, there is not much to debate. Most people accept that animals are at least partial members of the moral community and that we may use animals for human purposes; they believe it is morally wrong to inflict "unnecessary" harm on animals or to treat them in ways that are not considered "humane." This position is known as the *animal welfare* view, and it is reflected in anticruelty statutes and other laws that impose a legal obligation to treat animals "humanely." Yes, there are people who still defend the view that animals simply do not matter at all and that nothing we do to them raises a moral issue or should raise a legal issue. But there are people who defend the view that the earth is flat. The moral and legal significance of nonhuman animals is a settled matter.

This is also not a book about whether to defend the status quo with respect to animal use and treatment. Although we claim to take animal interests seriously and to include animals in the moral and legal community to some limited degree, the present state of our treatment of animals amounts in many instances to what would be considered torture if the same treatment were inflicted on humans. For example, the vast majority of animals exploited for food are raised in horrendous circumstances, exposed to considerable pain and suffering during their brief lives, and slaughtered in a way that can be described only as barbaric. We inflict suffering and death on billions more used for sport hunting, other entertainment purposes, clothing, and biomedical research. In sum, we humans suffer from a form of moral schizophrenia; we say one thing, that animals matter and are not just things, and we do another, treating animals as though they were things that did not matter at all. The traditional animal welfare approach has failed.

What the authors do disagree about—and what this book debates—is how to address the problem.

One of us (Francione) argues in favor of the animal rights approach, which, as it is presented here, maintains that we have no moral justification for using nonhumans at all, irrespective of the purpose and however "humanely" we treat them, and that we ought to abolish our use of nonhumans. Moreover, because animals are property—they are economic commodities—laws that require that we treat them "humanely" will, as a general matter, fail to provide any meaningful level of protection for animal interests. Regulation, the animal rights approach argues, may help to increase the production efficiency of animal exploitation but will not result in our recognizing that animals have inherent value, that is, value that goes beyond the economic value of animals as commodities. Further, welfare regulation makes people think that animal exploitation has been made more "humane" and causes them to become more comfortable with animal exploitation, which perpetuates and may even increase the use of animals. The animal rights position that will be defended here focuses on strict vegetarianism (also known as veganism) and on creative, nonviolent education about veganism as the primary practical strategy for the gradual shift away from the property paradigm and as the foundation of a political movement that will support measures consistent with the ultimate goal of abolition.

The other author (Garner) argues in favor of the protectionist approach, which maintains that although the traditional animal welfare approach has failed, this does not mean that it cannot be reformulated theoretically and used more effectively in a practical sense. Animals are different from humans, and other things being equal, the moral value of animal life is less than the moral value of human life, this approach argues. At least some uses of animals may be justifiable, but we should better regulate our treatment of animals consistent with the recognition that although animals may not have a right not to be used by humans, they have a morally significant interest in not being made to suffer incidental to our use of them. The property status of animals is not an inevitable obstacle to better treatment, considering that in some countries, such as Great Britain, animals are property but receive better treatment than they do in the United States and other countries. Further, even if we think that abolition is the desired long-term goal, we should pursue welfare regulation as a means to that end as part of a diverse approach to the problem. In a protectionist approach, there is nothing inconsistent about having an abolitionist ideology but pursuing reform to ensure more "humane" treatment.

In the first part, the animal rights or abolitionist position is presented and defended. The case for animal protectionism follows in the second part. In the third part, we engage in a discussion about our respective positions.

The theoretical debate between the abolitionist approach and protectionist approach—the latter of which Francione calls "new welfarism"—is not merely an academic one. The practical strategy of animal advocates must necessarily be informed by theory, and their political, legal, and social campaigns will be determined by whether they seek ultimately to abolish exploitation or regulate it and whether they believe that regulation will lead to abolition. The debate between abolition and regulation is at the center of modern animal advocacy. This book is our attempt to explore and evaluate these different approaches and to provide what we hope is a clear context for this important debate.

Gary L. Francione
Robert Garner

The Animal Rights Debate

1

The Abolition of Animal Exploitation
Gary L. Francione

Terminology

Throughout this chapter, I refer to the position I defend as both the "animal rights" position and the "abolitionist" position. This alternative usage reflects two concerns. First, it is my view that rights theory, properly understood, requires the *abolition* of animal use, and it is thereby distinguished from the welfarist position, which focuses on the *regulation* of animal exploitation.[1] For the most part, when I refer to animal rights, I am really referring to *one* right: the right not to be treated as the property of humans. The recognition of this one right would require that we (1) stop our institutionalized exploitation of nonhuman animals; (2) cease bringing domesticated nonhumans into existence; and (3) stop killing non-domesticated animals and destroying their habitat. I am not arguing that animals ought to have the same rights as humans, many of which would not even be applicable to nonhumans. My position differs in considerable ways from those of Tom Regan,[2] Bernard Rollin,[3] and others who have attempted to apply a liberal rights approach to nonhumans in ways that do not necessarily or clearly require the abolition of the use of all sentient nonhumans.

Second, misuse of the animal rights label by animal advocates, institutionalized exploiters, and the media to refer to any measure rightly or wrongly thought to benefit animals, including what are clearly and unequivocally welfarist regulations, has caused a great deal of confusion in the social discourse concerning animal ethics. For example, People for the Ethical Treatment of Animals (PETA) claims to be an animal rights organization, but its campaigns focus primarily on making animal use more "humane" through regulatory changes. Randy Strauss, President and CEO of Strauss Veal and Lamb International, Inc., a large American meat processor, is seeking to increase veal consumption by allowing people to "fully enjoy veal with the satisfaction of knowing that veal calves are raised in a humane manner."[4] Strauss states, "Animal rights are important."[5] When meat processors are saying that they recognize and accept animal rights, it is time to sharpen terminology.

Focus

I discuss the variety of contexts in which we exploit nonhuman animals, but I focus primarily on the use of animals for food. The reason for this emphasis is that the use of animals for food is, by far, the most numerically and culturally significant animal use. According to the Food and Agriculture Organization of the United Nations, we kill and eat approximately 56 billion animals every year.[6] That breathtaking number does not include the billions of fish and other aquatic animals we kill and eat. As I discuss here, we cannot morally justify this slaughter. Our use of animals for food is the primary practice that, in effect, legitimizes all other forms of exploitation. As long as we regard it as acceptable to kill and eat animals—however "humanely" we may treat or slaughter them—we will never take animal rights seriously. We will never find our moral compass while their flesh or eggs are on our plates or while their milk is in our glasses.

A Personal Note

Throughout this chapter, I am sharply critical of the welfarist position in all of its forms. I want to make it clear from the outset that I do not in any way question the personal sincerity of those who support the welfarist perspective. Indeed, I know many welfare advocates personally and have affection and respect for many of them as individuals. I do, however, reject the notion that it is somehow divisive or otherwise undesirable to debate the relative moral and strategic merits of the abolitionist and welfarist approaches. On the contrary, given the extent of animal exploitation and what I regard as the manifest failure of the welfarist approach, I maintain that the debate is not only desirable but essential.

I stress that I am not making any moral judgment about welfarists as individuals, just as I hope they are not making a moral judgment about me even though they disagree strongly with the abolitionist approach to animal rights that I have developed and defend.

A Summary of the Discussion

This chapter is divided into three sections. In the first section, I reject the fundamental premise of the animal welfare approach—that animal life has a lesser moral value than human life and that, therefore, it is morally justifiable to use animals for human purposes as long as they are treated "humanely." I argue that, for the purpose of being used as human resources, all sentient nonhumans have the same moral value as humans and that we have a moral obligation to abolish animal use irrespective of how "humane" our treatment of animals may be.

In the second section, I respond to the claim that the regulation of animal use provides significant protection for animal interests. I argue that because animals are chattel property—they are economic commodities—animal welfare regulation provides very

limited protection for animals and does not reduce animal suffering in any significant way. Moreover, there is absolutely no empirical evidence that welfare regulation will, as some claim, lead to
either the reduction or the abolition of animal use. The animal
welfare approach does, however, make the public feel more comfortable about animal exploitation; indeed, that is an explicit goal
of many large animal advocacy organizations. The animal welfare
approach has also resulted in the creation of a disturbing partner-
ship between animal advocates and institutionalized exploiters.

In the third section, I respond to claims made by welfarists that
the animal rights position is unrealistic because it rejects the notion
of incremental change to reduce animal exploitation and does not
provide any practical guidance for what we should do now to help
animals. I argue that the animal rights position does offer a plan
for practical incremental change that has ethical veganism, or the
rejection on moral grounds of the consumption of animals as food
and for other uses, as its foundation. The abolition of animal exploitation necessarily requires a paradigm shift away from the status
of animals as property and to the position that animals are moral
persons. Personhood is inconsistent with the property status of animals and with any animal use, however "humane." Ethical veganism is itself a recognition of the moral personhood of animals.

Animal Rights and Animal Welfare: The Moral
Value of Animal Life

Many animal advocates maintain that any rights/welfare debate
is beside the point because these approaches are not inherently
opposed, and a social movement concerned about animal ethics
can accommodate both, simultaneously promoting both animal
rights and animal welfare. That is, these advocates maintain that
there is nothing confused or inconsistent in arguing that we should

support abolishing or at least significantly reducing animal use but that we should also support reforms that supposedly make animal use more "humane." For example, Professor Robert Garner argues that animal welfare regulation can serve as a means to the end of the abolition of animal use or at least to a significant reduction of animal use and animal suffering.[7] I have previously described Garner's position, which is embraced by many, if not most, of the large animal protection organizations, as the "new welfarist" position because it purports to combine the rights and welfare positions into a theoretically and practically consistent package.[8]

The problem is that the welfarist and rights positions are in fundamental and irreconcilable tension both as a theoretical and a practical matter. The welfarist approach—however it is packaged or presented—regards the lives of animals as having less moral value than the lives of humans. The defining feature of the rights position as I defend it involves a rejection of the notion that animal life has a lesser value than human life. My position maintains that all sentient beings—human or nonhuman—are equal for the purpose of not being treated as resources, just as an intellectually gifted human and a mentally disabled human are equal for the purpose of not being used as a forced organ donor or as a nonconsenting subject in a painful biomedical experiment.

This difference between the welfarist position and the rights/abolitionist position has important practical implications. The welfarist position maintains that it is acceptable for humans to use animals for at least some purposes for which we would never consider it acceptable to use any humans, as long as we treat animals "humanely" and do not impose "unnecessary" suffering on them. This position is implied logically by the view that animal life is of lesser moral value than human life. There are certainly differences between and among welfarists in that some are more progressive than others in what they view as "humane" treatment. But all welfarists share in common the belief that animal use and suffering incidental to our using animals as our resources can be morally justified because animals matter less morally than humans.

In the first part of this section, I discuss the view, present in welfarist theory since its emergence in the nineteenth century, that nonhumans have a lesser moral value than do humans. I then discuss the rejection of this view by rights/abolitionist theory and the defense of the moral equality of human and nonhuman life.

Animal Welfare

Before the nineteenth century, animals were regarded as things.[9] Neither our use nor our treatment of animals mattered morally or legally. There were some who, like French philosopher René Descartes, claimed that animals were literally nothing more than machines created by God. Descartes denied that animals were sentient; that is, he did not believe as a factual matter that animals were perceptually aware and able to have conscious experiences, including the experience of pain. For the most part, however, it was accepted that animals were sentient and had an interest in avoiding pain and suffering but that we could ignore animal interests and treat animals as if they were machines because they were different from humans in that they were supposedly not rational or self-aware, not able to think in terms of abstract concepts or use symbolic communication, incapable of engaging in reciprocal moral relationships with humans, or not in possession of a soul. However, regardless of whether humans regarded nonhumans as machines that were not sentient and had no interests, or as sentient and with interests that could be ignored because of supposed cognitive or spiritual defects, the bottom line remained the same: we could not have moral or legal obligations that we owed directly to animals. We could have obligations that concerned animals, such as an obligation not to damage our neighbor's cow, but that obligation was owed to the neighbor as the owner of the cow, not to the cow. The cow simply did not matter morally or legally.

In the nineteenth century, an ostensible paradigm shift occurred, and the animal welfare theory was born.[10] Two primary architects of this theory were utilitarian philosophers Jeremy Bentham and John Stuart Mill. Utilitarianism is the moral theory that what is right or wrong depends on consequences; the right act or policy is that which will result in the most pleasure or happiness of all affected. In assessing consequences, we must be impartial and give equal consideration to everyone's happiness or pleasure without regard to race, sex, sexual orientation, intellectual or physical abilities, and so on. Utilitarians reject the notion of moral rights because, as we see as this discussion continues, rights protect the right holder even if the balance of consequences does not favor that protection.

Bentham and Mill maintained that the requirement of impartial consideration entailed ignoring the species of a being as a determinant of moral significance just as it required ignoring race. They argued that even if animals were not rational or self-aware or otherwise did not have minds that were similar to those of humans, these cognitive differences were irrelevant to the moral significance of animal suffering. For example, Bentham argued that although a full-grown horse or dog is more rational and more able to communicate than a human infant, "the question is not, Can they *reason*? nor, Can they *talk*? but, Can they *suffer*?"[11] Humans and nonhumans may be different in many respects, but they are relevantly similar in that they are both sentient; they are perceptually aware and able to experience pain and pleasure.

Both Bentham and Mill were opposed to the race-based slavery that existed at the time on the ground that it violated the principle of impartiality or equal consideration by according greater weight to the pleasure or happiness of the white slave owners than to that of the black slaves. They were staunch advocates of the abolition of human slavery. They saw a similarity between slavery and animal exploitation in that both slaves and animals were treated as things; that is, they were excluded completely from the moral community and were "abandoned without redress to the caprice" of their respective tormentors.[12] Just as race did not justify our ignoring the principle of impartiality and according greater weight to the happiness of whites than to that of blacks, species did not justify our ignoring the suffering of animals.

Did this mean that Bentham and Mill advocated the abolition of animal use just as they advocated the abolition of human slavery? No, they did not. The fact that animals were supposedly not rational and otherwise had minds that were dissimilar to those of humans did not give humans a license to do whatever they wanted with animals, but it did mean that it was morally acceptable to use and kill them for human purposes as long as we treated them well. According to Bentham, animals live in the present and are not aware of what they lose when we take their lives. If we kill and eat them, "we are the better for it, and they are never the worse. They have none of those long-protracted anticipations of future misery which we have."[13] Bentham also maintained that we actually do animals a favor by killing them, as long as we do so in a relatively painless manner: "The death they suffer in our hands commonly is, and always may be, a speedier, and by that means a less painful one, than that which would await them in the inevitable course of nature. . . . [W]e should be the worse for their living, and they are never the worse for being dead."[14] If, as Bentham apparently maintained, animals do not as a factual matter have an interest in continuing to live, and death is not a harm for them, then our killing of animals would not per se raise a moral problem as long as we treated and killed animals "humanely."

Moreover, Bentham and Mill opposed human slavery not only because it abrogated the liberty of humans who, unlike animals, had an interest in their lives, but also because the pain and suffering caused to the slaves outweighed any pleasure or happiness that slave owners derived from the practice. The same analysis did not hold for animals. It was, according to the welfarists, possible to minimize animal pain and suffering so that our pleasure would outweigh their pain. Mill argued that in balancing human and animal interests, it was important to keep in mind that humans had supposedly superior mental faculties so that they had a higher quality of pleasure and happiness; human interests had a greater weight in any balancing. For example, he maintained that in calculating pleasure and pain as part of any weighing process, we must take into account that humans "have faculties more elevated than the animal appetites," and he expressed agreement with those ethical views that assign "to the pleasures of the intellect, of the feelings and imagination, and of the moral sentiments, a much higher value as pleasures than to those of mere sensation."[15] According to Mill, "[a] being of higher faculties requires more to make him happy, is capable probably of more acute suffering, and is certainly accessible to it at more points, than one of an inferior type . . . he can never really wish to sink into what he feels to be a lower grade of existence."[16] Animals lack a "sense of dignity, which all human beings possess in one form or other."[17] Moreover, humans have "a more developed intelligence, which gives a wider range to the whole of their sentiments, whether self-regarding or sympathetic."[18] As a result, "[i]t is better to be a human being dissatisfied than a pig satisfied."[19]

So although the early utilitarians responsible for the emergence of the animal welfare approach maintained that the principle of impartiality required that we give serious consideration to animal interests when assessing the consequences of actions, they believed that animals did not have an interest in continuing to live and that their interests in not suffering had lesser value than competing human interests. Because animals did not have an interest in continuing to exist, and because they supposedly had inferior sentient experiences, it was acceptable for humans to treat animals as property and to use and kill them for human purposes as long as humans treated animals "humanely" and did not impose "unnecessary" suffering on them.[20] Bentham and Mill favored legislation aimed at preventing the "cruel" treatment of animals, and the anticruelty laws and other animal welfare laws that presently exist in Britain, the United States, and most other Western countries can be traced directly to the utilitarian philosophers of nineteenth-century Britain. But it is clear that the historical basis of the animal welfare approach is that animals have a lesser moral value than humans.

This notion about the supposed moral inferiority of nonhumans is also represented in contemporary animal welfare theory, the leading figure of which is Peter Singer.[21] Singer is also a utilitarian and maintains that the morally correct action is that which will maximize the satisfaction of preferences (as distinguished from happiness or pleasure) of those affected, including nonhuman animals. But like Bentham and Mill, Singer very clearly regards animal life as having less value than human life. For instance, like Bentham, he maintains the following position:

> While self-awareness, the capacity to think ahead and have hopes and aspirations for the future, the capacity for meaningful relations with others and so on are not relevant to the question of inflicting pain ... these capacities are relevant to the question of taking life. It is not arbitrary to hold that the life of a self-aware being, capable of abstract thought, of planning for the future, of complex acts of communication, and so on, is more valuable than the life of a being without these capacities.[22]

Singer also states,

An animal may struggle against a threat to its life, even if it cannot grasp that it has "a life" in the sense that requires an understanding of what it is to exist over a period of time. But in the absence of some form of mental continuity it is not easy to explain why the loss to the animal killed is not, from an impartial point of view, made good by the creation of a new animal who will lead an equally pleasant life.[23]

That is, Singer, like Bentham, argues that because animals do not know what it is they lose when we kill them, they do not have any interest in continuing to live and, therefore, death is not a harm to them. They do not care that we use and kill them for our purposes. They care only about not suffering as a result of our using and killing them. Singer describes himself as a "flexible vegan" who will eat animal products when he travels, visits the home of others, or is in the company of people who would find his insistence on not eating animal products to be annoying or disconcerting,[24] and he argues that as long as we take seriously the interests of animals in not suffering, our use of them may be ethically defensible:

If it is the infliction of suffering that we are concerned about, rather than killing, then I can also imagine a world in which people mostly eat plant foods, but occasionally treat themselves to the luxury of free range eggs, or possibly even meat from animals who live good lives under conditions natural for their species, and are then humanely killed on the farm.[25]

Singer maintains that similar human and nonhuman interests in not suffering ought to be treated in a similar fashion, as required by the principle of impartiality, or, as Singer refers to it, the principle of equal consideration. He claims that because humans have "superior mental powers,"[26] they will in some cases suffer more than animals and in some cases suffer less, but he acknowledges that making interspecies comparisons is difficult at best and perhaps even impossible. That is, although Singer does not adopt Mill's more categorical position that the pleasures of the human intellect are almost always to be given greater weight, Singer's view about the relationship between "superior" human cognition and assessments of suffering comes very close and undercuts the ability to make impartial assessments of competing interests, virtually guaranteeing that human interests will always prevail.

Moreover, as a utilitarian, Singer is committed to permitting animal use at least in some circumstances. For example, if humans derive great satisfaction from eating animal flesh and animal products, and we were able to produce these with a minimal amount of pain and suffering, then he would be committed to the position that the institution of animal use would be morally acceptable, particularly if death is not a harm for animals. Indeed, given that utilitarians regard happiness, pleasure, the satisfaction of interests, and so on as good, and given that humans obviously enjoy animal use, it would seem that if we could provide a reasonably pleasant life and a relatively painless death for animals, we would be morally obligated to bring into existence as many animals as we could, kill them as quickly as we could, bring more into existence and kill them, and so forth, so that we could maximize the total amount of happiness, pleasure, or preference satisfaction in the world. In any event, like Bentham and Mill, Singer does not object to the use per se of animals, he does not advocate the abolition of the property status of animals, and he is a strong supporter of reforming and improving animal welfare through laws and voluntary modifications of industry practices.

Singer's view that nonhuman animals do not have an interest in their lives because they are not self-aware leads him to distinguish among species of nonhumans and to treat as special or privileged those animals who are closer to humans because they are at least arguably self-aware in a way relevantly similar to humans. Singer coedited *The Great Ape Project: Equality Beyond Humanity*, which proposed that the nonhuman great apes "have mental capacities and an emotional life sufficient to justify inclusion within the community of equals."[27] Because these nonhuman animals are genetically and cognitively similar to human animals, Singer argues that they deserve greater legal protection than other nonhumans, who he, along with Bentham and others, believes live in "a kind of eternal present."[28]

Finally, the position that animal life is of lesser value than human life is one that permeates the welfare position as it has been developed by utilitarian philosophers, such as Bentham, Mill, and Singer. But this position also surfaces in the work of rights theorist Tom Regan. Regan rejects both utilitarian moral theory and the theory of animal welfare. He maintains that we have no moral justification for treating at least adult mammals exclusively as means to the ends of humans, so he does not rely on the lesser moral value of nonhumans to justify animal use as did Bentham and Mill and as does Singer. Regan does, however, argue that in a situation in which there is a conflict, such as a situation in which we are in a lifeboat and must choose whether to save a dog or a human, we should choose to save the life of the human over the dog because death is a greater harm for the former than for the latter. According to Regan, "the harm that death is, is a function of the opportunities for satisfaction it forecloses," and death for an animal, "though a harm, is not comparable to the harm that death would be" for humans.[29]

In sum, although the welfarists, who are utilitarians, maintain that what is right or wrong is dependent on consequences and that in assessing consequences we should equally favor the equivalent interests of nonhuman animals, they believe it is permissible to use animals as resources for humans either because animals do not have an interest in their lives or because their interests generally are of lesser weight relative to those of cognitively superior humans. In other words, nonhuman animals, unlike at least normal adult humans, do not have an interest in not being used as resources; as long as they have a reasonably pleasant life and a relatively pain-less death, we may continue to own and use them. We should, how-ever, endeavor to do so in the most "humane" way possible.

The welfarists are committed to the position that animal life is of lesser moral value than human life. The welfarists talk about the "luxury" of eating meat and animal products and about "flexible" use of nonhuman animals in situations in which we would never use humans. Given that welfarists do not talk about the "luxury" of killing humans or about being "flexible" when it comes to practices that involve the intentional killing of humans, they *must* maintain that there are morally relevant differences between humans and nonhumans that make the use of animals by humans morally justi-fied. If they deny that there is a moral difference between human and animal life, then their support for animal use, however "humane," is nothing more than outright discrimination based only on species.

Animal Rights

The welfarist position rests on the notion that there is a qualitative distinction between the minds of humans and nonhumans and that this qualitative distinction means both that nonhumans do not have an interest in their lives and that there is a morally relevant distinction between the sentient experiences of humans and other animals. As a preliminary matter, this notion ostensibly conflicts with the theory of evolution, which, at least according to Darwin, maintains that the differences between humans and other animals is a matter of degree and not of kind. On an almost daily basis, an article shows up, sometimes in a popular magazine or newspaper and sometimes in a respected scientific journal, about how animal minds are really like human minds.[30] We can, however, concede for purposes of argument that given that humans are, at least as far as we know, the only animals who use symbolic communication and whose conceptual structures are inextricably linked to language, it is most probably the case that there are significant differences between the minds of humans and the minds of nonhumans.[31] But the rights/abolitionist response to any such observation is, "So what?"

The rights/abolitionist position rejects the notion that any differences that may exist between human and animal minds mean that animals have no interest in continuing to exist or that the sentient experiences of nonhumans have a lesser weight than those of humans.[32] It applies the notion of equal consideration to animal *use* and not merely to animal *treatment* and maintains that we cannot justify using nonhumans as human resources, irrespective of whether we treat animals "humanely" in the process. It is not necessary to come to any conclusion about the precise nature of animal minds to be able to assess the welfarist view that death itself does not harm nonhuman animals because, unlike humans, they live in what Singer describes as an "eternal present." The only cognitive characteristic that is required is that nonhumans be *sentient*— that is, that they be perceptually aware.[33] Sentience is necessary to have interests at all. If a being is not sentient, then the being may be alive, but there is nothing that the being prefers, wants, or desires. There may, of course, be uncertainty as to whether sentience exists in a particular case, or with respect to classes of beings, such as insects or mollusks. But the animals we most routinely exploit— the cows, chickens, pigs, ducks, lambs, fish, rats, and so on—are all, without question, sentient.

To say that a sentient being—any sentient being—is not harmed by death is decidedly odd. After all, sentience is not a characteristic that has evolved to serve as an end in itself. Rather, it is a trait that allows the beings who have it to identify situations that are harmful and that threaten survival. *Sentience is a means to the end of continued existence*. Sentient beings, by virtue of their being sentient, have an interest in remaining alive; that is, they prefer, want, or desire to remain alive. Therefore, to say that a sentient being is not harmed by death denies that the being has the very interest that sentience serves to perpetuate. It would be analogous to saying that a being with eyes does not have an interest in continuing to see or is not harmed by being made blind. The Jains of India expressed it well long ago: "All beings are fond of life, like pleasure, hate pain, shun destruction, like life, long to live. To all life is dear."[34].

Singer recognizes that "[a]n animal may struggle against a threat to its life," but he concludes that this does not mean that the animal has the mental continuity required for a sense of self. This position begs the question, however, in that it assumes that the only way that an animal can be self-aware is to have the sort of autobiographical sense of self that we associate with normal adult humans. That is certainly one way of being self-aware, but it is not the only way. As biologist Donald Griffin, one of the most important cognitive ethologists of the twentieth century, notes, if animals are conscious of anything, "the animal's own body and its own actions must fall within the scope of its perceptual consciousness."[35] We nevertheless deny animals self-awareness because we maintain that they cannot "think such thoughts as 'It is *I* who am running, or climbing this tree, or chasing that moth.'"[36] Griffin maintains that "when an animal consciously perceives the running, climbing, or moth-chasing of another animal, it must also be aware of who is doing these things. And if the animal is perceptually conscious of its own body, it is difficult to rule out similar recognition that it, itself, is doing the running, climbing, or chasing."[37] He concludes that "[i]f animals are capable of perceptual awareness, denying them some level of self-awareness would seem to be an arbitrary and unjustified restriction."[38] It would seem that any sentient being must be self-aware in that to be sentient means to be the sort of being who recognizes that it is that being, and not some other, who is experiencing pain or distress. When a sentient being is in pain, that being necessarily recognizes that it is she who is in pain; there is some*one* who is conscious of being in pain and who has a preference, desire, or want not to have that experience.

We can see the arbitrary nature of the welfarist assumption if we consider humans who have a condition known as transient global amnesia, which occurs as a result of a stroke, a seizure, or brain damage. Those with transient global amnesia often have no memory of the past and no ability to project themselves into the future. These humans have "a sense of self about one moment—now—and about one place—here."[39] Their sense of self-awareness may be different from that of a normal adult, but it would not be accurate to say that they are not self-aware or that they are indifferent to death. We may not want to appoint such a person as a teacher or allow her to perform surgery on others, but at least most of us would be horrified at the suggestion that it is acceptable to use such people as forced organ donors or as non-consenting subjects in biomedical experiments, even if we did so "humanely." Even if animals live in a similar "eternal present," that does not mean that they are not self-aware, that they have no interest in continued existence, or that death is not a harm for them. A similar analysis holds for what Singer identifies as "any other capacity that could reasonably be said to give value to life."[40] Some humans will not have the capacity at all, some will have it less than other humans, and some will have it less than other nonhumans. This deficiency or difference may be relevant for some purposes, but it does not allow us to conclude that a human lacking the capacities that Singer identifies as giving value to life does not have an interest in continuing to live or that death is not a harm for her.

Moreover, to the extent that we, like Regan, regard death as a harm for animals, but as a lesser harm because animals have fewer "opportunities for satisfaction," we also beg the question in favor of our own species. There is much about life that I enjoy, and I derive many satisfactions from life. But I cannot with any confidence say that I have more opportunities for satisfaction than does one of the rescued dogs who share our home, any more than I could say with any confidence that I derive more satisfaction from life than does another human.

Also arbitrary is the welfarist notion that humans have "superior mental powers" and that in assessing animal pain, or in trying to determine whether human pleasure or the avoidance of human pain justifies imposing pain and suffering on animals, we should keep in mind Mill's notion that "[i]t is better to be a human being dissatisfied than a pig satisfied." What, apart from self-interested proclamation, makes human characteristics "superior" or allows us to conclude that we experience more intense pleasure when we are happy than a pig does when she is happily rooting in the mud or playing with other pigs? Just as in the case about the harm of death, such an analysis works only if we assume what we are setting out to prove. The analysis works only if we commit the logical fallacy of begging the question.

The problem with the welfarist approach becomes clear if we restrict our analysis to human beings. Assume we have two humans: a philosophy professor and a factory worker who has no higher education and has no interest in having any discussions that would be regarded by the philosopher as intellectually stimulating. If we were to say that it is better to be a philosophy professor dissatisfied than a factory worker satisfied, such an assertion would, quite rightly, be viewed as arbitrary and elitist. Although there is certainly a tradition in Western thought that assigns a higher value to intellectual pursuits than to other sorts of activities, that tradition was shaped almost exclusively by academics and others who valued intellectual pursuits and was not the result of any democratic or impartial assessment of competing pleasures. The notion that nonhuman animals have pains and pleasures that are different from and lesser than those of humans is no different from asserting that the pleasures and pains of a less intelligent or less educated human are inferior to those of a more intelligent or better educated one.

To the extent that humans and nonhumans have different sorts of minds, those differences may be relevant for some purposes, just as differences between and among humans may be relevant for some purposes. Mary's greater ability at math may justify our giving her a scholarship over Joe, who lacks ability at math. The rescued dogs who live with my partner and me very much like to sit with us when we watch movies, but we do not consider their likes and dislikes in movies when we go to the video store because, at least as far as we can tell, they do not have any. So there are relevant differences between the minds of humans and the minds of nonhumans. Any differences, however, are not logically relevant to, for instance, whether we use dogs in painful experiments or kill them for other purposes, just as Joe's inability to do math is not relevant to whether we should take his kidney to save Mary or use him in an experiment to obtain data that may benefit Mary. We cannot claim that humans are superior based on their having more interests, or more intense interests, than nonhumans without begging the question and engaging in reasoning that, if applied in the human context, would quite rightly be seen as blatantly arbitrary and elitist.

The rights position, as I have developed it, rejects the notion that some nonhumans, such as the nonhuman great apes, are more deserving of moral status or legal protection than other animals because they are more like humans. The fact that an animal is more like us may be relevant to determining what other sorts of interests the animal has, but with respect to the animal's interest in her life and the harm that death constitutes to her, or her interest in not being made to experience pain and suffering, her being similar to humans is not relevant at all.

To be clear: if a being is sentient—that is, if she is perceptually aware—she has an interest in continuing to live, and death is a harm to her. It is not necessary to have the autobiographical sense of self that we associate with normal adult humans. Moreover, we cannot say that her interests in her life or the quality of her pain or pleasure are of lesser moral value because her cognitions are not the same as those of normal adult humans. The fact that the minds of humans differ from nonhumans does not mean that the life of a human has greater moral value any more than it means that the life of a human who has normal mental capacities has greater moral value than the life of a mentally disabled person or that the life of an intelligent person has greater moral value than the life of a less intelligent one. Although the differences between humans and animals may be important for some purposes, they are completely irrelevant to the morality of using and killing animals, even if we do so "humanely."

As we saw earlier, the welfarist tradition does not challenge the property status of animals. Welfarists propose regulation that they maintain will raise the price of animal products and thereby reduce consumption (a matter that is addressed in the following section), but, for the most part, they do not propose the abolition of the institution of animal property. The rights position advocates that animals should have the right not to be treated as the resources of humans.

We should be clear here about the meaning of "right."[41] A right is merely a way of protecting an interest; the interest is protected even if the general welfare would be increased or improved if we ignored that interest. To explain what a right is in these terms should make clear why utilitarians reject rights. As we saw previously, utilitarians are consequentialists; what is right or wrong depends on consequences. To say that an interest is protected by a right means that we must protect that interest even if the consequences would weigh against that protection. For example, to say that I have a right to my life is to say that my interest in continuing to live is protected even if using me in a painful biomedical experiment that would result in my death might lead to a cure for cancer. Many utilitarians would have no problem with using humans in biomedical experiments if it were reasonably certain that good consequences would ensue. Most rights theorists would have a problem with such use.

To say that a right protects an interest from being sacrificed for consequential reasons is not to say that the interest is protected absolutely. For example, to say that I have a right to liberty does not mean that I cannot forfeit my interest in liberty by being found guilty of committing a crime. It means only that my interest in liberty will be protected even if others would benefit from my imprisonment.

There is a great deal of controversy about what human interests ought to be protected by rights, particularly legal rights, which involve an interest being protected by the power of the state. But there is general agreement that humans have an interest in not being treated exclusively as the resources of another and that this interest ought to be protected by a basic, pre-legal right not to be treated as a slave. We certainly do not treat everyone equally—for instance, we often pay more money to people who are considered more conventionally intelligent or who are better baseball players. But for purposes of treating humans exclusively as the resources of others, as far as human slavery is concerned, we regard all humans, irrespective of their individual characteristics, as having equal inherent value. That is, we regard all humans as having a moral value that, though not necessarily requiring that we treat them all equally for all purposes, does require that we treat them equally with respect to their interest in not being treated exclusively as the resource of others. We protect this interest with a right in that we do not regard it as morally justifiable to enslave humans or use them as forced organ donors even if to do so would increase overall social welfare. Slavery involves letting another, the slave owner, decide the value of the fundamental interests of the slave, including her interests in life, liberty, and not suffering various forms of pain and deprivation. Not being a chattel slave is a prerequisite to having other rights. The laws of every nation, as well as the norms of customary international law, prohibit slavery. This is not to say that chattel slavery does not still exist—it most certainly does—but no one defends it, and it is universally condemned. If animals matter morally, then we must apply the principle of equal consideration— the moral rule that we treat similar cases similarly—and ask whether there is a good reason not to accord the right not to be treated as property to nonhumans as well. Is there a justification for using animals in ways that we would consider inappropriate ever to use any humans?

The answer is clear. There is no rational justification for our continuing to deny this one right to sentient nonhumans, however "humanely" we treat them. As long as animals are property, they can never be members of the moral community. The interests of animal property will always count for less than the interests of animal owners. We can fall back on religious superstition and claim that animal use is justified because animals do not have souls, are not created in God's image, or are otherwise inferior spiritually. Alternatively, we can claim that our use of animals is acceptable because we are human and they are not, which is nothing more than speciesism and is no different from saying that it is acceptable for whites to discriminate against blacks because of differences in skin color or for men to exploit women because of differences in gender.

The animal rights position does not mean releasing domesticated nonhumans to run wild in the street. If we took animals seriously and recognized our obligation not to treat them as things, we would stop producing and facilitating the production of domestic animals altogether. We would care for the ones whom we have here now, but we would stop breeding more for human consumption, and we would leave non-domesticated animals alone. We would stop eating, wearing, or using animal products, and we would regard veganism as a clear and unequivocal moral baseline.

If we stopped producing domesticated animals, we would avoid the overwhelming number of conflicts that so trouble those who advance the animal welfare position.[42] To put the matter simply, if we did not keep bringing domesticated animals into existence for our use, we would not have to worry about how we treat them and whether our standards are "humane." There is no real conflict between a human who wants to eat a steak or drink a glass of milk and the cow who must be exploited to produce these products. There is a conflict only because we assume that the cow is there to be used as a resource. The cow is property, and there is a conflict between the property owner and the property sought to be exploited. Once we see that we cannot morally justify using animals—however "humanely"—then these conflicts disappear. Even if the use of animals in biomedical research benefits humans—and this is highly questionable at best—there is no more a conflict between humans who would receive the benefit and the animals whose use would provide any benefit than there is a conflict between humans who would benefit from the use of other humans as non-consenting subjects in experiments or as forced organ donors and those humans who would be used.[43] The existence of the conflict between the humans and nonhumans in this context begs the question about the moral justification of animal use in the first place.

But what about the situation in which there is a genuine conflict? What do we do in the unlikely situation in which we are passing by the burning house that contains a human and a nonhuman, and there is time to save only one? If we would save the human over the nonhuman, does that not mean that we think that animals have less moral value? It would depend on the reason for the choice. If we thought that death was a lesser harm to the animal because humans are "superior," then that decision would certainly reflect a judgment about relative moral value. If, however, we chose to save the human not because we thought that death was a lesser harm to the animal but because, as humans, we have a greater understanding of the meaning and consequences of death for our own species than we do for other species in terms of disruption of other relationships and so on, this would reflect our own limitations of knowledge and not reflect any judgment about the moral value of the animal.

There are all sorts of situations in which we prefer the interest of one human over another, and this does not necessarily mean that we are making a negative judgment about the moral value of humans whose interests are not favored in these situations. Assume I pass by the burning house and see two humans therein—a very young person and a very old person—and I have time to save only one. I decide to save the young person because she has not yet lived her life, and the old person appears to be very near the end of hers. Does that mean that I regard older people to be of less moral value or that I can use them for experiments or as forced organ donors? Of course not. In any event, these hypotheticals are of little use because they invariably involve situations in which we will feel that we have failed morally no matter what we do; they are poor places in which to formulate moral principles that go beyond the actual situation.

Conclusion

There is a fundamental theoretical difference between the rights/abolitionist position and the welfare/regulationist position. The latter maintains that animal life matters less morally than human life and that it is acceptable to use nonhumans for human purposes, under at least some circumstances, as long as we treat animals "humanely." Death is not a harm for nonhumans. Animals do not care *that* we kill and eat them or use them for other purposes. They just care about *how* we treat them and how we kill them.

The rights position as I propose it maintains that death is a harm for any sentient being and that we cannot make meaningful distinctions between the quality of sentient experiences between humans and nonhumans that would justify imposing any pain and suffering on nonhumans incidental to our use of them as our resources, any more than we can make such distinctions between or among humans for the purpose of justifying slavery or otherwise treating humans exclusively as resources.

Animal Welfare Does Not Work

Animal advocates often claim that even if there is a theoretical difference between the rights and welfare positions, any such difference is without practical import. These advocates claim that the animal rights/abolitionist position is "utopian" and does not provide any practical normative guidance that we can pursue now to help animals and that we need to do something practical to address the enormous animal suffering that presently exists. That "something practical" is animal welfare regulation that, despite any limitations, still offers what Robert Garner claims is "a great deal of scope for reform."[44] Proponents of welfare regulation claim three benefits. First, they argue that welfare reform will reduce animal suffering immediately by making exploitation more "humane." Second, welfare reform will reduce demand immediately by increasing production costs and making animal products more expensive. Third, welfare reform will help to raise consciousness about animal exploitation, and this will, in the future and gradually, lead us to stop exploiting animals altogether or at least will gradually lead to significantly reduced animal exploitation.

In the section following this one, we see that the rights/abolitionist position does, contrary to the claim just described, provide both practical normative guidance for the present and a strategy for the future. In this section, we see that the underlying assumption of the position that welfare reform is the only, the best, or even a desirable strategy for animal advocates to pursue now, is wrong. Putting aside matters of moral theory, as a practical matter, animal welfare regulation simply does not work.

Animals are property; they are treated as economic commodities with only extrinsic or conditional value. To the extent that we protect animal interests, we do so only when it provides a benefit— usually an economic benefit—for humans. As a result, the protection of animal interests is, for the most part, very limited. Regulation does not decrease animal suffering in any significant way, and it does not decrease demand by making animal exploitation more expensive. On the contrary, welfare reform generally increases production efficiency so that it actually becomes cheaper to produce animal products. To the extent that a welfare regulation imposes any cost on animal production, that added cost is not significant.

Moreover, welfare reform makes the public feel more comfortable about using animal products and makes curious bedfellows out of institutional exploiters and animal advocates. When an industry agrees to the reform, which is generally in its economic interest anyway, animal advocates praise the industry, allowing it to represent to the public that it cares about animal interests. Animal advocates can then use the "victory" against industry for fundraising purposes. And there is absolutely no evidence—none whatsoever—that animal welfare reform will lead to abolition or to significantly decreased animal use in the future.

Welfarists maintain that animal advocates should support welfare reforms because it is better to inflict less suffering on animals than more suffering. Putting aside the factual matter of whether welfarist reform actually does reduce animal suffering or may actually increase overall suffering and death by making the public more comfortable about supposed "humane" animal treatment, this argument is flawed. It is, for instance, better in one sense to torture someone for one hour rather than two hours; it is better not to beat a victim in addition to raping her or him. But that does not mean that we should campaign for more "humane" torture or more "humane" rape or give awards to perpetrators who inflict unjustified harm in more "humane" ways. We certainly do not do so where issues of human rights are involved. So even if welfare reforms were effective—and I argue that they are not—the promotion of welfarist campaigns necessarily assumes the notion discussed in the preceding section: that nonhuman animals have a lesser moral value than human animals.

Animals as Property and the Economics of Welfare Regulation

It is imperative to understand that animals are property.[45] They are economic commodities; they have a market value. Animal property is, of course, different from the other things that we own in that animals, unlike cars, computers, machinery, or other commodities, are sentient and have interests. All sentient beings have interests in not suffering pain or other deprivations and in satisfying those interests that are peculiar to their species. It costs money to protect animal interests. As a general matter, we spend money to protect animal interests only when it is justified as an economic matter—only when we derive an economic benefit from doing so. For example, the Humane Slaughter Act in the United States, enacted originally in 1958, requires that larger animals slaughtered for food be stunned and not be conscious when they are shackled, hoisted, and taken to the killing floor.[46] This law protects the interests that animals have at the moment of slaughter but does so only because it is economically beneficial for producers and consumers.[47] Large animals who are conscious and hanging upside down and thrashing as they are slaughtered will cause injuries to slaughterhouse workers and will incur expensive carcass damage. Therefore, stunning large animals makes good economic sense. Of course, these animals have many other interests throughout their lives, including an interest in avoiding pain and suffering at times other than at the moment of slaughter, and these other interests are not protected because it is not economically effective to do so. Moreover, the Humane Slaughter Act has not been interpreted to apply to smaller animals, including birds, who account for about 95 percent of the animals slaughtered for food in the United States. The reason for this exclusion is that given the number of birds slaughtered, and their relatively smaller size and lesser value, it has not been considered economically efficient to protect the interests of chickens in the same way as the interests of cows. But as we see later in this chapter, welfarists are campaigning for more "humane" poultry slaughter on the basis that recent studies in agricultural economics indicate that the proposed reforms would be economically beneficial to the producers of animal products.

There are laws that require that we treat animals "humanely" and that we not inflict "unnecessary" suffering on them.[48] These laws, however, do not prohibit uses that are unnecessary; they supposedly prohibit only treatment that is not necessary to achieve a given use.[49] For example, as I mentioned at the outset, we kill and eat approximately 56 billion land animals every year. No one maintains that it is necessary to eat animals to lead an optimally healthy lifestyle, and an increasing number of mainstream health care professionals tell us that animal foods are detrimental to human health. Animal agriculture is a disaster for the environment because it involves a very inefficient use of natural resources and creates water pollution, soil erosion, and greenhouse gases. The only justification that we have for the pain, suffering, and death that we impose on these billions of animals is that we enjoy eating animal foods or that it is convenient to do so or that it is just plain habit. Our use of animals in entertainment and for sport hunting also cannot be considered as necessary. The only use of animals that cannot be dismissed as transparently trivial involves biomedical research that will supposedly result in cures for serious human illnesses (most of which are related to our consumption of animal products), and even in this context, which involves a miniscule number of animals relative to our other uses, there are serious questions about the need to use animals.[50]

Because animal welfare laws do not question use and purport only to regulate treatment, they generally explicitly exempt what are considered the "normal" or "customary" practices of institutionalized animal use, or courts interpret pain and suffering imposed pursuant to those practices as "necessary" and "humane."[51] That is, the law defers to industry to set the standard of "humane" care. This deference is based on the assumption that those who produce animal products—from the breeders to the farmers to the slaughterhouse operators—will not impose more harm on animals than is required to produce the particular product, just as the rational owner of a car would not take a hammer to her car and dent it for no reason. The result is that the level of protection for animal interests is linked to what is required to exploit animals in an economically efficient way. And that allows for a standard of treatment that, if applied to humans, would constitute torture. Animal welfare provides little protection for animal interests.

Contemporary Welfarist Campaigns: Reinforcing the Property Paradigm

It is, of course, possible as a theoretical matter to achieve protection for animal interests that goes beyond what is necessary to exploit them as economic commodities; however, it is highly unlikely as a practical matter. We must remember that it costs money to protect animal interests and, to the extent that we spend that money and do not derive an economic benefit, we increase the cost of using animals, which generates powerful opposition from producers and consumers alike. Contemporary welfarist campaigns promoted by animal advocates demonstrate that animal welfare remains firmly rooted in the notion of animals as economic commodities.[52] These campaigns do nothing to move animals away from the property paradigm or to accord value to animal interests that goes beyond their value as human resources. Here we examine several of what are literally dozens of campaigns that fit the same pattern.

Poultry slaughter: Animal advocates in the United States are campaigning to change the way that poultry are slaughtered. As mentioned previously, poultry are not included under the protection (such as it is) of the Humane Slaughter Act. They are slaughtered using a process that involves their being shackled upside down while still fully conscious and passed through electrically charged water that is supposed to stun them, and then their throats are slit. They are then "bled out" and placed into scalding water to facilitate feather removal. This method of slaughter risks injury and trauma to the birds as they are unloaded from crates and then shackled. Birds may suffer shocks before being stunned and are often inadequately stunned and conscious during the cutting, bleeding, and scalding processes. Animal welfare advocates are seeking to make poultry slaughter more "humane." The Humane Society of the United States (HSUS) filed a lawsuit to have the act apply to poultry, but the trial court rejected the challenge and the apellate court found a lack of standing.[53] HSUS, PETA, and other groups have been urging industry to adopt a method of slaughter known as "controlled-atmosphere killing," or "CAK." CAK involves either placing the birds, who are still in the crates in which they have been transported to the slaughterhouse, in a chamber that contains a nonpoisonous gas that is supposed to kill them by anoxia, or gassing them while they are still in the truck en route to the slaughterhouse. The dead birds are then shackled and processed. An alternative procedure, "controlled-atmosphere stunning," or "CAS," involves the birds being stunned but not killed, shackled while supposedly unconscious, and then killed by having their throats slit.[54]

Not all welfarists are enthusiastic about CAK/CAS systems. For example, Bernard E. Rollin, a prominent animal ethicist and advisor to the American Humane Association's humane certification label program, claims that suffocation creates severe distress, and he does not accept CAK as a "humane method of euthanasia."[55] Other advisors to the American Humane Association, which describes itself as the oldest national organization dedicated to protecting children and animals, have expressed the view that it is not clear that the use of gas is any more humane than the stunning process if stunning is properly performed.[56] The American Humane Association states that "[b]ased on our scientific experts and existing evidence, we are not aware of any science-based conclusive evidence that the distress chickens, turkeys or other species experience in existing electric stunning methods is greater, or less than that with gas anesthesia induction."[57] Sociologist Roger Yates has collected sources showing that there is a significant amount of debate among poultry scientists as to the welfare benefits of CAK and CAS.[58] Researchers have noted that poultry exposed to gas are often not killed, and the birds exhibit signs of significant pain, suffering, and distress during the gassing process.

Putting aside whether the actual method of killing provides a meaningful welfare benefit and is not simply replacing one horrible process with a different one that is equally horrible, the claim made by CAK/CAS supporters that "[w]ith CAK, all of the abuses that chickens currently suffer are eliminated" is false and outrageously so.[59] It is simply untrue to maintain, as PETA does, that CAK/CAS involves a death free of pain, suffering, or distress. Given the realities of CAK/CAS, it is not accurate to describe CAK/CAS as a system that puts "the birds 'to sleep' quickly and painlessly"[60] or that "gently put[s] them 'to sleep.'"[61] It is also untrue to say that "[w]ith CAK, workers never handle live birds, so there are no chances for abuse."[62] Yates notes,

PeTA have themselves documented how workers sadistically treat animal property such as chickens: being trapped inside a transportation crate hardly protects one from all abuses and rights violations—and this is only half of the story in the first place. The chickens and hens have still to be taken from battery cages, cage-free facilities and broiler houses and placed in the transportation crates. They are still subject to rights violations at the farm end of the process.[63]

Although there is a great deal of uncertainty as to whether CAK actually provides any significant welfare benefit to the animals, there is considerable economic evidence that CAK can increase the efficiency of the poultry production process. According to an HSUS report on the economics of poultry slaughter, "[l]ive shackling and electrical stunning reduce meat quality and yield. Rough handling during shackling and convulsions induced by electrical stunning cause broken bones, bruising, and hemorrhaging."[64] Moreover, "[d]uring electrical stunning, chickens can defecate and inhale water, contaminating carcasses," and "[t]hese factors lead to carcass downgrades and condemnations, decreasing processors' revenue. In 2004, 5 million U.S. poultry were condemned, post-mortem, due to bruising and contamination, alone."[65] Finally, "[s]hackling and electrical stunning take their toll on workers, as well. Slaughter facility employees suffer muscle strain, cuts from chickens' claws, and respiratory problems. The injury rates among poultry slaughterhouse workers are among the highest of any U.S. industry."[66] HSUS proposes CAK as a "practical alternative to electrical stunning [that] is being adopted by many European processors."[67] CAK will, according to HSUS, improve animal welfare. However, it will also help the economic bottom line.

Although "CAK involves large capital costs in the purchase of gas stunning equipment," HSUS explains, this method "results in cost savings and increased revenues by decreasing carcass downgrades, contamination, and refrigeration costs; increasing meat yields, quality, and shelf life; and improving worker conditions."[68] Moreover, it "results in fewer broken bones and less bruising and hemorrhaging" and "increases boning yield and deboned meat quality."[69] In addition to less carcass damage, producers will benefit because "CAK increases the rate of rigor development [and] ... results in faster carcass-maturation times and reduces handling, floor space, and refrigeration costs."[70] Contamination costs are reduced because the birds do not inhale contaminated water as they can during the stunning process, and "CAK can improve worker conditions and safety, decreasing labor costs due to production line inefficiencies, injuries, and turnover from handling conscious birds."[71] According to HSUS, "a plant that installs a CAK line at a cost of $1 million, with a capacity to slaughter 1 million birds per week, would have annual operating costs of between $265,200 and $436,800, and increased revenue of $1.87 million from increased meat yield. Payback would be achieved in less than one year, with increased profits thereafter."[72] In the United Kingdom, "producers adopting CAK were able to recoup their capital investment in one year."[73]

Although PETA is considered more radical than HSUS, its analysis of CAK/CAS is remarkably similar in its emphasis on economic benefits for producers and consumers. PETA maintains that electrical stunning "has serious negative implications with regard to carcass quality, yield, and contamination."[74] When the birds are dumped from the crates in which they are transported to the slaughterhouse and then shackled, they suffer "broken bones, bruising, and hemorrhaging, all of which lower carcass quality and yield."[75] During the dumping and shackling process, the birds "scratch and peck at—and vomit and defecate on—each other ... causing carcass contamination."[76] Stress prior to slaughter "increases the acidity of their flesh, reduces tenderness, and increases drip loss."[77] When the birds pass through the electrified water, they "often inhale pathogens in the electric water bath, causing carcass contamination."[78]

Birds who miss the knife that is supposed to cut their throat or who otherwise are not dead before going into the defeathering tanks where they are scalded to death defecate in the tanks, "contaminating all the birds submerged afterward."[79] And "[b]irds who are scalded to death are condemned and cannot be sold, further lowering yield."[80]

The electrical stunning method also involves increased labor costs. The lighting in the areas used for dumping and shackling is kept dim to calm the birds, and this creates "a poor working environment."[81] The terrified birds peck at workers and "flap violently during handling, kick up dust and debris, injure workers, and defecate and vomit on them. This increases illness and injury rates, lowering worker welfare and increasing costs for employers."[82] These "poor conditions result in an extraordinarily high turnover rate among slaughterhouse workers, averaging between 75 and 100 percent annually."[83]

A PETA headline promotes CAK as a "Less Cruel, More Profitable Method of Chicken and Turkey Slaughter."[84] Studies cited by PETA show that the use of gas results in fewer broken bones, less hemorrhaging, and reduced bruising. PETA notes that "each year approximately 400,000 to 1 million carcasses are condemned for bruises" and that "CAK would significantly reduce this problem, and the resulting reduction in bruising would have important implications for the producer because it would 'improve the yield and the value of products' and almost completely eliminate blood stains."[85] The CAK method "further increases yield by eliminating the possibility that live birds will enter the scalding tank and be condemned. Even a small increase in meat yield per bird can lead to a significant increase in revenue."[86] A plant processing 1.3 million birds per week "would earn an additional $2 million a year (3 cents per bird)."[87] Producers also benefit from reducing the number of birds killed in the rough pre-slaughter handling incidental to the electric immobilization method, and "the significant rearing costs associated with each bird (e.g., feeding, housing, lighting, transport) are completely lost when a carcass is condemned or discarded. By increasing meat yield, producers who use CAK would be able to recoup these otherwise wasted costs, providing yet another financial advantage."[88]

Moreover, CAK, according to PETA, almost completely eliminates both external contamination, which is caused when the birds are bruised or scratched and become prone to microbial contamination or when they come into contact with feces from birds who defecate in the scalding water of the defeathering tank, and internal contamination, which results from the inhalation of water when the birds spasm in the electrified water bath. "This has significant implications for producers since, according to the USDA . . . about 4 million chickens are condemned each year for being contaminated."[89]

CAK further "provides producers with improved quality when compared to electric immobilization methods."[90] In addition to reducing bruising and other problems, CAK provides "improved shelf life and quality, and unimpeded bleedout."[91] PETA states that CAK "is also reported to produce more tender breast meat than when electrical stunning is used"[92] and that "CAK produces better-quality meat that lasts longer—in terms of smell and color—than the meat of electrically immobilized birds."[93] CAK results in "faster carcass-maturation times" and enables "early filleting," and this has "important financial benefits, as refrigeration can be significantly reduced, thus saving on storage, energy, and refrigeration equipment and maintenance costs."[94] CAK provides further environmental benefits by reducing by-product waste and by using less water.[95]

According to the data presented by PETA, CAK results in considerable labor savings and improves conditions for workers, who "do not handle live, flapping birds."[96] The dim lighting used in the dumping and shackling areas is not necessary, and "[l]ights can be kept bright."[97] Further, "the air is not dusty with fecal matter and debris."[98] Overall working conditions are improved, fewer injuries are sustained by workers, and birds do not vomit or defecate on workers. Because the birds are dead when hung, CAK turns "hanging into a desirable job."[99] PETA reports that slaughterhouses in Michigan, France, and Germany, as well as the Canadian Food Inspection Agency, have reported improved labor conditions, including "improved ergonomics,"[100] as a result of adopting CAK.

As for the expense of the CAK system, PETA maintains that "the initial cost of switching from electric immobilization to CAK can be offset and quickly surpassed by gains achieved from improving carcass quality and meat yield and from lowering costs by reducing the need for refrigeration, storage, labor, and environmental cleanup."[101] Like HSUS, PETA notes that the cost of installing CAK can be recovered in about one year and also notes that even smaller producers will enjoy "an additional $1 million to $1.3 million in profit annually from improvements in meat yield alone when compared to an electric immobilization system."[102] A large producer, such as Tyson Foods, which processes 150,000 birds per day in each of its forty plants, would recover the start-up costs in 1–1.6 years and would then enjoy a profit of $47–64 million per year depending on the sort of gas that was used, and this profit increase includes only a 1 percent increase in meat yield and ignores all other economic benefits.[103] PETA concludes its analysis with "select poultry-industry endorsements of controlled-atmosphere killing."[104] These endorsements emphasize the many economic benefits of CAK/CAS. PETA provides contact information for suppliers of CAK/CAS systems and gases.

Gestation crates: HSUS, in conjunction with Farm Sanctuary and other groups, is leading efforts in the United States to have conventional gestation crates for pigs banned in favor of larger individual crates or group housing systems employing an electronic sow feeder ("ESF") to reduce aggression at feeding time. HSUS argues that studies indicate that "[s]ow productivity is higher in group housing than in individual crates, as a result of reduced rates of injury and disease, earlier first estrus, faster return to estrus after delivery, lower incidence of stillbirths, and shorter farrowing times. Group systems employing ESF are particularly cost-effective."[105] In addition, "[c]onversion from gestation crates to group housing with ESF marginally reduces production costs and increases productivity."[106] HSUS cites one study showing that "the total cost per piglet sold is 0.6-percent lower in group ESF systems, while the income to the piglet farmer is 8-percent higher, because of increased productivity,"[107] and another showing that "compared to gestation crates, group housing with ESF decreased labor time 3 percent and marginally increased income per sow per year."[108]

HSUS claims that "[s]avings at the sow farm can be passed onto the fattening farm, where the cost per unit weight decreases 0.3 percent."[109] This will result in a decrease in the retail price of pork and a small increase in demand. HSUS concludes that "[i]t is likely that producers who adopt group housing with ESF could increase demand for their products or earn a market premium."[110] HSUS claims that despite the greater efficiency of alternative production systems, pork producers in the United States are only slowly adopting those economically more desirable systems because of "inertia and producers' lack of familiarity with ESF."[111]

Industry agreement to more "humane" standards: As an example of "successful American campaigns," Peter Singer cites efforts by animal advocates and organizations, such as PETA, that led to agreement by McDonald's to "set and enforce higher standards for the slaughterhouses that supply it with meat" and to provide increased space to hens confined in egg batteries.[112] Singer claims that these actions by McDonald's, which were followed by Wendy's and Burger King, are "a ray of hope" and "the first hopeful signs for American farm animals since the modern animal movement began."[113] PETA claims that "[t]here's been a real change in consciousness"[114] concerning the treatment of animals used for food and praises McDonald's as "'leading the way' in reforming the practices of fast-food suppliers, in the treatment and the killing of its beef and poultry."[115]

The changes praised by Singer and PETA do not reflect any recognition that animals have interests that still should be protected even if there is no economic advantage to humans and do not in any way move animals away from the property paradigm. The slaughterhouse standards promoted by Singer and PETA were developed by Temple Grandin, designer of "humane" slaughter and handling systems.[116] Grandin's guidelines, which involve techniques for moving animals through the slaughtering process and stunning them, are based explicitly on economic concerns. According to Grandin,

> Once livestock—cattle, pigs and sheep—arrive at packing plants, proper handling procedures are not only important for the animal's well-being, they can also mean the difference between profit and loss. Research clearly demonstrates that many meat quality benefits can be obtained with careful, quiet animal handling.…Properly handled animals are not only an important ethical goal, they also keep the meat industry running safely, efficiently and profitably.[117]

In talking about stunning animals before slaughter, Grandin states,

> Stunning an animal correctly will provide better meat quality. Improper electric stunning will cause bloodspots in the meat and bone fractures. Good stunning practices are also required so that a plant will be in compliance with the Humane Slaughter Act and for animal welfare. When stunning is done correctly, the animal feels no pain and it becomes instantly unconscious. An animal that is stunned properly will produce a still carcass that is safe for plant workers to work on.[118]

She maintains that "[g]entle handling in well-designed facilities will minimize stress levels, improve efficiency and maintain good meat quality. Rough handling or poorly designed equipment is detrimental to both animal welfare and meat quality."[119]

In discussing as a general matter the slaughter and battery-cage improvements to which Singer refers, McDonald's states,

> Animal welfare is also an important part of quality assurance. For high-quality food products at the counter, you need high quality coming from the farm. Animals that are well cared for are less prone to illness, injury, and stress, which all have the same negative impact on the condition of livestock as they do on people.
>
> Proper animal welfare practices also benefit producers. Complying with our animal welfare guidelines helps ensure efficient production and reduces waste and loss. This enables our suppliers to be highly competitive.[120]

Wendy's also emphasizes the economic efficiency of its animal welfare program: "Studies have shown that humane animal handling methods not only prevent needless suffering, but can result in a safer working environment for workers involved in the farm and livestock industry."[121] In a report about voluntary reforms in the livestock industry, the *Los Angeles Times* stated that "[i]n part, the reforms are driven by self-interest. When an animal is bruised, its flesh turns mushy and must be discarded. Even stress, especially right before slaughter, can affect the quality of meat."[122]

Again, there is a question as to whether Grandin's reforms provide any significant welfare benefit. A slaughterhouse that complies with Grandin's guidelines is still a most hideous place, and many of the welfare benefits that Grandin touts are based on what she claims as her unique and almost mystical insight into animal cognition that comes from her being autistic.[123] Moreover, even Grandin has expressed concern that the audit process, which is the central focus of her program, is meaningless and fails to prevent even the worst abuses of animals being slaughtered.[124]

Minor Increases in Production Costs

It is important, however, not to lose sight of the fact that even on the rare occasion that a particular welfare reform does not increase production efficiency and results in an increase in production cost not offset by better product quality, reduction in worker injuries, or other benefits, welfare reform is still not likely to impose any significant opportunity costs on animal use, and animals will never receive a significant level of increased protection. For example, the leading animal welfare campaign in the United States seeks to abolish battery cages in favor of what is essentially one large cage that is benignly called a "cage-free" barn. The organization spearheading this effort is HSUS. Although the cage-free system will not increase production efficiency by lowering costs, it will not result in any significantly increased cost to producers either. HSUS acknowledges that conversion to cage-free systems would "increase production costs 3 to 12 cents per dozen eggs" but points out that at the lower end of this range, this conversion would increase production costs less than switching to larger battery cages, which is promoted by the leading American egg-industry trade association.[125] HSUS states that "[g]iven the marketing share of egg prices and the low price elasticity of egg consumption, cage-free producers more than compensate for increased costs through increased income. Consumers, in turn, increase their monthly average per capita expenditures on eggs by 4 to 24 cents."[126] HSUS concludes that "[i]t is little surprise that cage-free egg production is the fastest growing and most profitable segment of the industry."[127] Indeed, according to an essay published by HSUS, even if welfare reforms involve an increase of costs at the farm level, given that farm costs generally represent less than half of the retail price of animal products, and given that the demand for these products is inelastic, any increase in retail price, which will be very small in any event given the modest nature of the most ambitious of welfare reforms, will be passed along to the consumer.[128] If consumers purchased only free-range products, and even if those products increased production costs, average per capita spending for food would increase by only $3 per week.[129]

Moreover, it is ludicrous to suggest that cage-free eggs represent any significant welfare improvement for the hens. Cage-free hens are crammed into dark, industrial sheds that are filthy and filled with toxic gases that accumulate from the waste of thousands of hens. There can be up to 30,000 birds in one barn. Like hens in conventional battery cages, cage-free hens have their beaks burned off at one day of age. This procedure, which is extremely painful, is not performed with any anesthetic. Like hens in conventional batteries, most cage-free hens are starved to force their bodies into repeated laying cycles. Like hens in conventional batteries, cage-free hens are considered useless or "spent" after eighteen months of age. They are then killed, often by being stuffed in a drum and then gassed. Roosters are killed—usually by suffocation—at birth because they cannot produce eggs. Interestingly, Paul Shapiro, Director of the HSUS Factory Farming Campaign, was critical of cage-free and free-range eggs before he became employed by HSUS.[130] He now is spearheading the HSUS campaign for cage-free eggs.

It should also be noted that many consumers are willing to pay a premium for food that is perceived to be more wholesome or healthy, and what are characterized as higher-welfare products, such as cage-free or free-range eggs, are often marketed as being more healthy. Indeed, the market for these products is as closely related to concern about human health as it is to concern about animal welfare.

A Difference in Europe?

Some advocates argue that although animals are property, European countries provide a much higher level of animal protection, and they claim that this shows that, contrary to my position, the property status of animals is not as important as I maintain it to be. For example, Robert Garner states that British animal welfare laws are more stringent than laws in the United States and that "[t]he key point is that the explanatory variable cannot be property since in both countries animals are regarded as the property of humans."[131]

To the extent that Garner's claim is true, the practical results are not as great as Garner proposes in that animals are still treated badly in Britain, and any differences are marginal at best. Indeed, Garner claims that there have been "gradual erosions of factory farming," but he acknowledges that "the fundamentals remain."[132] He discusses the regulation of slaughter and claims that although "[i]n theory ... the suffering of farm animals in the last moments of their lives should be minimal," there are problems that "occur because animal welfare often takes second place to cost-cutting."[133] He acknowledges that the creation of the single market under the European Union "has been detrimental to British animal welfare because animals, or animal products, can be exported to, or imported from, countries whose animal welfare standards are poorer than those in Britain."[134] Although Garner claims that the importance of economic concerns "has begun to wane," his evidence for this is a relatively short list of claimed animal welfare improvements, some of which have not even been enacted and some of which have been enacted but are not enforced.[135] For example, Garner cites a 1999 Directive of the Council of Europe,[136] which requires that, by 2012, egg producers in member states stop using the conventional battery cage for laying hens, as proof that "the position of agribusiness is weakening."[137] Similarly, Peter Singer claims that "[b]attery cages are being phased out in Europe,"[138] and PETA claims that the supposed ban is "an incredible step for egg laying hens."[139] An examination of the Directive indicates, however, that it is not "an incredible step for egg laying hens," nor is it indicative that "agribusiness is weakening" or that "[b]attery cages are being phased out in Europe."

The Directive gives egg producers an option. They may switch from conventional battery cages to "enriched cages" that have a nest, a perching space, litter for scratching and pecking, and unrestricted access to a feed trough. Alternatively, producers can go to cageless system, such as "barn" (cage-free) or free-range eggs. Estimates are that free-range eggs will cost 2.6 eurocents more to produce than a conventional battery egg, cage-free or barn eggs will cost 1.3 eurocents more, and an egg from an enriched system will cost "less than 1 [euro]cent." more[140] According to a report submitted to the EU, the extant evidence "suggests that the enriched cage system will not operate at a significant cost disadvantage to the traditional battery cage."[141] Therefore, "many producers are likely to switch to enriched cage production."[142] The EU adds that any increased production cost will be offset in that "the higher animal welfare standards can serve as a valuable selling point for EU producers."[143]

Even moderate animal welfare organizations acknowledge that the enriched cage, which is permitted under the Directive and which most producers will choose because it is the least expensive of the three required options, does not improve animal welfare in any significant way. For example, Compassion in World Farming (CIWF) commissioned a report opposing the enriched cage, concluding that it "offers no worthwhile welfare benefits as compared with the conventional cage."[144] The Royal Society for the Prevention of Cruelty to Animals (RSPCA) stated that enriched cages "don't adequately meet even some of the most basic welfare needs of the birds. This includes not enough room to spread their wings properly or sufficient facilities to dustbathe effectively, leading to to [sic] frustration and distress," and an RSPCA farm animal scientist stated that "[e]nriched cages are little better than the notorious battery cages. Little will change from the hens' point of view."[145]

Moreover, even if producers go to the slightly more expensive free-range or cage-free systems, there is considerable controversy about whether those systems will be any better for the hens, who will still be subject to horrible abuse and bodily manipulation throughout their lives and who will end up in the same slaughterhouse after they are spent. Male chicks, who are of no use to the egg industry, will still be suffocated or crushed. And there have already been several exposés concerning the atrocious conditions at free-range and cage-free operations that have been awarded the RSPCA Freedom Food certification.[146]

Garner also cites the ban on fox hunting as another example of progress in Europe. The ban supposedly prohibits using hounds to hunt foxes but allows the use of hounds to follow a scent and flush out a fox. It is legal for hunters to use hounds to flush out a fox (or other wild mammal) and then shoot the animal or use a falcon to kill the animal. Supporters of hunting are flouting the law and encouraging exploitation of all loopholes and are claiming that more foxes are being killed than before the ban came into effect.[147] Four years since the ban went into effect, "[n]ot a single hunt has gone out of business, there are twice as many registered hounds as there were three years ago," and according to hunt supporters, "the number of people hunting is up by 11%."[148] Even if the law is not repealed, as many predict it will be, it can hardly be regarded as anything but a colossal failure.

It is difficult to find any area where there has been sustained improvement. Great Britain is the birthplace of the antivivisection movement, and the use of animals in experiments and testing has been a primary target of animal advocates. Although the overall number of animals used in experiments decreased from the mid-1970s to mid-1990s and then leveled off, the numbers of procedures involving live animals in Britain has increased by 18 percent since 2000, with a 6 percent increase from 2006 to 2007.[149] All indications are that the European Union is, as a general matter, resisting regulation of vivisection.[150] Indeed, whenever human interests are implicated, welfare reforms are ignored. For example, in 2006, in the wake of fear about the H5N1 virus—known as the "bird flu"—producers in Britain returned free-range poultry to traditional intensive confinement.

Finally, many of the animal welfare changes that have occurred in Europe have been based on increasing the efficiency of exploitation. For example, the adoption of alternatives to crates for sows and calves in Europe has been based on increased productivity and decreased costs. This may indicate that the Europeans are more competent at figuring out how to maximize the wealth represented by animal property, but it does not mean that Europeans are moving away from the property paradigm or deciding to accord inherent value to animal interests.

Producer Resistance

For the most part, producers of animal products derive a palpable economic benefit from making welfare reforms, completely apart from the separate benefit that comes from being able to assure members of the public that the animal products they are consuming have been produced in a "humane" fashion, a matter that is examined in the next section. So the question is, why have these welfare reforms not already been instituted if they are economically beneficial? The answer is that animal agriculture is not an efficient industry. Part of the reason for this is that intensive agriculture, which is the overwhelmingly dominant method of confining animals used for food, developed relatively recently—in the past fifty years or so. It was a system designed with the idea that producers could increase profit by maximizing the number of animals crammed into a particular space and by mechanizing the entire process as much as possible. There was no thought given to the fact that animals, unlike other production inputs, are sentient and that the stress caused by intensive confinement would result in damage to the animal property. Agricultural economists and scientists are only now beginning to identify inefficiencies in intensive systems, and animal advocacy organizations are using this information to identify practices that are vulnerable on economic grounds and that can be targeted in successful campaigns for fundraising purposes. Animal advocacy organizations have, in effect, become part of the mechanism that provides information to industry on how it can increase production efficiency while making changes that both industry and animal advocates can claim result in significant improvements in animal welfare.

A related question concerns why—if welfare reforms increase production efficiency or result in significant price increases that can be passed along to the consumer, given the inelastic nature of the demand involved—institutionalized exploiters not only fail to embrace these reforms voluntarily but even actively resist them, at least initially. There are at least four reasons. First, it is important as a strategic matter for any industry—particularly one that is regulated—to impose an opportunity cost on those who seek to introduce any regulatory reform, including those reforms that may ultimately be cost-efficient or that would not result in any significant price increase. To the extent that industry agrees without resistance to regulatory reform, it encourages subsequent efforts to impose more extensive regulation that may have a significantly negative financial impact. Second, because understanding of the economic inefficiencies of intensive agriculture is a relatively recent phenomenon, industry tends at least initially to respond negatively to being educated about these inefficiencies by the animal protection community. Third, there are often different interests within the community of institutionalized exploiters. There can, for instance, be no doubt that for anyone who was starting a poultry slaughtering business today, it would be economically irrational not to adopt a CAK/CAS method of slaughter. But established businesses often need to be persuaded to make the large capital investment in switching from electrical stunning to CAK/CAS. Fourth, to the extent that a regulatory reform results in any price increase—even a very small one—the ability to satisfy demand with cheaper imports may cause affected producers to suffer a competitive disadvantage.

A good example of these various factors is found in the campaign led by HSUS, Farm Sanctuary, and others to amend California law by a ballot referendum. In November 2008, California voters overwhelmingly approved of "Proposition 2," which was initially designated as the "Prevention of Farm Animal Cruelty Act" and which requires that, with certain exceptions, veal calves, breeding pigs, and egg-laying hens have more space. The law will not take effect until 2015, and debate over Proposition 2 focused almost exclusively on the egg issue. Although switching from a conventional battery cage to a cage-free system would increase the cost of egg production by less than 12 cents per dozen, producers using the conventional battery system would incur a capital cost in switching to cage-free systems and, because California could import eggs from out of state (which it already does with respect to approximately one-third of its shelled eggs) at little or no additional cost, those producers would suffer a competitive disadvantage. Although some farming organizations that use conventional cages opposed Proposition 2, approximately 100 farming organizations supported it. HSUS and other welfare advocates are supporting legislation that would require all eggs in California to come from cage-free systems, which would stop cheaper, conventional eggs from being imported and would result in a very small price increase for eggs sold in California and no competitive disadvantage for

California egg producers. HSUS "says it hopes the California egg industry remains viable so that other states won't see a switch to cage-free hens as an industry-killer."[151]

Reform Does Not Lead to Abolition or Significantly Reduced Use

Many animal advocates recognize that animal welfare regulation is limited but argue that welfare regulation will, at some point in the future, lead to the abolition of animal exploitation or at least to a significant reduction in animal use. I have referred to these advocates as "new welfarists."[152] Singer, Garner, PETA, and most of the large animal advocacy organizations in the United States, Britain, and Europe fall into this category. New welfarists differ from traditional welfarists in that they claim not to see animal welfare reform as an end in itself but rather to see it as a means to eventual abolition of some or all animal use or, at least, to significantly reduced animal use. Almost all of these organizations claim to want regulation that is far more extensive than would have been sought by traditional welfarists. It is, indeed, difficult to find animal advocacy organizations that are welfarist in the traditional sense, including the more conservative groups, such as HSUS and RSPCA. The primary difference between PETA and HSUS is that PETA supports welfare reform but claims that it would like to see an eventual end of animal use; HSUS supports welfare reform but explicitly denies that it wants to eliminate animal use or seeks to pose a threat to agriculture, claiming instead that it wants only to make improvements in the methods of animal exploitation.

The new welfarists are vague as to exactly how welfare reform will lead in an incremental way to abolition or to significantly reduced animal use. To the extent that they provide any insight into how they view the process, it appears as though they see two mechanisms at work. First, they maintain that welfare reform will sensitize people to the problem of animal suffering and that this greater sensitivity will lead people gradually along a path to abolition. Second, new welfarists maintain that welfare reform will increase the price of animal products, and this will result in a decrease in demand for animal products.

The problem with the new welfarist position is that there is absolutely *no* empirical evidence to support it. We have had animal welfare, both as a prevailing moral theory and as part of the law, for more than 200 years now, and we are using more nonhuman animals in more horrific ways than at any time in human history. Animal welfare reform has not led to the abolition of any institutionalized uses of animals. It is, of course, true that some particular practices are no longer extant; some forms of animal use for purely entertainment purposes, for example, are no more, but we still use animals for entertainment, and these animals are often treated every bit as brutally as they were in practices that are no longer extant. In any event, there is absolutely no evidence to support the position that welfare reform sensitizes people in a way that makes society move closer in an incremental way to abolition.

There is certainly no evidence to support the view that welfare reform decreases demand for animal products by making those products more expensive. There are, however, reasons to draw the exact opposite conclusion. First, as discussed previously, welfare reform generally lowers production costs. Even in those cases where it raises production cost, any increased cost is marginal.

Second, even if welfare reform did increase production cost, and did so in a way that required the increased cost to be passed along, in part or in whole, to consumers, it is unlikely that this would affect demand in any significant way. Demand for many animal products is highly inelastic; that is, demand is not particularly sensitive to price increase. For example, although cage-free or free-range systems for laying hens may increase total costs, any such increase may be partly offset by increased production per hen, and any net price increase is unlikely to affect the relatively inelastic demand for eggs. Interestingly, Austria has banned conventional battery cages ahead of the 2012 European Union deadline, and Austrian animal welfare advocates claim that Austrian egg production has dropped by 35 percent.[153] But according to *Statistics Austria*, overall egg production in Austria was 89,271 tons in 2005 and 90,613 tons in 2006. That is an *increase* of 1.5 percent. Overall production jumped to 95,197 tons in 2007, an *increase* of 5.1 percent.[154]

Third, even if costs were increased to the point where consumers were willing to switch to another product, they would in all likelihood be able to get a cheaper product produced under a less stringent welfare standard. This is a consequence of single-market systems, such as those created by the European Economic Community and treaties, such as GATT and NAFTA; member nations cannot, for the most part, prohibit the importation of products because lower welfare standards were employed in the production of those products. For example, Britain supposedly has better welfare standards for pigs, and whether the higher price of British pork is related in whole or part to those welfare standards or to other economic aspects of the industry, Britain is importing cheaper pork and pork products, and these imports are mostly from countries where the welfare standards would violate UK law.[155] In any event, it should be understood that, as a general matter, campaigns that target individual producers, groups of producers, or producers in a geographical region are problematic in that even if the campaign succeeds in affecting the targeted producers or region, if the demand persists, the campaign may be without practical effect.

Fourth, even if costs increased to the point where consumers were no longer willing to purchase a particular animal product, this does not mean that consumers would switch to buying vegetables or tofu. If the price of a particular animal product is sufficiently high to result in a change in demand, consumers will seek another form of animal protein. In a sense, the market for animal protein is infinitely inelastic in that there will always be a cheaper form of animal protein that consumers can switch to if the price of another product becomes too high.

What new welfarists conveniently ignore in claiming that welfare reform will lead incrementally to reduced animal use or even to abolition in the long term is that not only does animal welfare not reduce demand or sensitize society in a way that moves it incrementally in a positive direction, but welfare reforms actually make people feel more comfortable about continuing to exploit animals by reassuring them—falsely—that standards have been improved in meaningful ways. This false reassurance reinforces the notion, which is deeply embedded in our speciesist culture, that it is morally acceptable to use animals as long as they are treated "humanely." The welfarist approach actually supports and strengthens the property paradigm and does not move away from it.

Making society feel more comfortable about animal exploitation is more often than not an explicit goal of animal welfare campaigns and organizations. For example, many of the large animal advocacy groups in the United States and Britain are involved in promoting labeling schemes under which the flesh or products of nonhumans is given a stamp of approval. For example, Humane Farm Animal Care (HFAC), with its partners HSUS, the American Society for the Prevention of Cruelty to Animals, *Animal People*, the World Society for the Protection of Animals, and others, promotes the "Certified Humane Raised & Handled" label,[156] which it describes as "a consumer certification and labeling program" to give consumers assurance that a labeled "egg, dairy, meat or poultry product has been produced with the welfare of the farm animal in mind."[157] HFAC emphasizes that "[i]n 'food animals, stress can affect meat quality . . . and general [animal] health,'"[158] and that the label "creates a win-win-win situation for retailers and restaurants, producers, and consumers. For farmers, the win means they can achieve differentiation, increase market share and increase profitability for choosing more sustainable practices."[159] Retailers win as well because "[n]atural and organic foods have been among the fastest growing grocery categories in recent years. Now grocers, retailers, restaurants, food service operators and producers can benefit from opportunities for sales and profits with Certified Humane Raised & Handled."[160]

The Humane Society International, an arm of HSUS, has launched a "Humane Choice" label in Australia that it claims "will guarantee the consumer that the animal has been treated with respect and care, from birth through to death."[161] A product bearing the "Humane Choice" label assures the consumer of the following:

> [T]he animal has had the best life and death offered to any farm animal. They basically live their lives as they would have done on Old McDonald's farm, being allowed to satisfy their behavioural needs, to forage and move untethered and uncaged, with free access to outside areas, shade when it's hot, shelter when it's cold, with a good diet and a humane death.[162]

Whole Foods Market, Inc., a chain of supermarkets located in the United States, Canada, and Great Britain, claims to be working "with our knowledgeable and passionate meat and poultry providers as well as with forward thinking humane animal treatment experts" in order to "not only improve the quality and the safety of the meat we sell, but also support humane living conditions for the animals."[163] Whole Foods also claims that "species-specific Animal Compassionate Standards, which require environments and conditions that support the animal's physical, emotional, and behavioral needs, are currently being developed. Producers who successfully meet these voluntary Standards will be able to label their products with the special 'Animal Compassionate' designation."[164]

The RSPCA in Britain has the "Freedom Food" label, which is "the farm assurance and food labelling scheme established by the

RSPCA, one of the world's leading animal welfare organisations. The scheme is a charity in its own right, set up in 1994 to improve the welfare of farm animals and offer consumers a higher welfare choice."[165] The RSPCA provides "certification for farmers, hauliers, abattoirs, processors and packers and the scheme approves well-managed free-range, organic and indoor farms."[166] The Freedom Food label "gives consumers the assurance that the scheme is backed by the RSPCA, one of the most respected animal charities in the world."[167] The RSPCA advises that consumers can show their support for improving farm animal welfare and higher welfare standards "by choosing products with the Freedom Food logo."[168] Producers can add value to their animal products because the Freedom Food label "differentiates your product and can give you a competitive advantage. Displaying the Freedom Food logo enables consumers to identify your products as higher welfare."[169] Producers also benefit because of increased margins, the development of a "niche" for "higher welfare" products that allows producers to "widen . . . [the] target market," and "[a]ssociation with the RSPCA, one of the most well known animal welfare charities in the world."[170] Moreover, producers can "[g]ain credibility within the supply chain" and get other economic benefits, including cheaper farm insurance provided through the RSPCA.[171] And the RSPCA will actually help producers to market their animal flesh and other animal products: "We use a variety of marketing tools including advertising, pr, website, exhibitions, sampling and in-store promotions. We also work closely with national retailers to develop joint promotional activities, undertake joint campaigns with the RSPCA and offer marketing support to our members."[172]

Putting aside the matter that these labeling schemes are intended by animal advocates to make the public feel more comfortable about animal exploitation, there are serious questions as to whether these schemes translate into any significant welfare benefit for nonhuman animals. For example, a number of producers who have the RSPCA Freedom Food label have been exposed as engaging in heinous animal abuse.[173] One scholar who has looked at the Whole Foods Animal Compassionate Standards has raised serious questions about whether they will amount to anything more than deceptive corporate branding.[174]

In addition to labeling schemes, animal welfare groups give awards to animal exploiters. For example, PETA gave a "Best Animal-Friendly Retailer" award to Whole Foods, claiming that the corporation "has consistently done more for animal welfare than any retailer in the industry, requiring that its producers adhere to strict standards,"[175] and a "Visionary" award to slaughterhouse designer and meat-industry consultant Temple Grandin, who, according to PETA, has made "improvements to animal-handling systems found in slaughterhouses [that] have decreased the amount of fear and pain that animals experience in their final hours" and who "is widely considered the world's leading expert on the welfare of cattle and pigs."[176] PETA, HSUS, Farm Sanctuary, Peter Singer, and others issued a statement to "express their appreciation and support for the pioneering initiative being taken by Whole Foods Market in setting Farm Animal Compassionate Standards."[177] A leading vegetarian magazine in the United States, *VegNews*, featured Whole Foods CEO John Mackey on its cover[178] and declared him "Corporate Exec of the Year" in 2005.[179] CIWF gives "Good Egg Awards" to those who use, sell, or promote cage-free eggs. Recipients include McDonald's, Sainsbury's, Carrefour, Hellman's Mayonnaise, and Whole Foods.[180]

Animal welfarists also praise animal exploiters who adopt welfare reforms that improve production efficiency. For example, PETA announced a boycott of Kentucky Fried Chicken (KFC) until the company agrees to switch from the electrical stunning of poultry to controlled-atmosphere killing.[181] The Canadian division of KFC agreed to phase in, over an eight-year period, a requirement that suppliers of its chickens use CAK.[182] PETA was "thrilled to announce that KFC Canada has agreed to a historic new animal welfare plan that will dramatically improve the lives and deaths of millions of chickens killed for KFC Canada" and announced that it was "ending its Kentucky Fried Cruelty boycott in Canada."[183] After all, KFC in Canada has, according to PETA, agreed to kill chickens by "gently put[ting] them 'to sleep.'"[184] By lifting the boycott of KFC Canada, PETA implied that it is once again morally acceptable to consume KFC chicken, as long as it is done in Canada and even though the CAK process will not be implemented in Canada for eight more years. Indeed, PETA explicitly urges those concerned to boycott KFC outside Canada *until* it adopts the CAK plan.[185] This clearly encourages people to patronize KFC once the CAK process is adopted. KFC Canada also announced that it would start marketing a vegetarian faux-chicken sandwich, which is fried in the same oil as the real chicken and which comes with mayonnaise. PETA promoted the sandwich, including a "buy one, get one free" downloadable coupon (in English and French) on the PETA Web site, along with a link to locate KFC stores. KFC Canada president Steve Langford stated that once he sat down with the PETA people, "we found out that we had no differences of opinion about how animals should be treated."[186] Matt Prescott of PETA said he believed "that KFC in Canada is genuinely concerned about animal welfare."[187] Prescott added that "[a]ll we want is for KFC worldwide to do what KFC Canada has done."[188] PETA praised McDonald's, claiming that it is "leading the way"[189] in reforming the practices of those who supply fast-food restaurants because it endorsed Temple Grandin's handling and slaughter methods, which Grandin promotes on the basis of economic efficiency. HSUS characterizes as "socially responsible" institutions that serve cage-free eggs.[190] California's Proposition 2, promoted by HSUS and other welfare organizations, was styled as the "California Prevention of Farm Animal Cruelty Act," and upon its passage, HSUS President and CEO Wayne Pacelle said, "California voters have taken a stand for decency and compassion and said that the systemic mistreatment of animals on factory farms cannot continue. All animals deserve humane treatment, including animals raised for food."[191] Putting aside that Proposition 2 will not even come into effect until 2015, this measure will provide no meaningful improvement in animal welfare, let alone the elimination of "the systemic mistreatment of animals on factory farms."[192]

All of this is intended to make people feel better about the exploitation of nonhuman animals, and that is precisely the effect that it is having. There is increasingly abundant media coverage about how people are feeling better about eating meat because they have become "compassionate carnivores."[193] *Reuters* featured an article noting that "[s]ome vegetarians, and those who have reduced their meat consumption because of their conscience or politics, are beginning to eat sustainable meat, choosing products that are not the result of industrial farming practices."[194] Celebrity chefs, such as Wolfgang Puck and Hugh Fearnley-Whittingstall, are leaders in promoting "happy" meat and animal products.[195] A popular author who raises animals for slaughter, Catherine Friend, writes about her "respect" for animals and, in an almost unfathomable expression of moral schizophrenia, shares a "Letter to My Lambs" that she wrote to her lambs being sent to slaughter: "I wish you a safe journey, and I honor your role in my life."[196] A "safe journey" to the slaughterhouse? Friend argues that by not "remaining 'at the table,'"[197] those who do not consume animal products do nothing to shift animal production away from intensive farming and toward "humane," sustainable practices, such as those Friend claims to use. In other words, those who do not consume "happy" animal flesh and products are actually harming animals. Similarly, in promoting the KFC faux-chicken sandwich, PETA was asked about the fact that the patty was cooked in the same oil as the non-faux chicken. PETA responded that advocates should not complain because "we run the risk of making vegetarianism/veganism appear to be difficult, unpleasant, or outright annoying, which will likely turn off others from even considering adopting a vegetarian diet—and that does harm animals."[198]

That this is not recognized as outright absurdity is attributable in large part to the fact that Peter Singer, often referred to as the "father of the animal rights movement" and described by Garner and others as a "radical,"[199] describes being a "conscientious omnivore" as a "defensible ethical position"[200] and claims that those concerned about animal ethics can indulge in "the luxury of free range eggs, or possibly even meat from animals who live good lives under conditions natural for their species, and are then humanely killed on the farm."[201] It is, of course, not the case that these "happy" products represent any significant improvement in the protection of animal interests, and in any event, it is clear that the welfarist approach is not taking incremental steps toward abolition or reduced animal use. On the contrary, we are consuming more animals than ever before on a per capita basis. And we should not be surprised that PETA is telling people that they should eat a non-vegan sandwich fried in the same oil as chicken because otherwise they will be harming animals by making veganism "appear to be difficult, unpleasant, or outright annoying." After all, as we saw earlier and as we see in the next section, Singer explicitly argues that we may have a moral obligation not to be vegan in situations in which others will be annoyed or disconcerted by insistence on veganism.[202]

In sum, the new welfarists have enthusiastically embraced the position that the moral issue is not *that* we are using animals, but only *how* we use them, and that our use of nonhumans is morally justifiable as long as our treatment is acceptable. Rather than representing incremental steps toward abolition or reduced animal use, the new welfarist approach perpetuates and perhaps even increases animal exploitation by encouraging an uninformed public to believe that our treatment of animals has improved and that they can now consume animals without a guilty conscience and by reinforcing the traditional welfarist notion that animal use is morally acceptable as long as the level of treatment is acceptable. Institutionalized exploiters recognize this. For example, Randy

Strauss of Strauss Veal and Lamb International, Inc., who was mentioned at the outset of this chapter, claims to want "to revolutionize the veal industry" by replacing the traditional veal crate with group stalls over the next several years.[203] Strauss, citing the European experience, where consumers increased their consumption of veal when Europe converted from the crate to the group stalls, recognizes that "[t]here are a growing number of people who, if they feel good about what they're eating, will eat veal."[204] Strauss wants to "capture that market" so that he can "increase the 0.6-pound per capita consumption market resulting in a healthier veal industry."[205] HSUS described Strauss's decision as "historic."[206] A consistent theme that runs through the literature of industrial suppliers of animal products is the recognition that the public perception of increased animal welfare can only help the particular industry by boosting demand. Given that most welfare reforms actually increase production efficiency, welfare reform is very smart business.

The new welfarists are in error in that welfare reform does not move us away from the property paradigm; on the contrary, welfare reform relies on and reinforces the property status of animals in at least two respects. First, welfare reform is, as we have seen, always predicated on the notion that we may use animals as long as we treat them reasonably well and kill them in a relatively painless way. That is, welfarism does not challenge our use per se of animals; it challenges only our treatment of them. Second, welfare reform is almost always limited by the economic benefits that producers or consumers will enjoy if the reform is adopted. That is, welfare reform perpetuates the notion that animals are economic commodities without inherent or intrinsic value. Animal welfare will never be an incremental step toward anything but more animal exploitation and greater acceptance of that exploitation by a public that mistakenly believes, as a result of the propaganda of animal advocates, that it has been made more "humane."

Garner argues that only those who are willing to pursue moderate reforms and who are willing to negotiate with politicians and institutional animal users can get what he calls "insider status" that allows them to influence government policy or industry practice.[207] If the preceding discussion shows anything, it is that the animal advocacy movement has embraced the pursuit of moderate reforms and actively seeks insider status and that the result has been disastrous. Simply put, the animal advocacy movement—from traditionally conservative groups, such as the RSPCA and HSUS, to newer, supposedly more progressive groups, such as PETA—has merged into an enterprise that has embraced Singer's position that suffering and not killing, treatment and not use, is the moral problem and that "compassionate consumption" is the answer.

Garner claims that a number of advocacy groups are abolitionist as a philosophical matter and seek abolition in the long term but advocate welfare reforms in the short term as a strategic or pragmatic matter.[208] He cites CIWF as an example of such an organization.[209] In addition to giving awards to those who use or market "humane" products, CIWF has a campaign that promotes supposedly higher welfare standards as a way of strengthening the British pork industry.[210] Therefore, CIWF, which Garner argues has an abolitionist philosophy, implements that philosophy by promoting supposed welfare reforms that CIWF maintains will rescue and cause to prosper an industry that is presently "under serious threat." Perhaps this makes sense to Garner; it makes absolutely no sense to me. Garner also cites PETA as an example of a "radical" organization.[211] Again, this is perplexing given that PETA's campaigns very explicitly and deliberately reinforce the property status of animals. To say that such groups as CIWF and PETA really want abolition as a long-term goal is no different from saying that a political leader who starts a war really wants to achieve world peace as a long-term goal.

Conclusion

The new welfarist approach has made business partners out of the animal advocacy movement and institutional exploiters. The animal advocacy groups get to declare victory—and to fundraise—when legislation or voluntary industry agreement results in a change in practice that was inefficient and that would have been changed anyway, or in a change that adds a de minimis amount to production costs but that has no real effect on the bottom line either because demand for the product is inelastic or because "compassionate consumers" will actually increase demand for the product. Industry gets to reassure the public that they really do care about animals and that consumers can, in the words of Randy Strauss, "fully enjoy veal with the satisfaction of knowing that veal calves are raised in a humane manner." Corporations such as McDonald's, KFC, and Whole Foods can point to the endorsement of large animal advocacy organizations and prominent animal advocates, and they can even get direct marketing help from animal advocates if they adopt one of the increasing number of the labeling schemes sponsored or approved of by animal organizations.

Wayne Pacelle of HSUS attempts to show abolitionists the error of their ways by positing an analogy in the field of human rights. He argues that the abolitionist critique of animal welfare is analogous to saying that Amnesty International should not oppose the torture of political prisoners because those people should not be in jail at all.[212] Pacelle's argument assumes that welfare reform actually does stop the torture of nonhuman animals or at least mitigates that torture in some significant way. That assumption is not only unsupported but even contradicted by the facts. But assuming that welfare reform actually did provide a meaningful welfare benefit, the appropriate analogy would be to ask whether Amnesty International would praise and support a repressive regime because it substituted one form of torture for another that was actually less painful. As was discussed in the first section, it is, of course, always better to inflict less harm than more. If Joe decides to murder Jim, it is better that Joe not torture him as well as kill him and, if Joe does torture him, it is better if he does so only by shocking Jim rather than by both shocking and burning him. We would, however, be appalled if Amnesty International campaigned for more "humane" murder or gave Joe an award for shocking Jim rather than burning and shocking him. Pacelle's example proves the abolitionist point.

Humane Farm Animal Care, which, with HSUS and its other partners, promotes the "Certified Humane Raised and Handled" label, hits the nail on the head when it says that its label "creates a win-win-win situation for retailers and restaurants, producers, and consumers." How true. Only the animals lose.

Animal Rights: Utopian or Pragmatic?

New welfarists often argue that the animal rights/abolitionist approach is utopian or idealistic and does not provide any practical normative guidance. According to these critics, abolitionists want nothing short of the immediate abolition of exploitation, and they reject any sort of incremental or practical change as a means to the end of achieving that abolition.[213] The new welfarists are certainly correct to say that abolitionists want to end all animal exploitation and would like to see it all end tomorrow, or even later today. But no one thinks that is possible, and the welfarists are wrong to say that abolitionists reject incremental change. The abolitionists reject regulatory change that seeks to make exploitation more "humane" or that reinforces the property status of animals; they instead seek change that incrementally eradicates the property status of nonhumans and recognizes that nonhumans have inherent value. The abolitionist position provides definite normative guidance for incremental change both on an individual and social level.

Veganism

On the individual level, rights theory prescribes incremental change in the form of ethical veganism.[214] Although veganism may represent a matter of diet or lifestyle for some, ethical veganism is a profound moral and political commitment to abolition on the individual level and extends not only to matters of food but also to the wearing or using of animal products. Ethical veganism is the personal rejection of the commodity status of nonhuman animals, of the notion that animals have only external value, and of the notion that animals have less moral value than do humans. Indeed, ethical veganism is the *only* position that is consistent with the recognition that for purposes of being treated as a thing, the lives of humans and nonhumans are morally equivalent. Ethical veganism must be the unequivocal moral baseline of any social and political movement that recognizes that nonhuman animals have inherent or intrinsic moral value and are not resources for human use.

The more people who become vegan for ethical reasons, the stronger will be the cultural notion that animals have a moral right not to be treated as commodities. If we are ever going to effect any significant change in our treatment of animals and one day end that use, it is imperative that there be a social and political movement that actively seeks abolition and regards veganism as its moral baseline. As long as a majority of people think that eating animals and animal products is a morally acceptable behavior, nothing will change. There may be a larger selection of "happy meat" and other fare for affluent "conscientious omnivores" or "compassionate consumers," but this will not abolish animal exploitation or do anything other than make society more comfortable with exploitation and thereby entrench it more deeply.

The welfarist says, in essence, "if we are going to eat or use an animal product, then this is the morally better one to choose." This position sidesteps whether the behavior in the "if" clause is morally acceptable. The rights position maintains clearly that there is no normal circumstance under which the behavior in the "if" clause is morally acceptable. The rights position promotes veganism because only when people see that the "if" is problematic will they even recognize our use of nonhuman animals as the fundamental moral issue and appreciate the problem with animal welfare, which focuses only on treatment. We will never even be able to see the moral problem with animal use as long as we are continuing to use animals. We will never find our moral compass as long as animals are on our plates, on our backs or feet, or in the lotions that we apply to our faces. We will never adequately address our moral schizophrenia as long as animals are nothing more than resources or economic commodities whose interests, including their interest in continuing to exist, can be ignored if we get some benefit from doing so.

Animal advocates who claim to favor animal rights and to want to abolish animal exploitation but who continue to eat or use animal products are no different from those who claimed to be in favor of human rights but who continued to own slaves. We marvel that people who campaigned so passionately for the "rights of man" could exclude slaves and women. Those campaigners were locked in their eighteenth-century "if" clause in that they assumed that it was acceptable to deny personhood to women and slaves and that the only question was how they were treated. Just as slavery represented the institutionalized commodification of humans, meat, dairy, eggs, animal clothing, and animal products represent the institutional commodification of nonhumans.

Moreover, there is no coherent distinction between meat and dairy or eggs. Animals exploited in the dairy and egg industries live longer, are treated worse, and end up in the same slaughterhouse as their counterparts killed for meat. There is as much suffering and death in dairy and egg products as in flesh products, if not more, but there is certainly no morally relevant distinction among them. To not eat beef but still drink milk makes as little sense as eating flesh from large cows but not from small cows. Moreover, there is also no morally relevant distinction between a cow and a fish or other sentient sea animal for purposes of treating either as a human resource. We may more easily recognize the pain or suffering of a cow because, like us, she is a mammal. But that is not a reason to ignore the suffering or death of the billions of sentient fish and other sea animals whom we kill annually.

The most important form of incremental change on a social level is creative, nonviolent education about veganism and the need to abolish, not merely regulate, the institutionalized exploitation of animals. The animal advocacy movement in the United States has seriously failed to educate the public about the need to abolish animal exploitation. Although there are many reasons for this failure, a primary one is that animal advocacy groups find it easier to promote welfarist campaigns aimed at reducing "unnecessary" suffering that have little practical effect and where the reforms are ultimately embraced by the industry involved. Such campaigns are easy for advocates to package and sell, and they do not offend anyone. It is easier to tell people that they can be morally conscientious omnivores than it is to take the position that veganism is a moral baseline. That, however, is precisely the problem. No one disagrees with the principle that it is wrong to inflict "unnecessary" suffering and that we ought to treat animals "humanely." But, as 200 years of animal welfare have made plain, these are merely platitudes in light of the property status of animals.

Veganism and creative, positive, nonviolent vegan education provide practical and incremental strategies both in terms of reducing animal suffering now and in terms of building a movement in the future that will be able to obtain more meaningful legislation in the form of prohibitions of animal use rather than mere "humane" welfare regulation. If, in the late 1980s, when the animal advocacy community in the United States decided very deliberately to pursue a welfarist agenda rather than an abolitionist one, a substantial portion of movement resources had been invested in vegan education and advocacy, there likely would be many hundreds of thousands more vegans than there are today. That is a very conservative estimate given the many millions of dollars that have been expended by animal advocacy groups to promote welfarist legislation and initiatives. The increased number of vegans would reduce suffering more by decreasing demand for animal products than all of the supposed welfarist successes put together.[215] Increasing the number of vegans would also help to build a political and economic base required for the social change that is a necessary predicate for legal change. Given that there is limited time, and there are limited financial resources available, expansion of animal welfare is not a rational and efficient choice if we seek abolition in the long term. Indeed, traditional animal welfare is not an effective way of reducing animal suffering in the short term.[216]

Moreover, it is important for animal advocates to be engaged in efforts to educate society at all levels and through all media about animal exploitation and the moral basis for its abolition. At the present time, the prevailing moral norm, reflected in the law, is that it is morally acceptable to use nonhumans for human purposes as long as animals are treated "humanely." As a result, the social debate focuses on what constitutes "humane" treatment, and many advocates spend their time trying to convince members of the public that larger cages are better than smaller cages or that gassing chickens is better than slitting their throats. The debate should be shifted in the direction of animal use and the indisputable fact that humans have no coherent moral justification for continuing to use nonhumans, however "humanely" they are treated. This requires that advocates educate themselves about the ethical arguments against animal use and that they engage in creative ways to make those arguments accessible to the general public. Given that most people accept that nonhumans are members of the moral community in some sense—that is, they already at least think that they reject the notion that animals are merely things—it is challenging, but not impossible, to get people to see that membership in the moral community means that we stop using animals altogether.

Educational efforts can take myriad forms, such as the following:

- Giving presentations at local educational institutions at all levels (grammar schools, high schools, community colleges, and colleges and universities) and engaging in other educational campaigns
- Distributing accessible literature about veganism and abolition
- Providing samples of vegan food at local community events
- Writing editorials and essays for newspapers and magazines
- Doing Web sites, blogs, podcasts, and other online activities concerning veganism and abolition
- Organizing lawful boycotts of companies not because they sell meat or dairy or eggs that are less "humanely" produced than the animal parts or products of other companies but because they are selling meat, dairy, or eggs at all

These activities represent a small fraction of what can be done. The opportunities are limited only by imagination. It is not necessary to have a great deal of money or to be part of a large organization to be an effective educator. Indeed, the sort of pervasive social change that is necessary requires a strong grassroots movement where neighbors educate neighbors. The paradigm shift will not occur as the result of a highly salaried corporate welfarist coming to town, giving a lecture, and flying out. As I have discussed elsewhere, the corporate movement has very deliberately eviscerated grassroots activism in the United States and is well on the way to doing so in Europe as well.[217] Activism has become writing a check to an organization that, most of the time, already has a great deal of money. But the pendulum is swinging back, largely as the result of the Internet, which has lowered the opportunity costs of communication and has facilitated networking among similarly minded activists, who can bypass the large organizations and their efforts to control the discourse about issues. These activists, often from different countries, can work together to create materials and provide mutual support and can take the fruits of their efforts into their local communities. Advocates do not have to have graduate degrees or be professional educators to be able to engage in effective abolitionist education. They need only have the willingness to learn some basic ideas and to think about how to bring those ideas to life in a creative way that will resonate with the public, much of which already cares about animals and is surprisingly receptive to arguments about animal rights and the abolition of animal use.

Because welfarists have a vested interest in perpetuating the status quo, they almost always miss the opportunity to help shift the paradigm. An example of this occurred in the 2007 scandal involving American football player Michael Vick's prosecution for his involvement in a dogfighting enterprise. The amount of media coverage about this in the United States and abroad was remarkable, and the animal advocacy community predictably chimed in about the need to increase penalties for dogfighting and the need to ensure that Vick was adequately punished. Vick's actions were clearly reprehensible, but how was he any different from the rest of us who participate in perhaps more removed but equally culpable forms of animal exploitation? For example, is there any morally meaningful difference between watching dogs fight and sitting around the summer barbecue grilling the flesh of animals who were tortured every bit as much as Vick's dogs? Those who barbecue did not observe with enjoyment the slaughter of those animals. But so what? Neither activity can be claimed to be justified morally. Both activities involve a reason no greater than pleasure: Vick derived pleasure from watching dogs rip each other part;

most of us derive pleasure from eating meat or other animal products. There is no necessity or even plausible claim of necessity in either case. But Vick's activity was treated as some sort of aberration meriting various sorts of punishment rather than as something that is very similar to what is regarded as normal. The Vick case presented a marvelous opportunity for animal advocates to highlight our moral schizophrenia about nonhuman animals, but this opportunity was lost in favor of a welfarist feeding frenzy focused on Michael Vick and dogfighting. The very best that can be said is that the Vick case raised public consciousness about dogfighting, but very few people approved of that activity before the Vick matter. An educational opportunity concerning the relationship between dogfighting and forms of animal exploitation that most people regard as acceptable was lost.

I wrote an essay titled "We're All Michael Vick," published in a major American newspaper, that argued that non-vegans should think more carefully before assuming a holier-than-thou attitude about Michael Vick.[218] I received over one thousand e-mails and letters about the essay, which clearly had provoked thinking about the issue of eating animal products. There were some who agreed with my position and some who disagreed. But most important was the large number of messages I received from people who said, in essence, that they had never before thought about the issue in this way and that I had gotten them to consider veganism as a rational and not an extreme reaction to the moral schizophrenia that characterizes the human–nonhuman relationship. Some wrote subsequently to say that they had become or were in the process of becoming vegans. But the experience made clear that if the animal advocacy community, with its billions of dollars and access to media, had used the Vick case as an opportunity to teach and educate, rather than to condemn Michael Vick for dogfighting and to fundraise on that narrow issue, it could have started an interesting discussion that, while probably falling on many deaf ears, would have fallen on receptive ears as well. And it would have served the important function of provoking people to think differently about the matter of animal ethics.

Rather than embrace veganism as a clear moral baseline, the animal advocacy movement has instead adopted the notion that we can consume animal products in a morally conscientious way. To the extent that welfarists promote veganism, they promote "flexible veganism," which they see as a way of reducing suffering along with welfarist reforms that they promote as reducing suffering. That is, welfarists restrict the scope of animal ethics to suffering. Therefore, anything that reduces that suffering—from being what Singer calls a "conscientious omnivore" to being vegan (but not all of the time) to being vegetarian to promoting cage-free eggs—is morally desirable. Welfarists do not accept veganism as a moral baseline because veganism is just one way of reducing suffering, and if someone is not a vegan but is supposedly reducing suffering in some other way, such as by promoting or eating cage-free eggs, then that is a defensible ethical position as well. Vegan Outreach, a group that promotes welfare reform and campaigns on college campuses to get dining halls to serve cage-free eggs, maintains that veganism "is not an end in itself. It is not a dogma or religion, nor a list of forbidden ingredients or immutable laws—it is only a tool for opposing cruelty and reducing suffering."[219] And there may even be times when we have an obligation not to be vegans. For example, Singer, who describes himself as a "flexible vegan" who does not eat vegan when traveling or visiting others, argues that when one orders a vegan meal in a restaurant, but it comes with animal products in it, sending it back results in wasting food, and "if you're in company with people who are not vegan or not even vegetarian, I think that's probably the wrong thing to do. It'd be better off just to eat it because people are going to think, 'Oh my god, these vegans ...'"[220] This welfarist position on veganism is problematic for a number of reasons.

First, the welfarist position on veganism assumes that the welfarist measures that are promoted as reducing suffering actually do reduce suffering. But we established here that most welfare reforms do not significantly (or at all) reduce animal suffering. For example, the notion that enriched cages or cage-free barns represent a significant improvement over conventional battery eggs is highly questionable at best. Moreover, welfarist reforms often make the exploitation of animals more economically efficient as well as make the public feel more comfortable about animal exploitation.

Second, the welfarist/new welfarist position on veganism reflects the view, discussed in the first section of this chapter, that animal life has a lesser moral value than human life. That is, welfarism from Bentham to Singer is clear on the point that although nonhumans suffer, and their suffering should not be discounted solely on the basis of species (although species may be relevant to our qualitative assessment of animal suffering), animals do not have the sort of self-awareness that gives them an interest in their lives. Killing animals is not the problem; animals do not care *that* we use them; they care only about *how* we use them. In connection with his support for the Whole Foods Animal Compassionate Standards and the use of the word "compassionate" in this context, Singer stated, "There might be some people who say, 'You can't be compassionate if you end up killing the animals.' I just think that's wrong. . . . I think as long as the standards really are compassionate ones, that do as much as they can to give the animals decent lives before they're killed, I don't have a problem with it."[221]

If one accepts that animals do not have an interest in continued existence that is separate and apart from their interest in not suffering—and I have provided reasons in the first section of this chapter that merit the rejection of any such view—then it is understandable that one would see anything that reduces suffering as morally indistinguishable from anything else that reduces suffering. Something that is done to respect life per se is not meaningful if the being whose life is respected does not care about her life. Given that welfarists generally are—and Singer certainly is—utilitarian, it seems that there would be some assessment of whether particular ways of reducing suffering are, as a consequential matter, more effective than others. That is, if, as I maintain, veganism not only respects animal life but also reduces suffering more effectively through reducing demand for animal products, one would think that even a utilitarian would urge veganism as having a greater benefit than, say, promoting a welfarist reform that may not reduce suffering at all and may indeed increase net suffering by lowering production costs and increasing demand or making consumers feel better about continuing to eat animal products or eating more of them. But welfarists, including Singer, do not seem to accept this analysis.

Third, the welfarists draw a line between being vegetarian, which generally means not eating animal flesh (although many vegetarians seem somewhat oddly to think that fish flesh is not the flesh of an animal), and being an omnivore. They assume in a utilitarian sense that it is better to be a vegetarian than to be an omnivore. The truth of that assumption is not at all clear. As I discussed earlier, a very good argument can be made that dairy products and eggs may involve more suffering than meat. It is very common for those who give up flesh to eat more dairy and eggs. So in a consequential sense, being a vegetarian may actually result in more suffering. Moreover, it is simply wrong as an empirical matter to say, as some do, that flesh is the result of death and that eggs and dairy products can be produced without killing an animal. Death is a necessary part of the production of *any* animal product.

Fourth, new welfarists often argue that because no one can be a perfect vegan, given that it is impossible to avoid all animal products, which are present in many things with which we come into contact and over which we have no control, insistence on veganism as a moral baseline is meaningless. For example, PETA points out that bicycle tires and road surfaces may contain animal products and that the production of vegetables and fruits results in harm to animals; therefore, PETA claims that adherence to veganism as a matter of principle is a matter of "personal purity," "narcissistic cultural fad," and "fanatical obsession."[222] Singer also describes being a consistent vegan as "fanatical."[223] Although it is impossible to avoid all contact with animal products, it does not follow that it makes no difference whether we are vegans. The welfarist position in this regard is no different from the position that because we will never completely eliminate horrible violations of human rights, it makes no difference whether we respect the rights of another human in situations in which we have control. Presumably, Singer would not choose to stay in a restaurant if he learned that those who worked in the kitchen were human slaves, even if the slaves had finished working for the evening.

The choice of materials used in road surfacing is not a matter within my control; the choice of what I eat, wear, or use on my body *is* under my control. Moreover, the new welfarist position fails to recognize the distinction between direct and indirect harm. When we build a road, we know that humans will be killed on that road. But that is surely different from our murdering a particular person. Similarly, the fact that animals are accidentally or incidentally killed in the cultivation of crops is different morally from intentionally killing individual animals.

Like Singer, PETA maintains that if we adhere to veganism in situations in which others will be discouraged from becoming vegan, then we actually have done something morally wrong and have an obligation *not* to be vegan in those circumstances: "If you do something that prevents another person from adopting a vegan diet, if your example puts up a barrier where you might have built a bridge, that hurts animals."[224] The PETA/Singer position is problematic on its own consequentialist terms because it assumes that not observing veganism will make it easier to persuade others to go vegan. But it is as likely that the opposite is true. By eating the dish covered in cheese or sprinkled with pork bits, or not inquiring of the server whether the dish has butter or cream or chicken stock, so as not to make a fuss, the animal advocate reinforces the notion that we should not take seriously that our consumption of animal products violates the fundamental moral rights of animals. Her behavior reinforces the notion that the lives of animals have less moral value than the lives of humans and that morality, as it applies to animals, is a matter of convenience. It is just as likely as a matter of consequence alone that such an event may serve as an opportunity for the animal advocate to educate her companions about why she views the moral issue as she does and thereby influence their thinking about the issue.

The PETA/Singer position is also problematic because, once again, it reveals the underlying welfarist notion that nonhumans matter less morally than humans. Would anyone, including the welfarists, maintain that, in order to establish a connection with pedophiles or rapists, we should participate in an act of pedophilia or rape? Should we, in order to build a bridge to racists, participate in a white power march? Should we, in order to have greater influence with our friends on the issue of sexism, patronize strip clubs? Of course not. But where animals are involved, welfarists have no problem advising conduct that they would never propose in the context of human rights violations.

Fifth, welfarists often claim that veganism is a matter of personal choice or lifestyle and should not be identified as a baseline moral principle of the rights movement. But that claim is incoherent. If eating or otherwise consuming or using animal products is merely a matter of personal choice, then why aren't rodeos or hunting or animal fighting all matters of personal choice or lifestyle? This is similar to the antislavery movement maintaining that the ownership of slaves was a matter of personal choice or lifestyle, or the women's rights movement maintaining that equal pay for equal work is properly a matter of the employer's personal choice. If animal exploitation is a matter of lifestyle or personal choice, it is not a matter of moral principle, and if it is not a matter of moral principle, then the notion of animal ethics is without meaning.

Sixth, it is clear that the welfarist rejection of veganism as a moral baseline is also related to the purely pragmatic self-interests of large, wealthy animal organizations that are more concerned with the size of their donor bases than with the moral message that they promote. For example, according to PETA, half of the PETA membership is not even vegetarian.[225] An organization whose membership is half non-vegetarians and half vegetarians (but not necessarily vegans) is not likely to respond favorably to the position that veganism is a moral baseline. This may account, at least in part, for why PETA's campaigns are welfarist and why it gives awards to sellers of "happy" meat and animal products and to slaughterhouse designers. While talking out of one side of its organizational mouth about veganism, PETA talks out of the other side about compassionate consumerism. The result is tremendous confusion, but that confusion allows PETA to seek a donor base that includes people who eat at McDonald's or buy "Animal Compassionate" meat at Whole Foods. This may make terrific business sense for PETA, but it does nothing to stop animal exploitation. If anything, it encourages people to believe that eating at McDonald's, which, according to PETA, is "leading the way" in fast-food animal welfare, or at KFC, which, according to PETA, "is genuinely concerned about animal welfare," is a form of activism for animals. Moreover, to the extent that animal advocates continue to support the consumption of animal products as the normal or default position, they necessarily keep veganism marginalized and facilitate its characterization as radical or extreme or as a matter of lifestyle choice, rather than as a nonnegotiable moral baseline.

Single-Issue Campaigns

In the preceding section, I argued that the claim that the rights/abolitionist approach does not provide any normative guidance as to incremental change is wrong. I argued that change at the individual level should take the form of ethical veganism, and change at the social or political level should take the form primarily of creative education concerning veganism and why we should seek to abolish, and not merely regulate, animal exploitation. The need for such education is particularly urgent at the present time when the overwhelming number of people regard animal use as normal or natural.

Many animal advocates, including ones who are committed to veganism, believe that incremental change on the social or legal level is best achieved by the old standby of the animal movement, the "single-issue" campaign, which focuses on some particular use or practice. Single-issue campaigns can involve efforts to get legislation to address the issue or efforts to motivate industry to make voluntarily changes, or they may involve general educational activities designed to get people to change their behavior. Organizations use single-issue campaigns as a primary vehicle for fundraising.

To the extent that any single-issue campaign focuses on regulating some use or practice to make it more "humane," the rights or abolitionist approach would, for the reasons that I have discussed previously, reject the campaign. Welfarist single-issue campaigns, whether promoted by large animal corporations or enacted at the grassroots level, do nothing to move nonhumans away from property status and, for the most part, reinforce that status and the cornerstone of welfarist ideology—that animals are resources to be used by us as long as we treat them "humanely."

But what about a single-issue campaign that seeks to prohibit or abolish a particular use or practice? For example, what about a campaign that maintains that we should abolish the use of animals for the purposes of making fur garments, without regard to what animals are involved (some campaigns focus on dogs and cats) or how the animals are raised or killed (some campaigns distinguish between animals raised on fur farms and those trapped or snared in the wild)? Although such a campaign does not present the same problems as those that propose making a use or practice more "humane," any single-issue campaign, including those that seek to prohibit something rather than regulate it, runs the risk of conveying the impression that certain forms of exploitation are worse than others. In the context of the fur campaign, the problem is that fur is characterized as involving some greater degree of exploitation than, say, wool or leather. But any such characterization would be inaccurate. Both wool and leather are every bit as morally objectionable as fur, in terms of both the horrible suffering involved and the fact that irrespective of any differences in suffering, all three forms of clothing involve killing animals for human purposes.

A campaign against meat conveys the impression that there is a meaningful moral distinction between flesh and other animal products, such as milk or eggs. The single-issue animal campaign cannot be analogized to, for example, a campaign to end genocide that focuses on Darfur but not Somalia. Genocide is regarded as wrong; a campaign to end genocide in one place does not imply that genocide in the other is morally distinguishable or acceptable. But in a society that regards eating all animal products as normal and acceptable, a campaign against meat most certainly implies that there is a moral distinction between meat on one hand and other animal products on the other. To find proof of this, we need look no further than the large number of people who claim to be vegetarians on moral grounds but who are not vegans. Finally, all single-issue campaigns tend to undermine the idea that is central to the rights position: that *any* instrumental use of non-humans violates the interests that animals have in not being treated as human resources.

In addition to being unsound as a matter of theory, single-issue campaigns, including those that purport to go beyond making exploitation more "humane" and to prohibit or abolish some particular use, have not had much practical effect. The fur campaign, which is the longest-standing single-issue campaign in the history of animal protection, is an excellent example of a campaign that has failed miserably. The fur industry is as strong as it ever has been, both as a matter of sales and as a matter of public opinion.[226] The campaign against foie gras in the United States resulted in legislation in California that was so weak that it was actually supported by California's only foie gras producer[227] and resulted in an ordinance in Chicago that was subsequently repealed.[228]

The practical difficulties with single-issue campaigns are related to their theoretical problems. That is, single-issue campaigns suggest that there is a distinction to be made among animal uses. The fur campaign, for instance, suggests that there is a moral distinction between fur and wool or leather or between using animals for clothing and using them for food. But there is no meaningful distinction to be made, and this point is not lost on those who oppose the fur campaign and claim that animal advocates who oppose fur are really out to end the use of animals for all clothing, food, and other purposes. Most animal advocates respond to this sort of challenge by denying the existence of an overall goal of abolishing all animal use and by trying to isolate fur as a discrete animal use that is unnecessary or cruel and should be prohibited. Animal advocates may think that this is an effective strategy, but it assumes that the public is much less intelligent than it is. Anyone who thinks about the matter even superficially realizes that there is no distinction and, because the animal advocacy movement has very deliberately refused to take the position that any animal use is morally unjustifiable, the public quite correctly regards targeting the use of animals for fur (or other particular purpose) as arbitrary.

This situation repeats itself over and over. In opposing particular instances of hunting, animal advocates are usually very careful to make clear that they do not oppose the consumption of all animal products, but that they oppose only the hunting event in question. Again, most people who think about the matter for more than a minute recognize that the animals whose corpses are sold in the supermarket suffer as much as or more than animals who are hunted and killed. Because rejecting all animal products is not on the table (so to speak)—the animal advocacy movement has very deliberately chosen not to place it there—opposing hunting quite correctly appears as arbitrary.

To the extent that advocates want to pursue single-issue campaigns, and I advise strongly against these campaigns, they should at least pursue prohibitions of significant animal uses rather than regulations that supposedly ensure more "humane" treatment, and they should do so in a context that explicitly recognizes the inherent value of nonhumans and makes clear that *no* animal exploitation can be justified morally.[229] A campaign that seeks to stop all animal use in circuses based on the inherent value of animals and as an explicit part of an overall effort to end all animal exploitation may at least represent some movement away from the property paradigm in a way that a campaign that seeks larger cages for circus animals does not. A campaign by university students to stop the use of animals in the classroom as part of an overall opposition to vivisection and animal exploitation generally is better than a campaign that seeks more "humane" treatment for animals used in the classroom. In other words, for a single-issue campaign to avoid conveying the impression that some forms of exploitation are less objectionable than others, the campaign should always be explicitly linked with an abolitionist message. Such campaigns may not have a realistic chance of success at this point in time, given the level of social discourse about animal ethics, but they might help to move that discourse in an abolitionist direction and thereby serve to raise consciousness about animal rights.

I reiterate, however, that I strongly advise against single-issue campaigns because they almost always reinforce the notion that certain forms of animal exploitation are better than others. Indeed, part of the appeal of these campaigns is that they permit large organizations to promote the notion that we can discharge our individual moral obligation to nonhumans by doing something less than embracing ethical veganism and discharge our overall obligation to them by doing less than abolishing all animal use. It is not coincidental that single-issue campaigns are the stock-in-trade of almost all large animal organizations.

Companion Animals

Welfarists often claim that the animal rights/abolitionist position is inconsistent with sharing one's home with dogs, cats, and other "companion animals." The recognition that animals have a right not to be treated as the property of humans would most certainly mean that we should stop bringing domesticated nonhumans into existence, and this would include dogs and cats. Although some humans treat their nonhuman companions well, many do not. Again, although bad treatment is worse than good treatment, the focus on treatment misses the point. However well we treat our nonhuman companions, they are completely dependent on humans for every aspect of their existence, and the best of living situations still involve what is a very unnatural situation for these animals.[230] Moreover, in the end, they are still our property.

But the rights/abolitionist position does not hold that we should not engage in and support efforts to find good homes for those nonhumans who exist now. Rescue and adoption efforts that lead to situations in which nonhumans are accorded inherent value are not analogous to efforts to make animal exploitation more "humane," and they constitute a form of incremental change that is consistent with a rights or abolitionist approach. Sterilization programs, although not ideal, are consistent with the abolitionist approach, as are programs where feral cats are trapped, sterilized, and returned to managed colonies.

The rights position does reject the position promoted widely by welfarists that the "humane" killing of healthy animals is morally acceptable. For example, PETA kills the overwhelming number of animals that it takes in at its animal facility.[231] The welfarist movement generally supports and has historically supported the idea that unwanted animals can be killed if the method of death is "humane." This position is not surprising given that, as discussed earlier, welfarists, following Singer, do not regard the killing of animals, as opposed to the suffering of animals, as a moral problem.

Violence as Incremental Change

The rights/abolitionist approach as I have developed it rejects the notion that violence is an appropriate way of effecting incremental change.[232] In the interest of disclosure, I embrace a nonviolent ethic as a general matter. There is, however, a more narrow and generally accepted basis from which to derive the conclusion that the use of violence cannot be justified. This alternate basis concerns the view that it is wrong to use violence in an arbitrary way or against those who are no more related to the targeted injustice than others.

Those who advocate violence in the context of animal exploitation maintain that it is acceptable to use violence against institutional exploiters, such as farmers, furriers, vivisectors, and so on. But these institutional exploiters do what they do because the rest of us demand that they do so. If we stopped demanding animal products, the producers of those products would put their capital into other activities. Although government and industry presently help to create and support the demand for animal products, we can choose to ignore their encouragement, and as a political matter, we can reject government policies that support animal products. If a sufficient number of people became vegan, the incentive for government support for animal use would diminish. So the responsibility for animal exploitation rests, to a very considerable degree, on those who demand animal products. This includes all of those "conscientious omnivores" or non-vegan animal advocates who consume cage-free eggs and "happy" meat. I suppose that it is easier to characterize farmers as the "enemy," but that ignores the reality of the situation.

What about the vivisector, a common target of those who advocate violence? Putting aside the debate about whether vivisection actually produces data useful to address problems of human health, most of the illnesses for which vivisectors are supposedly using animals to find cures are conditions that could be avoided entirely or drastically reduced if humans would stop eating animal foods and engaging in such destructive behaviors as smoking, excessive alcohol consumption, drug use, and failure to exercise. Again, who is the real culprit? I certainly do not think that vivisection is justifiable for any reason, but I find it curious that those who advocate violence can see vivisectors as detached from the social conditions that give rise to the illnesses that supposedly require vivisection—and in these conditions we are all complicit.

In addition, we must not forget that there are always multiple ways of addressing health problems. Vivisection is one way and, in the view of many (including myself), is not a particularly effective choice. The decision to invest social resources in vivisection, rather than in other, arguably more effective ways, reflects a political decision as much as, and probably more than, a scientific one. For example, the considerable expenditure on AIDS research using animals has produced little of use to humans suffering from AIDS, and most of what has resulted in longer and better lives for those suffering from HIV and AIDS has come from clinical trials with humans who have consented to those trials. It is certainly plausible that if the money spent on animal research were instead spent on public safe-sex education campaigns, needle exchanges, and condom distribution, the rate of new HIV cases would drop dramatically. The choice to use animal experiments to address the problem is, in many ways, a political and social decision. Animal experiments are considered an acceptable way of solving the AIDS problem, whereas needle exchanges, condom distribution, and safe-sex education are politically controversial. So again, the vivisector is not the only culprit here. Indeed, it may well be argued that those primarily responsible for the use of animals in AIDS research are the reactionary politicians who respond to a reactionary political base that rejects more effective ways of dealing with AIDS.

There is a sense in which the welfarist position and the pro-violence position are theoretically similar. Welfarists characterize institutional users as the primary problem and focus their attention on getting these users to reform their practices. Institutional users are economic actors who will do what they regard as efficient; they will make changes that increase production efficiency, and they will cater to niche markets, but they are not going to be the catalyst in widespread institutional change. If there are going to be significant and pervasive changes in animal treatment, these changes will occur only if there is a widespread demand for significantly higher-welfare products and a willingness both to pay the resulting much higher costs that significant change would entail and to keep lower-welfare products out of the market. Those who support violence similarly focus on the institutional exploiter and fail to recognize that as long as there is ubiquitous demand for animal products and no acceptance of the moral personhood of nonhumans, violence will do nothing as a practical matter. If you destroy five slaughterhouses, and the demand for meat remains the same, the demand will be met, and new slaughterhouses will be built (or existing ones expanded). If you shut down a company that supplies animals used in vivisection, but the demand for animals remains the same because the public supports vivisection, someone else will supply those animals. The only way that animal use will stop or be reduced significantly is if the paradigm shifts and demand drops.

Those who promote violence are certainly not creating any change in public sentiment concerning the legitimacy of animal use. If anything, the contrary is true. We live in a world where virtually anyone who can afford to eat animal products does so. In such a world, there is no context in which violence can be interpreted in any way other than as negative. In other words, in a world in which eating animal products is considered by most people as normal or natural in the way that drinking water or breathing air is, violence will quite likely be seen as nothing more than an act of simple criminality and will do nothing to further progressive thinking about the issue of animal exploitation. The fact that at least some animal advocates who endorse violence are not even vegan is truly bewildering. These people care so much about animals that they advocate violence but seem unable to stop exploiting nonhumans themselves.

A Note About Human Rights

In the early 1990s, I was invited to a meeting of leaders of the large animal protection organizations to speak about my view that the animal rights position entailed a rejection of racism, sexism, heterosexism, and other forms of discrimination and human rights violations. I was told by most of these leaders that the animal rights movement had no position on human rights issues.

I rejected that view then, and I reject it now. Speciesism is objectionable because, like racism, sexism, and heterosexism, it deprives beings with interests of equal consideration of their interests based on irrelevant criteria. To say that speciesism is objectionable because it is like these other forms of discrimination logically entails that animal rights advocates do—or at least should—have a position on these other forms of discrimination.

The issue of insensitivity to human rights is particularly a problem in the context of sexism. PETA has relentlessly promoted sexist imagery and campaigns to the point where it has become a primary form of street protest in the United States, South America, and Europe.[233] This reactionary approach is inconsistent with the position that it is wrong to commodify sentient beings, human or nonhuman. The choice is not between wearing fur and going naked. The choice is between wearing fur or some other animal product and not wearing fur or other animal product. As long as animal advocates continue to commodify women as things, as pieces of "meat," they can be certain that there will be no movement away from the paradigm that sees nonhuman animals as nothing but meat.

Conclusion

In any discussion about strategy, it is important to be mindful not only of basic moral principles but also of the practical consideration that all outreach involves a zero-sum enterprise. Animal advocates have limited time and limited resources. The time and resources spent on promoting "happy" meat and animal products is time not spent doing clear, unequivocal vegan education. The view for which I have argued is that such reforms are not only problematic as a matter of theory; they are also useless at best because they rarely go beyond what is necessary to make exploitation economically efficient and, in any event, the compromises required for animal advocates to achieve what Garner calls "insider status" invariably mean that legislation or even voluntary industry changes will provide little, if any, welfare benefit to animals. Welfare reforms are probably worse than useless in that they actually encourage people to feel more comfortable about animal exploitation and encourage the perpetuation of our moral schizophrenia.

It is ironic that advocacy for welfare reform is unnecessary in addition to being counterproductive. Most welfare reforms would be implemented by institutional users anyway because the reforms increase production efficiency. Welfare campaigns often target practices that are already identified by industry as possibly inefficient, and, if animal advocates promoted a clear message calling for the abolition of animal exploitation, the industry response would be to implement these reforms anyway so that industry could reassure the public that the welfare of animals was being taken seriously. The time and resources of animal advocates who really want to bring about a paradigm shift in our thinking about animals should be put into clear, unequivocal, and nonviolent vegan education targeted at abolishing all animal use. That is the best way to reduce use and suffering in the short term, and it is the *only* way to build an abolitionist movement in the long term that can shift the paradigm away from the status of animals as property.

Notes

Where cited materials were found on a Web site, citations include URLs. Web site content and URL addresses are, however, constantly changing. In order to ensure that the cited materials remain available to the reader, the URL cites have, where possible, been captured and are available in a file of notes on my Web site, at http://www.abolitionistapproach.com. Where the original URL citation is accurate as of the time that the book was completed, the original citation is provided, and the captured cite is provided following in parentheses. If the original URL should subsequently no longer contain the cited material, the reader can access that material through the captured cite. Where the original Web site content or URL citation was already changed, only the captured cite is provided.

1. *See* Gary L. Francione, *Animals as Persons: Essays on the Abolition of Animal Exploitation* (New York: Columbia University Press, 2008) (hereinafter *Animals as Persons*); Gary L. Francione, *Introduction to Animal Rights:*

Your Child or the Dog? (Philadelphia: Temple University Press, 2000) (hereinafter *Introduction to Animal Rights*); Gary L. Francione, *Rain Without Thunder: The Ideology of the Animal Rights Movement* (Philadelphia: Temple University Press, 1996) (hereinafter *Rain Without Thunder*); Gary L. Francione, *Animals, Property, and the Law* (Philadelphia: Temple University Press, 1995).

2. Tom Regan, *The Case for Animal Rights* (Berkeley: University of California Press, 1983).

3. Bernard E. Rollin, *Animal Rights and Human Morality*, 3d ed. (Buffalo, NY: Prometheus Press, 2006).

4. Bryan Salvage, "Revolutionizing the Veal Industry," *Meat Processing*, Dec. 2006, at 14 (quoting Randy Strauss).

5. *Id.* at 15 (quoting Randy Strauss).

6. *See* Food and Agriculture Organization of the United Nations: Animal Production and Health Division, *Global Livestock Production and Health Atlas*, at http://kids.fao.org/glipha/ (www.abolitionistapproach.com/animal-rights-debate/endnotes/6.pdf).

7. Robert Garner, *Animals, Politics, and Morality*, 2d ed. (Manchester: Manchester University Press, 2004), at 194–230.

8. *See generally Rain Without Thunder, supra* note 1.

9. *See Animals as Persons, supra* note 1, at 2–5, 28–30.

10. *See id.* at 5–9, 30–36, 129–47.

11. Jeremy Bentham, *An Introduction to the Principles of Morals and Legislation* (New York: Hafner, 1948), at 310–11 n. 1.

12. *Id.*

13. *Id.*

14. *Id.*

15. John Stuart Mill, "Utilitarianism," in *Utilitarianism and Other Essays: J. S. Mill and Jeremy Bentham*, ed. Alan Ryan (Harmondsworth: Penguin, 1987), at 279.

16. *Id.* at 280.

17. *Id.*

18. *Id.* at 324.

19. *Id.* at 281.

20. Interestingly, Bentham maintained that although some forms of slavery were more cruel than others, slavery, as an institution, would invariably become what H. L. A. Hart, in discussing Bentham's views, called "the lot of large numbers," in that Bentham recognized that "[i]f the evil of slavery were not great its extent alone would make it considèrable" (H. L. A. Hart, *Essays on Bentham* [Oxford: Oxford University Press, 1982], at 97). Bentham did not recognize that the institution of animal property would,

however "humane" it might be intended to be, become "the lot of large numbers" and invariably result in animals being treated as commodities. For a further discussion of Bentham's views on slavery and his failure to apply those views to the context of our use of nonhuman animals as property, see *Introduction to Animal Rights, supra* note 1, at 131–34, 146–48; *Animals as Persons, supra* note 1, at 145–46.

21. *See Introduction to Animal Rights, supra* note 1, at 130–50; *Animals as Persons, supra* note 1, *passim.*
22. Peter Singer, *Animal Liberation*, 2d ed. (New York: New York Review of Books, 1990), at 20.
23. *Id.* at 228–29.
24. *See* Dave Gilson, "Chew the Right Thing," *Mother Jones* (May 3, 2006), at http://www.motherjones.com/politics/2006/05/chew-right-thing (http://www.abolitionistapproach.com/animal-rights-debate/endnotes/24a.pdf); "Singer Says," *Satya* (Oct. 2006), at http://www.abolitionistapproach.com/animal-rights-debate/endnotes/24b.pdf.
25. Rosamund Raha, "Animal Liberation: An Interview with Professor Peter Singer," *The Vegan* (Autumn 2006), at 19.
26. Singer, *supra* note 22, at 16.
27. Peter Singer and Paola Cavalieri, eds., *The Great Ape Project: Equality Beyond Humanity* (London: Fourth Estate, 1993), at 5.
28. Raha, *supra* note 25, at 19.
29. Regan, *supra* note 2, at 324. For a discussion of Regan's view that death is a lesser harm for nonhuman animals, see *Animals as Persons, supra* note 1, at 210–29.
30. *See, e.g.,* Christine Kenneally, "What's So Special About Humans?" *New Scientist*, May 24, 2008, at 28.
31. For an excellent discussion of the nature of animal cognition and the confusion that it has caused in moral theory about animals, see Gary Steiner, *Animals and the Moral Community: Mental Life, Moral Status, and Kinship* (New York: Columbia University Press, 2008), at 1–55; Gary Steiner, *Anthropocentrism and Its Discontents: The Moral Status of Animals in the History of Western Philosophy* (Pittsburgh, PA: University of Pittsburgh Press, 2005), at 18–37.
32. For a further discussion of the abolitionist theory of animal rights, see *Introduction to Animal Rights, supra* note 1; *Animals as Persons, supra* note 1, at 25–66. *See also* Animal Rights: The Abolitionist Approach, http://www.AbolitionistApproach.com.
33. For a further discussion of the role of sentience in rights/abolitionist theory, see *Animals as Persons, supra* note 1, at 129–47, 165–66. Peter Carruthers maintains that because animals cannot think about their pain

in a reflective sense, they are not conscious of their pain and, therefore, animal pain is not morally significant. *See* Peter Carruthers, *The Animals Issue: Moral Theory in Practice* (Cambridge: Cambridge University Press, 1992), at 170–93. There are others who make similar claims—*see*, e.g., Peter Harrison, "Do Animals Feel Pain?" *Philosophy* 66 (1991): 25–40—but these claims are unusual to say the least.

34. "Âkârâṅga Sûtra," in *The Sacred Books of the East: Vol. 22, Jaina Sutras, Part 1*, trans. Hermann Jacobi, ed. F. Max Müller (Delhi: Motilal Banarsidass Publishers, 1989), at 19 (footnotes omitted). I recognize that Jainism, a tradition many of whose central tenets I am in agreement with, maintains that plants have one sense—the sense of touch. However, it appears that the sense in which the Jains use "sentience" in this context is different from the way that term is understood when it is applied to mobile, multi-sensed beings. Jains are forbidden from killing the latter but are allowed to kill and eat plants. Therefore, to the extent that Jains regard plants as sentient, they still draw a distinction between plants and other sentient beings. *See*, e.g., Jagdish Prasad Jain, *Fundamentals of Jainism* (New Delhi: Radiant Publishers, 2005), at 150–54; S. C. Jain, *Introducing Jainism* (Delhi: B.R. Publishing, 2006), at 71; Padmanabh S. Jaini, *The Jaina Path of Purification* (Delhi: Motilal Banarsidass Publishers, 1998), at 168; Vastupal Parikh, *Jainism and the New Spirituality*, 2d ed. (Toronto: Peace Publications, 2006), at 148.

35. Donald R. Griffin, *Animal Minds: Beyond Cognition to Consciousness* (Chicago: University of Chicago Press, 2001), at 274.

36. *Id.*

37. *Id.*

38. *Id.*

39. Antonio R. Damasio, *The Feeling of What Happens: Body and Emotion in the Making of Consciousness* (New York: Harcourt, 1999), at 16.

40. Singer, *supra* note 22, at 18.

41. For a further discussion of the concept of a right, see *Introduction to Animal Rights*, *supra* note 1, at xxvi–xxx; 92–100; *Animals as Persons*, *supra* note 1, at 49–52.

42. For a discussion of conflicts between humans and animals, see *Introduction to Animal Rights*, *supra* note 1, 151–62.

43. *See Animals as Persons*, *supra* note 1, at 170–85; *Introduction to Animal Rights*, *supra* note 1, at 31–49, 156–57.

44. Garner, *supra* note 7, at 41.

45. The property status of animals has been a consistent theme in my work and was the exclusive focus of *Animals, Property, and the Law*, *supra* note 1. For an excellent discussion of animal exploitation given the dynamics

of capitalism, see Bob Torres, *Making a Killing: The Political Economy of Animal Rights* (Oakland, CA: AK Press, 2007).

46. Humane Methods of Slaughter Act of 1958, Pub. L. No. 85–765, 72 Stat. 862 (codified at 7 U.S.C. §§ 1901–1907 (2000)).

47. The "[f]indings and declarations of policy" of the Humane Slaughter Act make clear the importance of economic considerations in assessing matters of animal welfare: "The Congress finds that the use of humane methods in the slaughter of livestock prevents needless suffering; results in safer and better working conditions for persons engaged in the slaughtering industry; brings about improvement of products and economies in slaughtering operations; and produces other benefits for producers, processors, and consumers which tend to expedite an orderly flow of livestock and livestock products in interstate and foreign commerce." 7 U.S.C. § 1901 (2000).

48. For a discussion of the necessity of animal use, see *Introduction to Animal Rights, supra* note 1, at 1–49. Courts have explicitly recognized that prohibitions against "unnecessary" suffering or "needless" killing must be interpreted by reference to institutional uses that are clearly unnecessary: "The flesh of animals is not necessary for the subsistence of man, at least in this country, and by some people it is not so used. Yet it would not be denied that the killing of oxen for food is lawful. Fish are not necessary to any one, nor are various wild animals which are killed, and sold in market; yet their capture and killing are regulated by law. The words 'needlessly' and 'unnecessarily' must have a reasonable, not an absolute and literal, meaning attached to them." *State v. Bogardus*, 4 Mo. App. 215, 216–17 (1877). Courts have also recognized that practices that are regarded as "cruel" as we normally use that term in ordinary discourse are permitted within the meaning of anticruelty laws. *See Introduction to Animal Rights, supra* note 1, at 58–63; *Animals, Property, and the Law, supra* note 1, at 146.

49. Robert Garner argues that the welfarist approach is "not trying to show that the use of animals is morally wrong regardless of the benefits to humans. Rather, the movement is trying to show that most, if not all, of the cruel and harmful techniques currently employed on animals are unnecessary in the sense that they do not produce human benefits or that such benefits can be achieved in other ways." Robert Garner, "Animal Welfare: A Political Defense," *J. Animal L. & Ethics* 1 (2006): 161, 167. Garner claims that I accept this analysis and that it is "somewhat ironic" that I do so given my criticism of Garner's defense of welfarism. Garner, *supra* note 7, at 41 n. 2. Garner fails to understand that my discussion of necessity concerns animal use per se and not the treatment of animals, which, as he correctly notes, is the focus of the welfarist approach.

50. Even if animal use in vivisection is "necessary" in that it cannot be dismissed as trivial and justified only by human amusement, pleasure, or convenience, animal use in this context cannot be justified morally. *See Animals as Persons, supra* note 1, at 170–85.

51. *New Jersey Society for the Prevention of Cruelty to Animals vs. New Jersey Department of Agriculture*, 196 N.J. 366 (2008), is one of the few cases that has questioned the interpretation of "humane" as conforming to "routine husbandry practices." The Court held as arbitrary and capricious administrative regulations that exempted from the anticruelty statute "routine husbandry practices" defined as those "commonly taught" at veterinary schools, agricultural colleges, and so on, where the agency did not even review what these institutions teach or consider whether what was commonly taught reflected welfare concerns. The Court made clear that if the agency had engaged in a proper review, its decision to exempt these practices would be immune from legal attack.

52. For a further discussion of reforms after 1995 and how these reforms have failed to provide a significant welfare benefit for animals and are generally linked to the efficient exploitation of animal property, see *Animals as Persons, supra* note 1, at 72–96.

53. *Levine v. Conner*, 540 F. Supp. 2d 1113 (N.D. Cal. 2008); *Levine v. Vilsack*, 587 F.3d 986 (9th Cir. 2009).

54. There appears to be a fair amount of confusion in that CAK and CAS seem to be used interchangeably so that systems that are intended to kill poultry and not merely stun them are described as CAS systems, and systems that are intended to stun but not to kill poultry are described as CAK systems. Moreover, although animal advocates note that CAS systems risk that stunned poultry may regain consciousness and seem to promote the CAK system, they also endorse those entities that have adopted a CAS system, often without making a distinction or highlighting the obvious additional welfare problem of regained consciousness.

55. "Research Incomplete on the Killing of Chickens—Controlled Atmosphere Stunning," *North Denver News*, Apr. 10, 2008 (quoting Bernard E. Rollin), at http://northdenvernews.com/content/view/1279/2/ (http://www.abolitionistapproach.com/animal-rights-debate/endnotes/55.pdf).

56. *See id.*

57. *Id.* (quoting American Humane Association).

58. Roger Yates, "On Controlling the Atmospheres of Chickens and Hens," *On Human-Nonhuman Relations: A Sociological Exploration of Speciesism*, July 7, 2008, at http://human-nonhuman.blogspot.com/2008/07/on-controlling-atmosphere-of-chickens.html (http://www.abolitionistapproach.com/animal-rights-debate/endnotes/58.pdf).

59. Sonja Barisic, "PETA, KFC Reach Deal on New Slaughter Method," *USA Today* (June 3, 2008) (quoting Matt Prescott), at http://www.usatoday.com/money/economy/2008-06-03-2318398055_x.htm (http://www.abolitionist approach.com/animal-rights-debate/endnotes/59.pdf).

60. "PETA Files Shareholder Resolution Calling on Brinker to Improve Chicken Slaughter," Apr. 27, 2006, at http://www.peta.org/MC/NewsItem .asp?id=8241&pf=true (press release) (http://www.abolitionistapproach .com/animal-rights-debate/endnotes/60.pdf).

61. Matt Prescott, "Historic Victory! PETA Wins KFC Campaign in Canada," *The PETA Files*, June 1, 2008, at http://blog.peta.org/archives/2008/06/ historic_victor_1.php (http://www.abolitionistapproach.com/animal-rights-debate/endnotes/61.pdf).

62. PETA, "The Case for Controlled-Atmosphere Killing," at http://www.peta .org/cak/ (http://www.abolitionistapproach.com/animal-rights-debate/ endnotes/62.pdf).

63. Yates, *supra* note 58.

64. HSUS, *An HSUS Report: The Economics of Adopting Alternative Production Practices to Electrical Stunning Slaughter of Poultry*, at 1, at http://www .hsus.org/web-files/PDF/farm/econ_elecstun.pdf (http://www.abolitionist approach.com/animal-rights-debate/endnotes/64.pdf).

65. *Id.* (citation omitted).

66. *Id.* (citation omitted).

67. *Id.*

68. *Id.* at 2.

69. *Id.* (citations omitted).

70. *Id.* (citations omitted).

71. *Id.*

72. *Id.*

73. *Id.* (citation omitted).

74. PETA, *Controlled-Atmosphere Killing vs. Electric Immobilization: A Comparative Analysis of Poultry-Slaughter Systems from Animal Welfare, Worker Safety, and Economic Perspectives* (hereinafter *PETA Analysis*), June 2007, at 5, at http://www.peta.org/cak/CAK+report.pdf (http://www .abolitionistapproach.com/animal-rights-debate/endnotes/74.pdf).

75. *Id.*

76. *Id.*

77. *Id.*

78. *Id.*

79. *Id.*

80. *Id.*

81. *Id.*

82. *Id.*

83. *Id.*

84. "The Case for Controlled-Atmosphere Killing," *supra* note 62.

85. *PETA Analysis, supra* note 74, at 20 (citations omitted).

86. *Id.* at 23–24.

87. *Id.* at 24.

88. *Id.*

89. *Id.* at 22 (internal citations omitted).

90. *Id.*

91. *Id.*

92. *Id.* (quoting Canadian Food Inspection Agency).

93. *Id.*

94. *Id.* at 24.

95.. *Id.* at 25.

96. *Id.* at 18.

97. *Id.*

98. *Id.*

99. *Id.*

100. *Id.* at 19.

101. *Id.* at 26.

102. *Id.* at 28.

103. *See id.*

104. *See id.* at 29–31.

105. HSUS, *An HSUS Report: The Economics of Adopting Alternative Production Systems to Gestation Crates,* at 1 (internal citations omitted), at
http://www.hsus.org/web-files/PDF/farm/econ_gestation.pdf (http://
www.abolitionistapproach.com/animal-rights-debate/endnotes/105
.pdf).

106. *Id.*

107. *Id.* at 2 (internal citation omitted).

108. *Id.* (internal citation omitted).

109. *Id.* (internal citation omitted).

110. *Id.*

111. *Id.* at 1.

112. Peter Singer, "Animal Liberation at 30," *N.Y. Rev. Books,* May 15, 2003, at 26.

113. *Id.*

114. Stephanie Simon, "Killing Them Softly: Voluntary Reforms in the Livestock
Industry Have Changed the Way Animals Are Slaughtered," *L.A. Times,* Apr.
29, 2003, at A10 (quoting Bruce Friedrich of PETA).

115. David Shaw, "Matters of Taste: Animal Rights and Wrongs," *L.A. Times,* Feb.
23, 2005, at F2 (quoting Lisa Lange of PETA).

116. For a discussion of Temple Grandin, see *Rain Without Thunder, supra* note 1, at 99–100, 199–202.

117. Temple Grandin, *Recommended Animal Handling Guidelines and Audit Guide 2007 Edition* (American Meat Institute Foundation), at 6, at http://www.animalhandling.org/ht/a/GetDocumentAction/i/1774 (http://www.abolitionistapproach.com/animal-rights-debate/endnotes/117.pdf).

118. Temple Grandin, "Humane Slaughter: Recommended Stunning Practices," at http://www.grandin.com/humane/rec.slaughter.html (http://www.abolitionistapproach.com/animal-rights-debate/endnotes/118.pdf).

119. Temple Grandin, "Stress and Meat Quality: Lowering Stress to Improve Meat Quality and Animal Welfare," at http://www.grandin.com/meat/meat.html (http://www.abolitionistapproach.com/animal-rights-debate/endnotes/119.pdf).

120. Bruce Feinberg and Terry Williams, "McDonald's Corporate Social Responsibility, Animal Welfare Update: North America," at http://web.archive.org/web/20031216173608/www.mcdonalds.com/corporate/social/marketplace/welfare/update/northamerica/index.html (http://www.abolitionistapproach.com/animal-rights-debate/endnotes/120.pdf).

121. "Wendy's Animal Welfare Program," at http://www.wendys.com/community/animal_welfare.jsp (http://www.abolitionistapproach.com/animal-rights-debate/endnotes/121.pdf).

122. Simon, *supra* note 114.

123. *See, e.g.*, Temple Grandin and Catherine Johnson, *Animals in Translation: Using the Mysteries of Autism to Decode Animal Behavior* (New York: Scribner, 2005).

124. Philip Brasher, "Recall Raises Questions About Food Audits; Firms Consider Cameras," *Tucson Citizen*, Mar. 25, 2008, at http://www.tucsoncitizen.com/daily/opinion/80611.php (http://www.abolitionistapproach.com/animal-rights-debate/endnotes/124.pdf). It should also be noted that there have been reports of widespread and serious violations of the Humane Slaughter Act. *See, e.g.*, General Accounting Office, *Report to Congressional Requesters: Humane Methods of Slaughter Act: USDA Has Addressed Some Problems but Still Faces Enforcement Challenges* (Jan. 2004); Joby Warrick, "'They Die Piece by Piece': In Overtaxed Plants, Humane Treatment of Cattle Is Often a Battle Lost," *Washington Post*, Apr. 10, 2001, at A01. *See also Animals as Persons, supra* note 1, at 96.

125. HSUS, *An HSUS Report: Human Health Implications of Cage and Cage-Free Egg Production—A Review of Food Safety*, at http://www.abolitionistapproach.com/animal-rights-debate/endnotes/125.pdf.

126. *Id.*

127. *Id.*

128. Jennifer Fearing and Gaverick Matheny, "The Role of Economics in Achieving Welfare Gains for Animals," in *The State of Animals IV: 2007*, ed. Deborah J. Salem and Andrew N. Rowan (Washington, D.C.: Humane Society Press, 2007), at 170.

129. *Id.*

130. *See* Jennifer Wolcott, "'Cage-Free' Eggs: Not All They're Cracked Up to Be?" *Christian Science Monitor*, Oct. 27, 2004, at http://www.csmonitor.com/2004/1027/p15s01-lifo.html (http://www.abolitionistapproach.com/animal-rights-debate/endnotes/130.pdf).

131. Garner, *supra* note 49, at 171.

132. Garner, *supra* note 7, at 118.

133. *Id.* at 112.

134. *Id.* at 204. *See infra* note 155.

135. *Id.* at 264.

136. Council Directive 1999/74/EC, OJ L 203, 3.8 (1999), at 53.

137. Garner, *supra* note 7, at 264.

138. Media Release, Animal Rights International, "This November, New Yorkers Will See What Egg Producers Don't Want Them to See," Oct. 25, 2007 (quoting Peter Singer), at http://www.abolitionistapproach.com/animal-rights-debate/endnotes/138.pdf.

139. PETA, "Victory for Hens: Battery Cages to Be Banned by 2012," at http://www.abolitionistapproach.com/animal-rights-debate/endnotes/139.pdf.

140. COM (2007) 865 final; SEC (2007) 1750 (2008), at 6.

141. Agra CEAS Consulting Ltd., *Study on the Socio-Economic Implications of the Various Systems to Keep Laying Hens, Final Report for the European Commission* (2004), at vi.

142. *Id.* at vii.

143. European Commission Press Release IP/08/19 (Jan. 8, 2008).

144. Philip Lymbery, *Laid Bare . . . The Case Against Enriched Cages in Europe: A Report Written for the Compassion in World Farming Trust* (2002), at 2, at http://www.ciwf.org.uk/includes/documents/cm_docs/2008/l/laid_bare_2002.pdf (http://www.abolitionistapproach.com/animal-rights-debate/endnotes/144.pdf). It is interesting to note that when, in 2008, the European Commission rejected calls from egg producers to postpone the implementation of the Directive (*see* Press Release, *supra* note 143), CIWF issued a press release describing the decision not to postpone the implementation of the Directive as "a huge success." But why? CIWF has campaigned on welfare grounds against the "enriched" cage, which is the option that most producers will likely choose. PETA and HSUS praised the Commission's decision, calling it a "[v]ictory for hens" and a "highly significant move for

animal welfare" without even mentioning the clear welfare problems with the "enriched" cage.

145. RSPCA, "News—Laying Hens: Barren Battery Cage Ban Upheld," Jan. 10, 2008 (quoting Alice Clark), at http://www.abolitionistapproach.com/animal-rights-debate/endnotes/145.pdf.

146. *See infra* note 173.

147. *See* "Calls to Scrap 'Derided' Hunting Ban," *BBC News*, Feb. 18, 2006, at http://news.bbc.co.uk/2/hi/uk_news/4726566.stm (http://www.abolitionistapproach.com/animal-rights-debate/endnotes/147.pdf).

148. *See* Flora Watkins, "Hope Grows for Repeal of Hunt Law," *BBC Today*, Apr. 7, 2009, at http://news.bbc.co.uk/today/hi/today/newsid_7985000/7985376.stm (http://www.abolitionistapproach.com/animal-rights-debate/endnotes/148.pdf).

149. Home Office, *Statistics of Scientific Procedures on Living Animals 2007*, HC 933 (July 2008), at 6.

150. Claire Thomas, "European Parliament Takes a Stand on Animal Research," *Science Magazine*, May 5, 2009, at http://blogs.sciencemag.org/science insider/2009/05/eu-parliament-t.html (http://www.abolitionistapproach.com/animal-rights-debate/endnotes/150.pdf).

151. *See* Jim Downing, "Bill Requires All Eggs Sold in California to Be From Cage-Free Hens," *Merced Sun-Star*, June 3, 2009, at http://www.mercedsunstar.com/275/story/880227.html (http://www.abolitionistapproach.com/animal-rights-debate/endnotes/151.pdf). Such a law would raise legal issues involving interstate commerce and trade.

152. *See generally Rain Without Thunder, supra* note 1.

153. Association Against Animal Factories, "Abolitionism versus Reformism," at http://www.vgt.at/publikationen/texte/artikel/20080325Abolitionism/index_en.php (http://www.abolitionistapproach.com/animal-rights-debate/endnotes/153.pdf).

154. *See* Statistics Austria, *Supply Balance Sheet for Eggs*, at http://www.statistik.at/web_en/statistics/agriculture_and_forestry/prices_balances/supply_balance_sheets/028973.html (http://www.abolitionistapproach.com/animal-rights-debate/endnotes/154.pdf).

155. *See* British Pig Executive (BPEX), *An Analysis of Pork and Pork Products Imported into the United Kingdom*, Apr. 2006, at 2, at http://www.bpex.org/members/files/13042006160592NRKXH20E.pdf (http://www.abolitionistapproach.com/animal-rights-debate/endnotes/155.pdf). *See infra* note 209.

156. HFAC, "Certified Humane Raised and Handled," at http://www.certified humane.org (http://www.abolitionistapproach.com/animal-rights-debate/endnotes/156.pdf).

157. HFAC, "What Is Certified Humane Raised & Handled?" at http://www
.abolitionistapproach.com/animal-rights-debate/endnotes/157.pdf.

158. *Id.* (quoting unspecified article in *Agricultural Research*).

159. HFAC, "Why Produce Certified Humane Raised and Handled?" at http://
www.abolitionistapproach.com/animal-rights-debate/endnotes/159
.pdf.

160. HFAC, "Why Carry Certified Humane Raised and Handled?" at http://www
.abolitionistapproach.com/animal-rights-debate/endnotes/160.pdf.

161. Humane Society International, "Humane Choice," at http://www.humane
choice.com.au/ (http://www.abolitionistapproach.com/animal-rights-
debate/endnotes/161.pdf).

162. *Id.*

163. Whole Foods Market, "Animal Welfare," at http://www.abolitionist
approach.com/animal-rights-debate/endnotes/163.pdf.

164. *Id.*

165. RSPCA, "Freedom Food—Welcome," at http://www.abolitionistapproach
.com/animal-rights-debate/endnotes/165.pdf.

166. RSPCA, "Freedom Food—Producer," at http://www.abolitionistapproach
.com/animal-rights-debate/endnotes/166.pdf.

167. *Id.*

168. "Freedom Food—Welcome," *supra* note 165.

169. RSPCA, "Freedom Food—Economic," at http://www.abolitionistapproach
.com/animal-rights-debate/endnotes/169.pdf.

170. *Id.*

171. *Id.*

172. RSPCA, "Freedom Food—Marketing," *id.*, at http://www.abolitionist
approach.com/animal-rights-debate/endnotes/172.pdf.

173. These exposés, which have been presented by BBC, ITV, Channel 4, and
other media, were investigated by Hillside Animal Sanctuary in Norwich.
Their Web site provides links to some of the media presentations. *See*
http://www.hillside.org.uk/ (http://www.abolitionistapproach.com/
animal-rights-debate/endnotes/173a.pdf). In at least one situation, the
RSPCA claimed that it had conducted an inspection of an egg producer
that had the Freedom Food stamp of RSPCA approval but had failed the
producer for various violations. Nevertheless, the RSPCA allowed the producer to keep its Freedom Food accreditation and continue to sell its
products with the logo. Chris Semple, "'Freedom Farm Cruelty' Exposed,"
The Sun, June 23, 2008, at http://www.thesun.co.uk/sol/homepage/news/
article1328275.ece (http://www.abolitionistapproach.com/animal-rights-
debate/endnotes/173b.pdf).

174. Darian M. Ibrahim, "A Return to Descartes: Property, Profit, and the Corporate Ownership of Animals," *Law & Contemporary Problems* 70 (2007): 89, 109–11.

175. 2004 PETA Proggy Award, "Best Animal-Friendly Retailer," at http://www.peta.org/feat/proggy/2004/winners.html#retailer (http://www.abolitionist approach.com/animal-rights-debate/endnotes/175.pdf).

176. 2004 PETA Proggy Award, "Visionary," at http://www.peta.org/feat/proggy/2004/winners.html#visionary (http://www.abolitionistapproach.com/animal-rights-debate/endnotes/176.pdf).

177. For a copy of the statement, see http://www.abolitionistapproach.com/animal-rights-debate/endnotes/177.pdf.

178. *VegNews*, Apr. 2004. The issue contained a lengthy interview with Mackey.

179. *VegNews*, Nov./Dec. 2005, at 36.

180. CIWF, "Good Egg Awards," at http://www.thegoodeggawards.com/ (http://www.abolitionistapproach.com/animal-rights-debate/endnotes/180.pdf).

181. PETA, "Kentucky Fried Cruelty: Cruelty Capital USA," at http://www.kentuckyfriedcruelty.com/index.asp (http://www.abolitionistapproach.com/animal-rights-debate/endnotes/181.pdf).

182. *See* Barisic, *supra* note 59. PETA neglected to mention that KFC Canada will phase in CAK over an eight-year period.

183. PETA, "KFC Canada Gives In to PETA's Demands," at http://www.abolitionist approach.com/animal-rights-debate/endnotes/183.pdf.

184. *See* Prescott, *supra* note 61.

185. *See* Barisic, *supra* note 59.

186. "KFC Canada Promises to Improve Chicken Welfare," CTV.ca (quoting Steve Langford), at http://www.ctv.ca/servlet/ArticleNews/story/CTVNews/20080601/kfc_chicken_080601/20080601?hub=Canada (http://www.abolitionistapproach.com/animal-rights-debate/endnotes/186.pdf).

187. *Id.* (quoting Matt Prescott).

188. *Id.* (quoting Matt Prescott).

189. *See* Shaw, *supra* note 115.

190. HSUS, "Guckenheimer Serves Up a Cage-Free Egg Policy" (quoting Paul Shapiro), at http://www.hsus.org/farm/news/ournews/guckenheimer_cage_free.html (http://www.abolitionistapproach.com/animal-rights-debate/endnotes/190.pdf).

191. HSUS, "Voters Approve Animal Protection Ballot Measures," Nov. 4, 2008, at http://www.hsus.org/press_and_publications/press_releases/voting_for_animals_110408.html (http://www.abolitionistapproach.com/animal-rights-debate/endnotes/191.pdf).

192. *Id.*

193. *See*, e.g., Connie Mabin, "Animal-Friendly Labels Appeal to Buyers," *Boston Globe*, Feb. 5, 2007, at http://www.boston.com/news/world/europe/articles/ 2007/02/05/animal_friendly_labels_appeal_to_buyers/ (http://www .abolitionistapproach.com/animal-rights-debate/endnotes/193a.pdf); Megan Lane, "Some Sausages Are More Equal Than Others," *BBC News Magazine*, Feb. 1, 2007, at http://news.bbc.co.uk/2/hi/uk_news/magazine/ 6295747.stm (http://www.abolitionistapproach.com/animal-rights-debate/ endnotes/193b.pdf).

194. Terri Coles, "Humane Farming Eases Pangs for Some Vegetarians," *Reuters*, Aug. 14, 2007, at http://www.reuters.com/article/healthNews/ idUSSCH47468520070814?sp=true (http://www.abolitionistapproach.com/ animal-rights-debate/endnotes/194a.pdf). *See also* Christine Lennon, "Why Vegetarians Are Eating Meat," *Food & Wine*, Aug. 2007, at http://www .foodandwine.com/articles/why-vegetarians-are-eating-meat (http://www .abolitionistapproach.com/animal-rights-debate/endnotes/194b.pdf).

195. For example, in the United States, "[c]elebrity chef Wolfgang Puck is cooking up kinder, gentler menus. As part of a new initiative to fight animal cruelty, Puck said Thursday he will no longer serve foie gras, the fatty liver produced by overfeeding ducks and geese." Moreover, his restaurants, casual eateries, and catering facilities "will use only eggs from hens that have lived cage-free; veal from roaming calves; and lobsters that have been removed from their ocean traps quickly to avoid crowded holding tanks." "Chef Wolfgang Puck Bans Foie Gras," *Washington Post*, Mar. 23, 2007, at http://www.washingtonpost.com/wp-dyn/content/article/2007/03/22/ AR2007032200954_pf.html (http://www.abolitionistapproach.com/ animal-rights-debate/endnotes/195a.pdf). In the United Kingdom, television chef Hugh Fearnley-Whittingstall led an unsuccessful effort to force Tesco, a supermarket chain, to carry poultry bearing the RSPCA Freedom Food label. *See* "TV Chef Loses Tesco Chicken Vote," *BBC News*, June 27, 2008, at http://news.bbc.co.uk/2/hi/business/7476829.stm (http://www .abolitionistapproach.com/animal-rights-debate/endnotes/195b.pdf).

196. Catherine Friend, *The Compassionate Carnivore: Or, How to Keep Animals Happy, Save Old MacDonald's Farm, Reduce Your Hoofprint, and Still Eat Meat* (Cambridge, MA: Da Capo Press, 2008), at 158, 160.

197. *Id.* at 247. In a review of Friend's book, one writer remarks that according to Friend, "[t]o be a compassionate carnivore, you don't have to cut out factory-farmed meat, you don't have to eat organic (her own small farm is humane, but non-organic) [and] you don't have to shun conventional farming. All you have to do is respect animals and be prepared to make a little effort to search for what Friend calls 'happy meat.'" Tim Lott, "How to Love Animals and Eat Them," *The Telegraph*, June 1, 2008, at http://www

.telegraph.co.uk/arts/main.jhtml?xml=/arts/2008/06/01/bofri101.xml (http://www.abolitionistapproach.com/animal-rights-debate/endnotes/197.pdf).

198. PETA2 Daily Blog, July 21, 2008, at http://blog.peta2.com/2008/07/calling_all_canadians_eat_some.html (http://www.abolitionistapproach.com/animal-rights-debate/endnotes/198.pdf). *See infra* notes 219–23.

199. Garner, *supra* note 7, at 59.

200. Patrick Barkham, "Alfalfa Male Takes On the Corporation," *The Guardian*, Sept. 8, 2006 (quoting Peter Singer), at http://www.guardian.co.uk/environment/2006/sep/08/food.ethicalliving (http://www.abolitionistapproach.com/animal-rights-debate/endnotes/200a.pdf). *See also* Peter Singer and Jim Mason, *The Way We Eat: Why Our Food Choices Matter* (Emmaus, PA: Rodale, 2006), at 81–183 ("The Conscientious Omnivores"). Singer's promotion of animal exploitation goes beyond endorsing eating "happy" animal products. For example, in *The Way We Eat*, Singer and Mason discuss the experience of working on a turkey farm "collecting the semen and getting it into the hen." The male turkeys were caught and restrained while another worker "squeezed the tom's vent until it opened up and the white semen oozed forth. Using a vacuum pump, he sucked it into a syringe." Singer or Mason then had to "break" the hens, which involved restraining the hen "so that her rear is straight up and her vent open." *Id.* at 28. The inseminator then inserted a tube into the hen and used a blast of compressed air to insert the semen into the hen's oviduct. So apparently, Singer's views about "animal liberation" are consistent with animal advocates inflicting harm on animals in order to satisfy their curiosity about the mechanics of animal exploitation. In an essay on bestiality, Singer maintained that "sex with animals does not always involve cruelty. Who has not been at a social occasion disrupted by the household dog gripping the legs of a visitor and vigorously rubbing its penis against them? The host usually discourages such activities, but in private not everyone objects to being used by her or his dog in this way, and occasionally mutually satisfying activities may develop." Peter Singer, "Heavy Petting," *Nerve.com*, 2001, at http://www.nerve.com/Opinions/Singer/heavyPetting/main.asp (http://www.abolitionistapproach.com/animal-rights-debate/endnotes/200b.pdf).

201. *See* Raha, *supra* note 25.

202. *See* "Singer Says," *supra* note 24; *infra* notes 219–23.

203. Salvage, *supra* note 4, at 15 (quoting Randy Strauss).

204. *Id.* (quoting Randy Strauss).

205. *Id.* (quoting Randy Strauss).

206. "Nations [sic] Top Veal Producer Eliminating Crates!!" Feb. 22, 2007 (quoting Paul Shapiro), at http://www.care2.com/c2c/groups/disc .html?gpp=9779&pst=728126 (http://www.abolitionistapproach.com/ animal-rights-debate/endnotes/206.pdf).

207. Garner discusses "insider status" in *Animals, Politics and Morality, supra* note 7. *See, e.g.,* 220–230.

208. *See id.* at 219–20.

209. *Id.* at 221.

210. CIWF, "Improving Pig Welfare Would Help Save British Farmers' Bacon," at http://www.ciwf.org.uk/news/pig_farming/improving_pig_welfare .aspx (http://www.abolitionistapproach.com/animal-rights-debate/end notes/210.pdf). *See supra* note 155.

211. Garner, *supra* note 7, at 61.

212. *See* Wayne Pacelle, "A New Dawn," at http://hsus.typepad.com/wayne/ 2008/06/karen-dawn-book.html (http://www.abolitionistapproach.com/ animal-rights-debate/endnotes/212.pdf).

213. Garner, *supra* note 7, at 221.

214. *See Animals as Persons, supra* note 1, at 107–151; *see also* http://www. AbolitionistApproach.com for essays and materials concerning the centrality of veganism to the animal rights/abolitionist approach.

215. An average omnivore in the United States is responsible for at least forty nonhuman deaths per year. This number is based on an estimate of 12 billion animals killed in the United States and consumed by a population of 300 million. The number of animals killed does not include fish or other aquatic animals and reflects only animals used for food and not for other purposes.

216. An example—one of many—of the futility of animal welfare campaigns concerns the federal Animal Welfare Act (passed originally in 1966 and amended on numerous occasions), which, among other things, purports to regulate the use of nonhumans in experiments. The law has historically been interpreted by the administrative agency charged with its enforcement (the Department of Agriculture) to exclude rats and mice, which are the animals most used in experiments. For thirty years, animal advocates campaigned to have rats and mice covered under the Act, spending what must have been many millions of dollars on these efforts, which included multiple lawsuits and administrative actions. If the effort had been successful, it would not have provided a significant welfare benefit to animals in that the Act very explicitly allows pain and suffering to be imposed on animals used in experiments if it is "necessary" to do so. Although there may be researchers with sadistic impulses who are inflicting pain and suffering on rats and mice that they do not think is

necessary, such people are surely a small minority. In any event, the effort was not successful. After the Secretary of Agriculture agreed to include rats and mice under the Act, Congress intervened and passed a law that specifically excluded rats and mice. *See Animals as Persons, supra* note 1, at 95–96. *See also Animals, Property, and the Law, supra* note 1, at 185–249; *Rain Without Thunder, supra* note 1, at 87–95.

217. *See Rain Without Thunder, supra* note 1.
218. *See* Gary L. Francione, "We're All Michael Vick," *Philadelphia Daily News*, Aug. 22, 2007, at 25.
219. Matt Ball, *A Meaningful Life: Animal Advocacy, Human Nature, and a Better World*, at 10 (Vegan Outreach, 2006), at http://www.abolitionist approach.com/animal-rights-debate/endnotes/219.pdf.
220. "Singer Says," *supra* note 24.
221. *Id.*
222. Bruce Friedrich, "Personal Purity vs. Effective Advocacy," at http://www.goveg.com/effectiveAdvocacy_personal.asp (emphasis in original removed) (http://www.abolitionistapproach.com/animal-rights-debate/endnotes/222.pdf).
223. "Singer Says," *supra* note 24.
224. Friedrich, *supra* note 222.
225. Steve Lowery, "How to Stuff a Lettuce Bikini," *Orange County Weekly*, July 31, 2003 (quoting Dan Mathews), at http://www.abolitionistapproach.com/animal-rights-debate/endnotes/225.pdf.
226. *See Animals as Persons, supra* note 1, at 93–94.
227. *See id.* at 87–90.
228. Phil Vettel, "Foie Gras Ban, We Hardly Knew Ye," *Chicago Tribune*, May 16, 2008, at http://www.chicagotribune.com/news/opinion/chi-foie-gras-ban-perspective,0,3199140.story (http://www.abolitionistapproach.com/animal-rights-debate/endnotes/228.pdf).
229. *See Rain Without Thunder, supra* note 1, at 190–219. I regret that some of the examples that I used in my discussion of incremental change in *Rain Without Thunder* have caused more confusion than elucidation, and I would approach the issue of incremental change differently if I were writing the book today.
230. *See* Richard Tompkins, "Paws for Thought," *FT Magazine*, July 7–8, 2007, at 15. This is another respect in which my position differs sharply from that of Tom Regan. Regan does not regard domestication as necessarily violating the rights of nonhumans. *See* Tom Regan, *The Case for Animal Rights*, 2d ed. (Berkeley: University of California Press, 2004), at 2.
231. Debra J. Saunders, "Better Dead Than Fed, Says PETA," *San Francisco Chronicle*, June 23, 2005, at http://www.sfgate.com/cgi-bin/article.cgi

?file=/c/a/2005/06/23/EDG11DC9BK1.DTL (http://www.abolitionist approach.com/animal-rights-debate/endnotes/231.pdf). *See also Rain Without Thunder, supra* note 1, at 106–109.

232. I agree with the Jain doctrine of Ahimsa, or nonviolence. *See, e.g.,* Jagdish Prasad Jain, *supra* note 34, at 145–69. I maintain, however, that Ahimsa requires veganism, which is a somewhat controversial position in Jainism. *See* Gary L. Francione, "Ahimsa and Veganism," *Jain Digest* (Winter 2009), at 9–10.

233. For a discussion of PETA's sexism, see *Rain Without Thunder, supra* note 1, at 74–76; Gary L. Francione, "The State of the Movement," Jan. 24, 2007, at http://www.abolitionistapproach.com/animal-rights-debate/endnotes/233.pdf.

2

A Defense of a Broad Animal Protectionism
Robert Garner

It is important to point out at the outset that I am not criticizing animal rights in this book. As I discuss in this chapter, a great deal of the ethics of animal rights is convincing. Rather, I want to challenge a particular version of animal rights that is held, in one form or another, by a section within the grassroots of the animal rights movement and that has been articulated skillfully and eloquently by Gary Francione in the first part of this book and elsewhere (1995, 1996; see also Dunayer 2004). This version of animal rights can be described as abolitionist because its major characteristic is the assertion that the abolition of the use of animals by humans is both ethically desirable and politically possible.

It is also fundamentalist, not just in the sense that it holds strongly to a particular set of beliefs, but also in its unwillingness to compromise those beliefs in order to achieve incremental short-term goals that fall short of the ideal end point.

"Fundamentalism" is a term that now has almost entirely negative connotations, but this is to overlook its advantages as a style of argumentation and as a political strategy. As one scholar (Heywood 2007, 288) has pointed out, "Fundamentalism is a style of thought in which certain principles are recognized as essential 'truths' that have unchallengeable and overriding authority." Defined in this way, it has, in particular, the great advantage of mobilizing political activism by offering certainty, simplifying the message, and creating a sense of identity among its adherents. Significantly, though, this kind of strategic fundamentalism also tends to be inflexible and dogmatic, finding it difficult to reconcile itself to the political art of the possible.

The position I seek to advocate in place of animal rights abolitionism is a version of a position that Francione himself has described as "new welfarism," although I prefer the label "animal protectionism."[1] This latter label is more accurate, partly because it can be distinguished from an old-style welfarism that has rightly been condemned ethically, if not politically, and partly because "new welfarism" fails to reflect the fact that I would support any measures that lead to the protection of animal interests, whether they be labeled animal welfare or animal rights.

In order to draw out the advantages of a broad animal protectionism over animal rights abolitionism, this chapter is organized into five main sections. In the first place, an attempt is made to clarify the ethical parameters of the debate. This is followed by an account of the ethical strengths and weaknesses of the positions in the debate. The third section provides a defense of animal protectionism against the charge that it is counterproductive and an endorsement of the position that it is the best available approach for the animal protection movement. Here, the unnecessary suffering principle is defended against both animal rights abolitionism and an alternative approach that focuses on an alleged inconsistency in the way animals are currently treated. Fourth, an attempt is made to outline a viable animal protection strategy. Here, it is argued that the emphasis placed by animal rights abolitionists on a vegan education campaign is flawed because it does not take enough account of the crucial importance of interests in the determination of public policy and the need for animal advocates to be engaged in a political, rather than a moral, struggle. The final section is a clarion call for the animal movement to be a broad church, not only on the grounds that this is a politically astute position to adopt but also on the grounds that any viable moral discourse must take into account more than rationalistic ethical principles.

The Continuum of Recognition

Our first task must be to establish accurately the ethical parameters of the debate and what follows for the treatment of animals from holding a particular set of ethical beliefs. It is important to distinguish here between what is prescribed by ethics and what is achievable politically or strategically. In the case of ethics, we are dealing with normative arguments that are a qualitatively different kind from empirical ones. Empirical arguments can be used to bolster normative ones, but ultimately—as David Hume (1739/1978), the great Scottish philosopher, most notably recognized—they cannot be used as their ultimate judge. We should therefore seek to avoid confusing pronouncements on the treatment of animals that our ethics lead us to suggest and pronouncements about what we think is politically feasible at any particular time.

In terms of the ethical debate, there have been, in theory and practice, important historical shifts in what is popularly deemed to be the correct way to treat animals. Up until the nineteenth century, it was common, in theory and practice, to regard animals as morally unimportant. The absence of moral standing meant that what was done to animals mattered little ethically.[2] This position is partly based on the view that animals are not moral agents in the sense that they are not capable of recognizing right from wrong or capable of participating in moral agreements (Kant 1965; Narveson 1987). The moral unimportance of animals has also been based on the assertion that they are not sentient, having no ability to experience pleasure and pain. This view is particularly associated with the seventeenth-century French philosopher René Descartes (1912), who held that animals are mere automatons, such that their apparent aversive reaction to negative stimuli is a mechanical response with no conscious intent. In particular, this provided a justification for experimenting on animals at a time when no anesthetic was available. A similar line of thought has been suggested by the contemporary British philosopher Peter Carruthers (1989), who argues, in at least some of his work on animal ethics, that animals do not have conscious awareness of their pain and therefore cannot suffer. For those who hold that animals have no moral standing, the only duties we have toward them are indirect ones. That is, harming animals becomes morally significant only if it harms the interests of humans who own them.

The advancement in animal ethics is revealed by the fact that few philosophers would deny now that animals are sentient, and few would deny that we owe at least something to them directly. What we do to animals, then, matters to them and not just to those humans with a vested interest in their protection. Indeed, this continuum of recognition has now gone a step further, with some philosophers challenging the view that animals are morally inferior to humans. As Francione rightly points out in this volume, the nineteenth-century utilitarian philosopher Jeremy Bentham (1948, 311) set the scene for this transformation in the moral status of animals when he wrote, in an oft-quoted passage, that "the question" of moral status is not "Can they reason? Nor, Can they talk? But, Can they suffer?" Animals' lack of moral agency is still, for some, philosophically important, but it is now more often than not invoked to deprive animals of an increase in moral status rather than to deny the existence of any moral standing. There is a consensus, in other words, that the sentience of animals means that we have some moral obligations to them.

It is the recognition of the moral significance of sentience that forms the basis of the concept of animal welfare. Indeed, animal welfare has reached such a degree of acceptability that it can be regarded as the moral orthodoxy. Its central feature is an insistence that humans are morally superior to animals but that, because animals have some moral worth, we are not entitled to inflict suffering on them if the human benefit thereby resulting is not necessary. The principle of unnecessary suffering, therefore, can be invoked if the level of suffering inflicted on an animal outweighs the benefits likely to be gained by humans. Robert Nozick (1974, 35–42) provides a concise but admirably effective definition of animal welfare when he writes that it constitutes "utilitarianism for animals, Kantianism for people." So sacrificing the interests of animals for the aggregative welfare is permissible provided that the benefit is significant enough, but treating humans in the same way is prohibited, regardless of what benefits might accrue from the sacrifice.

By contrast, a number of moral philosophers, writing mostly over the past forty years, have challenged the view that animals possess the inferior moral status that the animal welfare position prescribes. This position tends to be associated with the attempt to attach moral rights to animals, although the debate is much more nuanced than that suggests. In fact, one of the best-known pro-animal philosophers, Peter Singer (1990), argues from a utilitarian perspective. Singer suggests that we ought to treat like interests alike (the equal consideration of interests), and because at least some animals are sentient, it is morally illegitimate to always prioritize human interests in not suffering. In some situations, indeed, there may be a case for saying that animals can suffer more than humans and that therefore their interests should prevail.

It is a mistake, in my view, to label as welfarist Singer's ethical position (as opposed to his view on strategy, which might be characterized as "new welfarist"). It is true that other utilitarian thinkers, such as Bentham and John Stuart Mill, were influential in the theorizing of animal welfare. The emphasis placed by utilitarians on the moral value of sentience led to the conclusion that the suffering of animals ought to be taken into account in any valid moral theory. As Mill (1969, 184) wrote in 1874,

> Granted that any practice causes more pain to animals than it gives pleasure to man; is that practice moral or immoral? And if, exactly in proportion as human beings raise their heads out of the slough of selfishness, they do not with one voice answer "immoral," let the morality of the principle of utility be forever condemned.

To equate utilitarianism with animal welfare, however, is problematic and potentially misleading. This is because, for utilitarians, the benchmark for moral standing for *both* humans and animals is sentience. That is, although utilitarians (or, to be more precise, act utilitarians) find it difficult to incorporate the value of animal life into their theory, they also find it difficult to incorporate the value of human life. Following from this, utilitarians adopt an aggregative principle to determine the rightness or wrongness of an action. Thus, utilitarianism, or at least the version known as act utilitarianism, holds that the rightness or wrongness of an act can be determined by measuring the overall balance of pleasure (or, for Singer, preferences) over pain (or the denial of preferences). As we saw earlier, animal welfare amounts to applying utilitarianism for animals, but the ethical treatment of humans is to be judged in an entirely different way, in the sense that significant human interests cannot be traded off in a similar way.

The logic of Bentham's position is to equate the like suffering of humans and animals. Indeed, the emphasis he placed on the moral importance of sentience led his critics to claim that he was promoting the base pleasures and therefore encouraging individuals to live debased lives of sensual indulgence. In other words, in the critic's eyes, Bentham was encouraging humans to behave in an animalistic way and to regard such behavior as morally significant.

This was not strictly true. Bentham simply argued that pleasures could be measured quantitatively and that they did not differ qualitatively. It might be the case, after weighing the pleasures and pains involved in a particular act, that a more intellectual pursuit, on balance, would involve more pleasure than pain, but on the other hand, it might not. Critics, though, were not slow in claiming that Bentham's principle amounted to a "philosophy of pigs" because it might result in obligating people to pursue the pleasures of animals and sacrifice those of humans if by so doing we could maximize happiness or pleasure.

Mill, as a man who placed great store on intellectual pursuits, was so disturbed by the attempt to associate utilitarianism with what he called the lower pleasures that he revised Bentham's utilitarianism by distinguishing between higher and lower pleasures. For him, the "higher" pleasures (those that are peculiarly human) are infinitely preferable to the "lower" (animalistic) pleasures. "It is better to be a human being dissatisfied," Mill (1972, 10) famously wrote, "than a pig satisfied, better to be Socrates dissatisfied than a fool satisfied." It has been regularly suggested that Mill, by introducing a qualitative dimension to pleasure, undermines the utilitarian principle that only the quantity of pleasure is morally important. For our purposes, though, what is crucial is that the emphasis on sentience in the classical utilitarianism of Bentham put animals on the moral agenda in a big way. Bentham, for whatever reason, failed to draw the radical implications that seemed to follow from his ethical theory. Indeed, he seemed to settle on a version of animal welfare. Thus, in a letter to a newspaper in 1825, he wrote the following:

> I never have seen, nor ever can see, any objection to the putting of dogs and other inferior animals to pain, in the way of medical experiment, when the experiment has a determinate object, beneficial to mankind, accompanied with a fair prospect of the

accomplishment of it. But I have a decided and insuperable objection to the putting of them to pain without any such view.

(quoted in Clarke and Linzey 1990, 136)

Peter Singer, a later utilitarian, does draw such radical conclusions from utilitarianism. Because of this, his ethical position can be regarded as significantly different from animal welfare. It is true that Singer, all things being equal, does seem to regard animal life as less important morally than human life, and as discussed later in this chapter, I share this view. In a sense, though, this is not a theoretically significant observation for utilitarians because for them the morally important criterion is sentience, or the ability to suffer, and therefore the question of life and death for animals *or* humans is not of primary concern philosophically. The key point here is that Singer does not attach rights to either humans *or* animals. A morally correct action is one that maximizes pleasures or preferences. Singer's position is often, incorrectly, equated with animal welfare because he does not use the concept of rights for animals. For Singer, though, to prioritize human interests, in the way that the animal welfare ethic does, is speciesist because it is basing moral superiority on species membership rather than on a morally relevant characteristic. That is, present practices have a built-in assumption that nontrivial human interests are not to be counted as part of the utilitarian calculation, but merely defended, *whatever the cost to animals*.

Because of this, Singer can, and does, arrive at radical conclusions. Thus, he may be a "flexible vegan," as Francione points out in this book, but he does see himself philosophically as an inflexible vegetarian. Being a vegetarian, on the other hand, is not essential for animal welfarists. We might want to challenge Singer's argument for vegetarianism on utilitarian grounds (see subsequent paragraphs), but an animal welfarist could not engage in such a cost-benefit analysis where the interests of humans and animals are considered equally. Only if eating meat is unnecessary, in the sense that it does not serve any significant human benefit, can it be prohibited from an animal welfare perspective.

Singer's work is not immune from the general criticism of utilitarianism's aggregative principle. As it has been exhaustively noted, utilitarianism would appear to justify sacrificing the interests of individuals if this would result in an aggregative amount of the desirable objective. As a result, utilitarianism "entails very counterintuitive solutions to questions of distributive justice" (Carruthers 1992, 27). In Jones's words (1994, 62), "There is no end to the horror stories that can be concocted to illustrate the awful possibilities that utilitarianism might endorse." For example, utilitarianism might justify as moral the persecution of a racial minority in the interests of a racist majority or the killing of a healthy individual so that her organs can be transplanted into a number of sick individuals.

Although Singer's commitment to vegetarianism cannot be denied, the aggregative character of utilitarianism makes it debatable, to say the least, whether vegetarianism can be justified on utilitarian grounds. Such a justification would require the balancing of pains and pleasures or preference satisfactions, and therefore, meat-eating is not ruled out as it is if we grant to animals a right to life. Singer thinks utilitarianism does justify vegetarianism; others do not. Frey (1983, 197–206), for instance, provides an impressive list of the consequences of an end to animal agriculture—including the direct loss of jobs in the farming and food industries and knock-on effects in a number of other industries. Against this, however, we have to factor in the suffering inflicted on animals (particularly in intensive systems), the environmental consequences of raising animals for food, and the human health problems associated in particular with the increasing use of drugs in the meat-production process (Mason and Singer 1990, 72–127).

Genuine advocates of animal rights agree with Singer that animals deserve a higher moral status than the moral orthodoxy allows. However, they differ in their assertion that both humans and animals ought, individually, to be granted the protection offered by rights. Some animal rights philosophers suggest that rights can be granted to animals merely on the grounds that they are sentient (Rollin 1981). Others, most notably Tom Regan (1984), argue that it is the cognitive capacities of animals that are the key to their status as right holders.

Animal rights philosophers disagree with the view that animals (and humans) ought to be subject to the kind of cost-benefit analysis insisted on by utilitarians such as Singer. For them, it is not permissible to sacrifice the interests of some (humans or animals) in order to achieve an aggregate social benefit. To give an example, the rights view would not sanction the use of humans or animals in scientific experiments even if the consequence was that many other humans and animals benefited from it. Again, it is important not to misunderstand Singer's alternative position. An animal welfare view, as indicated previously, would sanction the use of animals in such scientific experiments if the benefit to other humans and animals was significant. The use of humans, as rights holders, is prohibited. Singer's view differs from the animal welfare position in the sense that he would be willing to consider a cost-benefit calculation provided that the interests of humans *and* animals are considered equally. This leaves open the possibility that it might be permissible to use both humans (at least some) and animals in scientific experiments, although Singer would then invoke the argument from marginal cases (see next section), which would rule out using either.

A Flawed Ethic

Philosophically, there are strong grounds for suggesting that the animal welfare ethic is flawed. Its defenders—those who accept human moral superiority—must be able to show why humans should be so regarded. This involves demonstrating that humans are different from animals in morally significant ways. Clearly, species membership alone is not sufficient without explaining what it is about humans that make them morally superior to animals. The usual answer to this question is the claim that humans possess a collection of mental characteristics—autonomy, memory, language, agency—that together constitutes personhood. Humans, therefore, are persons, and animals, though sentient, are not. Persons, it is said, can be harmed in much more fundamental ways than nonpersons and have lives that are qualitatively more worthwhile. As a result, it is morally permissible to sacrifice the interests animals have in not suffering in order to defend the much more profound interests humans have (see, for example, Townsend 1976).

Three responses to the personhood argument should be noted. First, it has been suggested that at least some animals do possess elements of personhood. This critique of the personhood justification for regarding humans as morally superior to animals is suggested in particular by Regan (1984). Regan seeks to show that at least some animals are what he calls "subjects-of-a-life," possessing enough mental complexity to be morally considerable. These capabilities are as follows:

Beliefs and desires; perception, memory, and a sense of the future, including their own future; an emotional life together with feelings of pleasure and pain; preference—and welfare—interests; the ability to initiate action in pursuit of their desires and goals; a psychophysical identity over time; and an individual welfare in the sense that their experiential life fares well or ill for them, logically independently of their utility for others.

(Regan 1984, 243)

Because at least some animals have these capabilities, Regan argues that they have a welfare that is capable of being harmed not only by inflictions of pain and deprivation but also by death because it forecloses all possibilities of finding satisfaction in life. The key point is that rights are not granted to animals by virtue of their sentience but because they are what Regan calls "subjects-of-a-life," beings with considerable cognitive capabilities.

There are two main problems with this critique of the personhood argument. First, some nonhuman species clearly have a greater claim to personhood than others, nonhuman primates being the prime candidates. This is the rationale behind the Great Ape Project, a movement that has sought to campaign for an extension of rights beyond the human species (Cavalieri and Singer 1993). However, the effect of achieving this goal would simply be to create another boundary line, with humans and some animals above it and the vast majority of animals below it. Second, it is equally clear that even the most intellectually able animals do not have the characteristics of personhood to the same degree as the average adult human. As a result, animals will always lose out in a direct application of the personhood argument if the personhood argument is applied without any further adaptation. To be sure that I am not misunderstood here, I am not claiming necessarily that animals are therefore morally less important than humans but claiming only that the adoption of the personhood argument, without any qualification, has that effect.

One such adaptation provides the second response to the personhood argument. This is the assertion that not all humans are persons. Thus, in the so-called argument from marginal cases, the following is asked: if we persist in justifying the exploitation of animals on the grounds that they are cognitively less able than humans, then what should we do with those humans—the seriously mentally disabled in particular—who do not themselves have the characteristics of personhood? Consistency would seem to demand either that we exploit human mental defectives as well as animals or that we exploit neither animals nor marginal humans (see Dombrowski 1997).

The argument from marginal cases has produced a burgeoning literature (see Garner 2005, 55–65), with by no means a majority supportive of the position. Against the position is the argument that infants can be excluded as marginal humans on the grounds that they are potential adults. Second, it has been suggested that kinship— the fact that we are genetically similar because we are all humans— is an important defense of treating marginal humans in the same way as normal adult humans (Midgley 1983). Finally, it is also suggested that the argument from marginal cases underestimates the capacity of marginal humans and that the capacities of even a severely damaged human are still greater than the most mentally developed nonhuman (Cohen 1986).

The third response to the personhood argument is the stronger argument—in my mind at least—that the mere fact that animals are sentient ought to result in animals being accorded a higher moral status than the animal welfare ethic allows. It is important to note that this follows *even if* we concede, as Singer (1993, 89–90), and others do, that animal lives are worth less morally than human lives. There are strong grounds for believing that this must be conceded. Indeed, there is a consensus among pro-animal philosophers that human life is more valuable than animal life. Even Regan (1984, 324–25), who does attach a right to life to mammals over the age of one, claims that in the event of a choice between saving the life of a human and the life of an animal, the human would normally win out.

The reason for the greater value placed on human life relates to the harm caused by death. There are two distinct ways in which harm might be caused by death. The first, what DeGrazia (2002, 59–61) calls the "desire-based account," postulates that death causes harm because it denies a desire to stay alive. DeGrazia is probably right to assert here that no animals, except perhaps the higher mammals, even understand the concept of staying alive, let alone the desire to do so. As a result, death is not a harm for animals according to this account of the harm caused by death. Normal adult humans, on the other hand, clearly do possess the concept of death, and most do have a desire to stay alive. "To take the lives" of such self-conscious beings, as Singer (1993, 90) points out, "is to thwart their desires for the future. Killing a snail or a day-old infant does not thwart any desires of this kind, because snails and newborn infants are incapable of having such desires."

DeGrazia (2002, 61) also identifies an "opportunities-based" account of the harm caused by death. Unlike the desire-based account, this view does not depend on an individual's awareness of the opportunities lost by death. Rather, "death is an instrumental harm in so far as it forecloses the valuable opportunities that continued life would afford." Thus, the nature of this thwarting of desires is not about individuals feeling frustrated, angry, or unfulfilled because they will not be alive to feel such things. Clearly, though, it is important to recognize that great anxiety is likely to be caused by a fear of death, a feeling that will not be present in a being that has no conception of his or her own future. But assuming the death was instantaneous and unexpected, it is the lost opportunities that are thwarted. In other words, there are harms of deprivation. So, laboring the point somewhat, it is wrong to claim that painless death causes no harm because we are not aware of it. We can clearly be harmed even though we are unaware of the fact.

For a person, death means that a future is taken away, consisting of "a constellation of experiences, beliefs, desires, goals, projects, activities, and various other things" (Rowlands 2002, 76). If the life is taken of a being who does not have this "constellation of experiences" or has them to a lesser degree, it is difficult to see that this being can be harmed to the same extent, provided the death is painless. As Sapontzis (1987, 218) remarks, "thanks to our superior intellect, we are capable of appreciating fine art, conceptual matters, moral fulfilment, flights of imagination, remembrance and anticipation, and so on in addition to what animals can experience" In Singer's (1990, 21) words, "to take the life of a being who has been hoping, planning and working for some future goal is to deprive that being of the fulfilment of all those efforts; to take the life of a being with a mental capacity below the level needed to grasp that one is a being with a future—much less make plans for the future—cannot involve this particular kind of loss."

All of this suggests that human lives are of greater moral importance than animal lives. It is important to recognize, however, that although the argument related to greater richness of opportunities means that animals (as well as marginal humans) have less to lose from death than do human persons, this is not to say that they lose nothing by death. Indeed, according to the opportunities-based account, to be harmed by death requires only sentience given that death prevents the future possibility of pleasurable experiences. This leads us to the conclusion that, although it is wrong to kill an animal, it is not as great a wrong as killing a human. So if we had to choose between saving the life of an animal and saving a human, then, all things being equal, we should choose the latter.

Similar arguments employed to justify the claim that it is a greater harm to take a human life than to take to an animal life might be used to deny animals a right to liberty. One interpretation would be that because humans are autonomous, liberty is intrinsically valuable to us. That is, it is valuable irrespective of the benefits—such as avoidance of frustration—that derive from it. For animals, on the other hand, liberty is valuable precisely because of the goods deriving from it. As a result, liberty is a means to the end of the achievement of other goals, whereas for humans it is intrinsically valuable. Liberty may therefore be beneficial to animals, but only when it has, say, the effect of alleviating suffering (Cochrane 2009a).

Another interpretation of the liberty argument is that for *both* humans and animals, the case for granting liberty is equally instrumental. That is, liberty is valuable to humans because of the benefits it produces in terms of the ability to perform the capabilities of autonomous beings. Therefore, what is wrong with human slavery, for example, is that it harms humans by so limiting them as to prevent them from performing many of the functions of autonomous beings. It makes less sense, on the other hand, to talk about animal slavery because there is not the same denial of autonomy through depriving animals of their liberty.

However, it seems sensible to further suggest that the same inequality between humans and animals does not apply to the issue of sentience. In some instances at least, the pain suffered by animals is at least as great as the pain suffered by humans, and this could also apply to other forms of suffering, such as fear or boredom. Indeed, it is possible to envisage situations where the suffering of an animal would be greater than that of a human in a similar situation. This "sentience position" therefore, does not rule out sacrificing animal lives in order to protect human lives, but it does clearly prohibit morally the infliction of suffering on animals for human benefit.

We are heading here toward a justification for according to animals a right not to suffer rather than a right to life or to liberty. This position would hold, for example, that where it can be shown that the use of animals in scientific research contributes significantly to the protection of human lives, and where such research does not involve causing animals to suffer, then it should be permitted. The consequence of accepting this sentience position is that many of the current practices justified by the animal welfare ethic become unacceptable. For instance, inflicting suffering on animals in order to provide food would, in almost all cases, no longer be sanctioned. There are two possible exceptions: One would be where depriving humans of the right to eat animals would be life-threatening, a scenario that does not exist now, at least in the developed world. The other would be an extensive system of animal agriculture where the suffering of animals is minimized. In an age of intensive animal agriculture, where factory farms are the norm, such a scenario is, at least at present, unlikely.

It is important to recognize that we have been focusing on ethical principles and not what is feasible politically. More specifically, it is being claimed here that *on ethical grounds* much of what is now permitted under the aegis of animal welfare ought to be prohibited. Equally, though, it is being claimed that *on ethical grounds* there may be a case for sacrificing the lives of animals if human lives will be protected as a result, and *on ethical grounds* there may be a case for using animals to the point where their lives are taken, provided that they do not suffer as a consequence. These are ethical principles and not arguments employed because it is thought they are more likely to be accepted by the general public and decision makers. It is a particular version of animal rights and by no means the only one. To reinforce a point made earlier, they are not principles that it is possible to defeat by the employment of empirical arguments or, to put it simply, by the use of facts.

It is important to note that the animal rights/liberation movement is not centered on demonstrating that animals have an intrinsic interest in life and liberty, although that may be for reasons of political convenience rather than ethical belief. More central to the animal rights/liberation movement is the assertion that animals have an interest in not suffering. This is why the two major issues in animal ethics are the treatment of animals on farms and treatment of animals in laboratories, where the greatest degree of suffering takes place. This is also why the keeping of pet or companion animals, as opposed to their treatment, is really on the periphery of the debate (despite the fact that it involves restrictions on liberty). Equally, zoos and circuses tend to be morally condemned by the animal rights/liberation movement not because of the loss of liberty such activity produces per se but primarily because the infringement of liberty causes suffering.

A Defense of Animal Protectionism Against Two Charges

Of course, as Francione and others have correctly observed, the animal protection movement has been prepared to campaign and lobby for political outcomes that fall short of an animal rights agenda, even if it is accepted that animals have a right not to suffer and not a right to life. Can we really object to this "new welfarism," as Francione and others do? Such an objection seems to be based on two main grounds, which I will discuss in order of importance. First, it is argued that animal welfare reforms are counterproductive because they make it more acceptable to exploit animals. In other words, they salve people's consciences. What is wrong, for instance, with eating humanely slaughtered and raised animals? Second is the argument that, in any case, animal welfare reforms are almost always unsuccessful. In particular, the property status of animals makes it impossible to achieve reforms that damage the interests of their owners. As a consequence of these two points, it is argued, animal rights advocates should focus on single-issue campaigns that are genuinely abolitionist, in the sense that they explicitly endorse the principle that exploiting animals is wrong, and predominantly on vegan education campaigns. This ensures that they will not be associated with campaigns and lobbying that focus on animal welfare improvements, thereby avoiding the impression that it is acceptable to eat animals or use them in scientific experiments provided that their treatment is humane. In addition, it enables the distribution of resources from pointless animal welfare campaigns to the task of promoting veganism.

Before these claims are considered in some detail, it is worth-while to point out that the critique of new welfarism, or animal protectionism as I prefer to call it, is intuitively odd. This is, first, because it seeks to challenge the operating practice of most animal rights groups. Most animal rights groups accept the need to engage in the contemporary political and legislative debate about animals, and this means, sometimes at least, advocating reforms to the way animals are treated that fall short of abolishing particular practices. Of course, Francione recognizes this. Indeed, it is a fundamental part of his case. As he argues (1996, 3), "the modern animal 'rights' movement has explicitly rejected the philosophical doctrine of animal rights in favor of a version of animal welfare that accepts animal rights as an ideal state of affairs that can be achieved only through continued adherence to animal welfare measures." The following question then arises: can all these organizations, and the people who work within them, be so wrong? It is, I concede, possible that they might be, but it is, I would suggest, unlikely. Second, animal rights abolitionism is intuitively odd because it asks us to accept the following proposition—that we should seek the complete abolition of practices that the animal protection movement has spent years trying, with only limited success, to reform. The question to ask here is, is such a position credible?

Animal Welfare Is Not Counterproductive

As we have seen, one objection to what has been described as new welfarism is the charge that it is a counterproductive strategy in that it hinders the achievement of abolitionist animal rights goals. An initial point to make here is that if this argument fails, as I think it does, then animal rights abolitionism is put immediately on the back foot. That is, if this argument fails, then the cost involved in pursuing a broader new welfarist, or animal protection, strategy all but disappears. The onus is then on the critics of animal protectionism to show that there have been no benefits to animals whatsoever from animal welfare measures that have been promoted by the animal protection movement. This, I would argue, is a difficult task.

A number of responses to the "counterproductive" argument can be made. In the first place, it might be argued that significant welfare reforms are not just a staging post toward the achievement of animal rights goals, but are in themselves ethically desirable. In other words, animal welfare measures that do reduce suffering *are* preferable to not acting from an ethical point of view. I argued earlier for an animal rights ethic based on the principle that animals have a right not to suffer. It is conceivable, in principle, that welfare reforms could minimize suffering to such a degree, without abolishing a particular practice, that ethical concerns could be allayed, although it is conceded that this would be difficult to achieve.

A more productive critique of the counterproductive argument is that it is a charge that is impossible to prove because it involves a speculative judgment: "*if* such and such is done, then a future objective will not be possible." It amounts to saying that *if* the public were not told that the welfare of animals was thriving, then they would be more likely to do something about it. As a corollary, it involves the judgment that *if* animal welfare reforms are pursued successfully, then animal rights goals will not be achieved because not enough people would want them. Equally speculative is the claim that *if* resources were diverted into vegan education campaigns, then more vegans would now exist. But how can we know all of this with certainty?

There appears to be anecdotal evidence that some people have been persuaded that the conditions of animals have been improved to the point that these people are no longer worried about the treatment of animals. At the very least, though, there needs to be more rigorous empirical research on this. Isn't it just as likely, if not more so, that the publicity given to the treatment of animals as a result of an animal welfare–based campaign will have the effect of mobilizing additional concern about the treatment of animals? Indeed, isn't this how concern for animals emerged in the first place? It is extremely likely, too, that those who are already committed to the abolition of the use of animals are unlikely to be persuaded of the error of their ways as a result of any one particular animal welfare campaign. If they were, it would be equivalent, in ideological terms, to saying that a slight improvement in the condition of the working class in a capitalist society would turn those on the extreme left into supporters of capitalism. Moreover, as I suggested earlier, decades of campaigning by animal rights groups— some, at least, of which has been concerned with abolishing particular uses of animals—has failed to produce more than minority support for abolitionist ends.

It is instructive here to take a historical view of how the animal issue has developed. Fifty years or so ago, vegetarianism was an alien concept for most. Now it is commonplace. This transformation, one can strongly speculate, has been at least partly the product of animal welfare–based campaigns, highlighting, for example, the evils of factory farming and the need to reform it. The only reason promoting veganism is now a more credible goal is exactly because of the work put in by the whole animal protection movement in the past, including those who have adopted an animal welfarist strategy.

There would also seem to be a built-in inconsistency with the counterproductive argument. If animal welfare reforms have been largely unsuccessful in genuinely improving the treatment of animals, then it is not clear how, for instance, it can be claimed that they can result in persuading people to continue eating them on the very grounds that their treatment has improved. If, on the other hand, animal welfare reforms have been successful in improving the treatment of animals, then are they not worth having for their own sake? Moreover, is it not the case that those reforms would not have been achieved without campaigning/lobbying? And if so, the following question then arises: is it worthwhile to sacrifice the benefits that have been achieved for an animal rights/abolitionist future that may not be realized? Is the animal rights abolitionist position really saying that if we had to choose between effective and ineffective animal welfare reforms, we should choose the latter because by so doing we make it less acceptable to eat or experiment on animals?

This kind of scenario is a familiar one for all fundamentalist positions. There is an instructive parallel in movements of the far left. It is often claimed—most notably by the Greek structuralist Marxist Nicos Poulantzas (1968)—that the capitalist system has survived, despite Marx's predictions of its inevitable downfall, because the ruling class offers compensations in the form of, say, free education and health care. These reforms may well serve the interests of the ruling class, it is argued, because free health care and education have the effect of creating a more productive workforce who will therefore increase the profits of the bourgeoisie. In addition, the reforms have the effect of buying off the working class, who, as a result, lose their revolutionary consciousness. The implication here is that the left should not support reforms to the capitalist system, irrespective of their capacity to increase the well-being of the working class, because to do so is to perpetuate the capitalist system and prevent a communist alternative.[3]

If we substitute humans for capitalists and animals for the working class in the preceding argument, we have a pretty accurate description of the abolitionist animal rights position. Both the unreconstructed Marxist position and the abolitionist animal rights position are predicated on the unprovable and unlikely assumption that if we stand back and let the position of the working class or animals deteriorate, then their ultimate liberation—from capitalism for the working class and from exploitation by humans for animals—will be made more likely. The fundamentalist leftist argument does not have much to commend it, but if anything, it is more plausible than the abolitionist animal rights position. This is because in the former case, at least there is a working class capable, at least in theory, of liberating itself. By contrast, animals, of course, are not capable of liberating themselves.

It is important to recognize what would be required to achieve the goals of the animal rights abolitionist. The agenda of the animal rights movement is abolitionist. One of the key features of rights is that they build protective fences around individuals. That is, there is a strong presumption that the interests of individuals should not be sacrificed in order to produce an aggregative social good. If animals are included as rights holders, then it follows that they too should be treated as ends and not as means to an end. If we accept that animals have a right to life, the consequence is that most, if not all, of the present ways we treat animals become morally illegitimate. We should certainly not continue to eat animals or experiment on them, the two main uses to which animals are put. Even if we accept the version of animal rights offered in this chapter, which does not advocate a right of life to animals, abolitionist outcomes would still seem to be the outcome of ethical inquiry.

It is not difficult to see that the achievement of this agenda presents enormous difficulties for the animal rights movement. No country in the world has prohibited the use of animals for medical research or as a source of food. The industries involved in these activities are extremely wealthy and have a great deal of political influence. Moreover, most consumers eat meat and benefit from the development of drugs that have been developed and tested on animals. Coupled with all of this is the use of animals to produce clothes, footwear, and entertainment in zoos, circuses, and horse and greyhound racing. The list is endless.

The animal rights movement is extraordinarily altruistic. Animal rights is a cause that seeks to advance the interests of nonhuman species, *even when* these interests are in conflict with the significant interests of humans. It is not surprising that research has found that concern for animals diminishes as the severity of conflict between animals and humans increases (Opotow 1993). So clearly, a movement that is painted as promoting a cause that will, rightly or wrongly, damage some human interests is going to face peculiar problems. This is particularly the case because, unlike other liberation movements—based, for instance, on race and gender—the beneficiaries cannot campaign for their own liberation. It therefore requires an unprecedented level of altruism for humans to act on their behalf. As Gray (1997, 162) astutely points out,

> There is little utility for practical men and women in observing that the demands of human well-being may be at odds with those of other animal species. After all, public policy is formed and implemented by human beings. No measure that does not promise a benefit to human is likely to gain a hearing.

Because of the inability of animals to liberate themselves, and because of the benefits humans get from exploiting animals, the animal protection movement needs to spend a great deal more time focusing on the question of agency. Merely assuming that a vegan education campaign is going to persuade enough, or the right, people to change their ways is naive in the extreme. Agency focuses not so much on what has to be done to achieve the objectives of animal advocates so much as on *who* is to do it. More specifically, it asks which groups of (human) individuals in society are more likely than others to support the objectives of animal rights. The animal protection movement has not done enough thinking about agency. More often than not, as with the emphasis on the vegan education campaign, there is an assumption that all we have to do is publicize the reality of animal exploitation, and once fellow humans come to see the rational case for animal rights, they will adopt it without question.

Animal Welfare Does Work, or Works Better
Than the Alternatives

The second feature of animal rights abolitionism is the claim that animal welfare does not work, so we are not really losing anything by demanding that the animal protection movement refocus its energy away from reformist animal welfare goals and to an abolitionist educational campaign. One initial point to make here, before considering this claim in detail, is that if it can be established—as I think I have done—that animal welfare reforms are not counterproductive, then the stakes are no longer as high. If campaigning and lobbying for animal welfare reforms does not have the effect of making future animal rights goals less likely, then all we now have to show is that, on balance, some, but by no means all, animal welfare reforms do improve the position of animals, however slightly.

Part of the case for the argument that animal welfare does not work is the property status of animals. This, it is argued by a number of legal scholars—including, most notably, Francione (1995, 1996), but also Kelch (1998) and Wise (2000)—is important because while animals remain the property of humans, not only is it impossible to achieve the elevated moral status for animals required by animal rights, but the status also ensures that animal welfare measures cannot be effective because legislation will not be allowed to infringe the rights of property owners.

It might be tempting to concede that there is much truth in the first assertion—that while animals remain property, they cannot have the full entitlement of rights, especially the right to be free from exploitation. They will always be, the argument goes, subordinate to their owners. Equality between humans and animals, in other words, is impossible while animals remain the property of humans, just as it was impossible for human slaves to achieve equality with those humans who were free. Even this position, however, can be challenged if we adopt the version of animal rights theory that I elaborated earlier. This is based on showing that animals have a right not to suffer rather than a right to life and liberty. Following Cochrane (2009b), it is possible to argue that equality between humans and animals can be consistent with ownership if we adopt the principle that we should treat the *interests* of animals equally with those of humans. Crucial to the success of this argument, which is worth exploring in some detail, is the acceptance of an interest-based conception of rights rather than a choice-based conception. The former sees rights as protecting individual interests whereas the latter sees rights as protecting an individual's autonomy to act. The choice of the former is consistent with the adoption of the position, suggested earlier, that animals do not have an interest in a right to life or to liberty because they lack autonomy, but that they do have an interest in not suffering.

The adoption of an interest-based conception of rights allows us to invoke the equal consideration of interests principle as the key indicator of human–animal equality. This is not the same, of course, as treating humans and animals in exactly the same way. It is for this reason that the oft-made comparison between human and animal slavery does not really work. Although it may be the case that human slavery infringes important human interests and therefore prevents slaves from achieving equality with other humans, the same is not necessarily the case with animals. To argue that it is the same is to imply that animals and humans have exactly the same interests. What we have to decide is whether ownership runs contrary to the interests of animals. Cochrane considers three incidents of ownership—the right to possess, the right to use, and the right to transfer—and argues in each case that ownership does not infringe the interests of animals. Here I consider the first two as the most important components of property, at least as they affect animals.

Possession clearly restricts the freedom of animals, but as we saw previously, lack of freedom does not necessarily infringe their interests, although—depending on the species and nature of the restriction—it might do so.[4] Thus, it may be that restricting the freedom of the great apes is to infringe their interests because of their greater level of autonomy. Equally, restricting the freedom of a wild animal may infringe her interests in not suffering. To give one more example, restricting a domesticated animal's freedom to the point (as in the battery cage) where she is unable to fulfill her natural functions is also likely to cause suffering and would therefore be inconsistent with the equal consideration of interests principle. The crucial point here is that I am rejecting the principle, held by Francione and others, that all animals have a level of autonomy that provides a blanket prohibition on their ownership.

What about the *use* of animals? The animal rights abolitionists are committed to the principle that the very fact that animals are used (a key component of ownership) is inconsistent with equality between humans and animals. Thus, only if animals cease to be property, and therefore can no longer be used, can they achieve equality. Clearly, if animals are used in a way that involves the infliction of suffering and death, then this is inconsistent with the equal consideration of interests because animals do have an interest in not suffering and might (notwithstanding my previous arguments) also have an interest in not dying. But the use of animals does not necessarily involve this outcome. As Cochrane (2009b) points out, equating their property status with inequality follows only if we add the additional claim that animals possess an interest in not being used against their will. If we conceive of animals as not being autonomous (and therefore not having an interest in developing and pursuing their own life plans), then they do not have that interest. Using animals per se, therefore, is not the problem. It is what they are used for that is the key.

The status of animals as property, it has been argued, is not necessarily inimical to treating their interests as equal to ours. Abolishing animals' property status is not therefore a necessary condition for the achievement of animal rights. It should also be pointed out that it is by no means a sufficient condition either. The abominable treatment of many supposedly free humans throughout the world is an important reminder that granting formal rights does not necessarily result in better treatment in reality. The imposition from above of edicts abolishing the property status of animals, therefore, is unlikely to have the desired effect without a concurrent change in social values relating to their moral status.

The second claim—that the property status of animals militates against the introduction of successful welfare measures—is even less convincing. In the first place, we can reject the claim that is sometimes made that the property status of animals robs them of *any* moral standing. Francione (1996, 131–32) compares anticruelty statutes with the protection of historical landmarks, the aim of which is to ensure that human enjoyment of this property continues. This is surely mistaken. If upheld, it would amount to saying that animals, in reality, are treated like inanimate objects with no intrinsic value. Not only, as we saw earlier, is this anathema to the principle of animal welfare, but more importantly, it is also not true that animals are regarded like this in practice.

Most modern animal welfare statutes recognize that animals can be harmed directly. Thus, in most developed countries, a plethora of animal welfare statutes and regulations exist whose aim is to limit property rights in order to benefit animals directly. As Tannenbaum (1995, 568) correctly points out, "if one were to ask legislators, prosecutors, judges, and employees of humane societies ... they would say, virtually *universally*, that the primary purpose of these laws is to protect animals." The reason for this, of course, is a recognition that animals are sentient. There would not seem to be a conflict between sentience and property status and no suggestion, therefore, that property must be inanimate.

It is also doubtful that the property status of animals exists as a barrier to meaningful animal welfare reforms. The property status of animals is not the only, or even the most important, reason for the undoubted existence of many inadequate animal welfare laws. Giving primacy to a legal construct is to incorrectly relegate the social and political context within which the law has to operate. Indeed, the fact that animals are regarded as the property of humans is itself a reflection, and not the cause, of the relatively low worth attached to animals. Rather than attending to the legal framework, we should pay our attention to public perceptions of the priority that ought to be given to animal protection, to the influence of powerful interest groups with a vested, usually economic, interest in animal exploitation, and to the ideological importance attached to individualism in liberal democratic political systems.

These social and political factors help to explain the fact that animal welfare achievements have been greater in some countries (such as Britain and other parts of Europe) than others (such as the United States and in many other parts of the world) and greater in some policy networks than others within the same country (see Garner 1998). The property status of animals cannot be an explanatory variable here because in both Europe and the United States animals remain the property of humans. It is clear that in the United States greater weight tends to be placed on protecting the individual against societal and state interference. As a result, it is much more difficult to justify intervening in the private sphere of individuals to protect animals than it is in a country such as Britain where a more utilitarian and pragmatic attitude to public policy exists. The explanatory role given to ownership as the cause of animal suffering can also be challenged if we compare the different ways in which animals are used. For example, levels of protection afforded to farm and laboratory animals differ, even within the same country. Even more marked is the fact that companion animals, despite being regarded as property, are generally treated much more favorably than domesticated animals in farms and laboratories.

Before we discuss the character of animal welfare reforms in practice, three contextual points are necessary. First, it is possible to confirm that reforms to the way animals are treated short of the abolition of particular practices can, in theory at least, be beneficial to animals, leaving aside the argument that they are counterproductive. It is self-evident, for instance, that genuine free-range poultry systems that allow birds to perform their natural behavior patterns are infinitely preferable to intensive poultry systems. Likewise, a policy on animal experimentation that seeks to promote the three Rs—reduction, refinement, and replacement—is, if successful, a worthy goal. For example, at the risk of laboring the point, a regulation that insists on environmental enrichment for all laboratory animals is, all things being equal, of greater worth than one that requires it only for particular species, which in turn is better than having no regulation at all, effective enforcement notwithstanding.

Second, it may be the case—although I do not know how we would go about measuring this accurately—that the pain and suffering endured by animals is greater now than it was, say, fifty years ago and that more animals are exploited now than in the past. This, however, does not prove that animal welfare measures do not work; it might be suggested that things would be worse still without these measures. Merely counting the number of animals that are exploited by humans is not an adequate measure of suffering. For example, the number of animals used in scientific procedures in Britain declined from the high point of the 1970s, but more recently there has been a slight increase, from 2.6 million in 1997 to 3.2 million in 2007 (HMSO 1997–2007). This increase, however, is caused almost entirely by the increase in genetically modified animals. At present, the Home Office (the British Government department responsible for administering animal experimentation) includes in the statistics *all* genetically modified animals bred, not just those used in scientific procedures. Not all genetically modified animals suffer, and as the recent House of Lords select committee report on vivisection concluded, their blanket inclusion is not a particularly useful exercise (House of Lords 2002, 42).

Third, there is so much animal welfare legislation now in the developed world that it is possible to find examples of weak animal welfare laws, reasonably strong laws that are poorly enforced, and those that are enforced effectively. Selectively choosing examples to support a particular case is, therefore, not difficult, whereas providing a balanced view is more so.

It can be readily conceded that animal welfare statutes are sometimes weak and enforced ineffectively, although this is not primarily because animals are regarded as property. Much criticism, for instance, is directed at general anticruelty statutes that depend on the difficult task of proving unnecessary suffering. It tends to be the case that relatively trivial human interests are sometimes allowed to outweigh the vital interests of animals, but it is sometimes the case too that many animals are excluded from coverage, most notably farm and laboratory animals. Having said this, anticruelty statutes are flexible and allow for the addition of activities that are subsequently deemed to be unnecessary without the need for further legislation.

However, the general anticruelty statute approach is not the only animal welfare model. Some measures are regulatory in tone but much more specific than general anticruelty statutes. Others have been abolitionist, rather than regulatory. In Britain, for instance, the value of the primary statutes governing animal agriculture and animal experimentation—the 1968 Agricultural (Miscellaneous Provisions) Act and the 1986 Animals (Scientific Procedures) Act, respectively—is not so much in the basic unnecessary cruelty provisions they both contain, but in the potential they afford for abolitionist regulations to be added. For example, regulations banning veal crates and sow stalls and tethers have been added as regulations under the 1968 Act, and a decision prohibiting cosmetic testing of finished products and the use of wild-caught primates was made under the auspices of the 1986 Act.

There have been other abolitionist measures too. The bill to ban fox hunting (and deer hunting and hare coursing) that came into law in 2005 was abolitionist in the sense that it has ended the practice of allowing hounds to kill foxes, deer, and hares (a ban on fox hunting had been introduced two years earlier in Scotland). Various attempts to challenge this legislation in the courts have also been defeated, and at least 30 people seeking to evade the ban have been successfully prosecuted (http://www.league.org.uk/convictions). It is true that the legislation is vulnerable to a Conservative victory at the next general election (although, at the time of writing, such an eventuality is by no means a foregone conclusion), but it should also be borne in mind that, as an issue of conscience, any future vote in the House of Commons is likely to be a free one with no whips enforcing party loyalties. Indeed, in the key vote on the issue in the run-up to the passage of the abolitionist bill, a number of Labour MPs voted against the ban, and a total of six Conservative MPs and twenty-six Liberal Democrat MPs supported it (BBC News 2003).

Britain also became the first country in the world to ban fur farming when it was prohibited under the Labor Government's Fur Farming Prohibition Order, which came into force on January 1, 2003. The production of fur from wild-caught animals is not prohibited, but the vast majority of British-produced fur came from farms. Likewise, the leghold trap has been banned across the EU and in Britain for about fifty years, and the EU also banned the import of products derived from animals caught by the leghold trap. In Britain, the fur trade has gone into a steep decline, before leveling off in recent years and showing some signs of a modest upturn. In other countries, the fur trade has not declined to the same degree.

The Strategy of Incremental Abolitionism

A great deal of debate has surrounded the degree to which animal rights abolitionism can be incremental. The possibility that animal rights abolitionists might be prepared to support a series of single-issue campaigns that can be organized concurrently with a vegan education campaign would help to counter the charge that their position is unrealistic. This prospect, however, seems unlikely. Dunayer (2004, 2007) has tried to claim bragging rights for putting forward a "purer" version of abolitionism than others, in particular Francione—a version that is unwilling to have much if anything to do with any kind of incrementalism. In reality, though, this is an erroneous interpretation of Francione's position. Although he spends some time setting out the tests that would be necessary for single-issue campaigns to be genuinely abolitionist (1996, 207–11), it is unlikely that any actual single-issue campaigns one can think of would pass them.

Take the case of battery cages. Francione (1996, 210) considers the possibility that the abolition of battery cages would be justified if it "replaces it with a rearing system that accommodates *all* of the hen's interests in freedom of movement and thereby fully recognizes the interest of the hen in bodily integrity." In reality, though, there would be at least two objections to this from the animal rights abolitionist. In the first place, the replacement criteria in the example above is set at such a high level that it is unlikely that any rearing system could ever achieve it. Second, even if a rearing system could meet all of the hen's interests, it would still fall foul of the test whereby a measure is not genuinely abolitionist if it "reinforces the notion that animal slavery itself is acceptable" (Francione 1996, 211). Dunayer (2007, 12) concurs: "A ban on caging hens invites the conclusion that caging (torture) is abusive but the egg industry per se (exploitive captivity) is not." In addition, not only would the abolition of battery cages fail to eradicate the property status of animals; it also would fall foul of the argument, discussed previously, that such a measure would be counterproductive because it would give the impression that it is okay to eat eggs provided that they are produced humanely. As a result, Francione argues, the animal rights movement should avoid single-issue campaigns in favor of those designed to promote ethical veganism.

For all intents and purposes, then, Francione's position is not really different from that offered at a later date by Dunayer, despite her protestations to the contrary. Her argument is that no abolitionist measures in animal agriculture that do not liberate the affected animals from human exploitation as sources of food can be consistent with animal rights theory. On these grounds, for example, the abolition of battery cages is not an animal rights measure and can never be because hens still remain exploited. Only the complete ending of the poultry industry will meet the requirements of this position (Dunayer 2004, 12–15). For her (2007, 16), only "banning the production or sale of eggs in a particular jurisdiction would be incremental abolition," as would "increasing the percentage of humans who are vegan."

Dunayer, like Francione, oscillates between two different justifications for her argument that the kind of abolitionism represented by the abolition of battery cages is inadequate. The first is that *however* hens are kept, they still remain the property of humans and therefore remain exploited. After all, the abolition of battery hens still results in the hens being confined. She points out (2004, 152),

Many activists misunderstand the term *abolitionist*. Bans aren't automatically abolitionist. Yes, a ban abolishes something. However, if it leaves the animals in question within a situation of exploitation (such as food-industry enslavement and slaughter), it isn't abolitionist in the sense of being anti-slavery. An abolitionist ban is consistent with nonhuman freedom. It prevents or halts, rather than mitigates, abuse.

The second justification Dunayer uses, again like Francione, is that it is a matter of empirical fact that no alternative system of poultry husbandry can possibly provide for hens the quality of life that will free them from suffering.

The first of these justifications is logically correct, but I would reject it on the grounds that I do not accept the premise that we should not accept reforms that fall short of banning the use of animals completely, even if that means animals remain exploited. In addition, as I indicated above, I do not accept the argument that we cannot apply the principle of the equal consideration of interests to animals who remain the property of humans, nor do I accept the argument that to reform the way animals are treated is to automatically prevent further welfare improvements or, indeed, future abolition. The second justification is more plausible but is an empirical matter that has not yet been proven. There are clearly models of poultry husbandry that do not require the replacement of battery cages with equally dense indoor systems. It is also extremely likely that most consumers are unaware that some so-called free-range eggs are in reality nothing of the kind. As a response to this, though, there is at least an equally valid case for the animal rights movement to publicize this misuse of the phrase and put pressure on retailers to stock only the genuine item, rather than to wash its hands of the issue and simply say that consumers should not buy them at all.

What about other abolitionist measures? Clearly, there are different forms of abolition in the sense that the animal rights advocate does not always have to consider the substitution of an alternative. For example, it is quite realistic to campaign for the abolition of the leghold trap used to catch animals for their fur without suggesting that a more humane alternative be used (even though I would argue that a humane alternative is better than the continued use of a device that causes more suffering and, in addition, that there is more chance of a successful reform if an alternative is suggested). Likewise, support for a campaign to ban the live export of animals (as has happened in Britain) is justifiable because it is not suggesting that animals be exported by any other, more humane means. Francione confirms (1996, 212, 217) that such objectives might be consistent with an incremental abolitionism. Even Dunayer (2007, 18) is prepared to accept that some incremental abolitionist measures—such as the banning of elephants in circuses and the use of primates in the laboratory—are consistent with an animal rights position.

However, there are at least two problems with Francione's and Dunayer's support for such objectives. First, accepting these forms of abolition as a viable objective for the animal rights movement is to suggest, implicitly, that it is okay to catch fur-bearing animals by other means, okay to eat animals that are not subject to the stresses of long-distance travel to the slaughterhouse, okay to keep other animals in zoos, and okay to use other animals in laboratories. Following the logic of the argument against new welfarism, does not the implementation of these incremental abolitionist measures make the catching of fur-bearing animals, the eating of meat from animals not exported long distances, the keeping of other animals in zoos, and the use of other animals in the laboratory more acceptable practices, thereby making their eventual abolition that much more difficult? Dunayer (2007, 12) comments in connection with the poultry industry, "I can't think of a better way to soothe the conscience of humans who eat animal-derived food than to suggest that food-industry enslavement and slaughter can be humane." In other words, only opposition to the whole practice of using the fur of animals, eating animals, keeping them in circuses, and experimenting on them seems consistent with the general argument being made against new welfarism.

Second, there have been a number of campaigns that have met with some success that, despite being abolitionist, do not meet all of the tests that Francione wants to apply. These include the ban on the leghold trap in Europe; the campaign against live exports in Britain, which caused huge problems for the agricultural industry; and some restrictions on the use of primates in the laboratory and the use of elephants in circuses. Would not this suggest that some campaigns that are consistent with "new welfarist" principles, if not animal rights abolitionist principles, have actually worked? This does not sit well with the claim by animal rights abolitionists that they cannot.

There are other forms of abolitionism that do not fall foul of all of the problems identified here. For example, the abolition of toxicity testing on animals does not involve suggesting, or even implicitly accepting, an alternative method that involves animals (although it may, of course, involve suggesting nonhuman-based alternatives). The abolition of toxicity testing on animals may, however, have the effect of further strengthening the use of animals in drug development by making it more acceptable. That this is the view of the British Research Defence Society (the body that lobbies government in support of the use of animals in scientific research) is clear by its reluctance to get involved in the issue of toxicity testing of products other than drugs, for fear of being associated with practices that it regards as less important (Garner 1998, 60–61). A campaign to support a ban only on a particular type of product testing (e.g., on cosmetics or on tobacco products) is also inconsistent with animal rights abolitionism because it gives the impression that it is okay to perform toxicity tests for other products on animals, and it makes animal testing itself more acceptable by removing its worst excesses. Presumably, then, the successful campaigns against cosmetic and tobacco testing on animals in Britain are not worth having if we accept animal rights abolitionism.

In a nutshell, the problem with the attempt to devise a form of incremental abolitionism is that it is difficult to identify abolitionist measures, short of abolishing all animal exploitation in a particular sphere of activity, that remain consistent with the animal rights abolitionist principle. This is the principle that only those abolitionist measures that end the use of animals, and therefore uphold their intrinsic value—by, in effect, abolishing their property status—are justified. As a result, no consistent incrementalist strategy derives from the abolitionist principle as conceived by the fundamentalist principle. Francione (1996, 218) does recognize this when he says the following:

> *Any* attempt to eradicate incrementally the property status of non-humans will *necessarily* have to confront the fact that all incremental measures are imperfect because none will succeed in securing the basic right of animals not to be regarded as property.

Added to this, at least if we follow the logic of the abolitionist perspective, is the likely effect such incremental abolitionism will have in making the exploitation of animals more acceptable, and therefore more difficult to abolish completely in the future. As a result, animal rights fundamentalists are condemned to relying exclusively on the vegan education campaign. My view is that this unduly restricts what animal rights activism should be about.

It is important to note that I am not rejecting such an educational campaign. There is certainly a place for it. Fundamental changes are unlikely to come about without extensive public campaigns designed to alter the public's consciousness. But it is a very different matter to say that the animal rights movement should rely *exclusively* on such a campaign. Surely the animal rights movement cannot stand idly by and refuse to involve itself in campaigns to abolish battery cages or the use of primates or campaigns for the better treatment of animals in any sphere in which they are used. And of course—by and large—it has not done so, much to its credit. In addition, the stipulation that support for incremental reforms cannot involve the advocacy of alternatives to present practices (the replacement of one trap, for instance, with a more humane alternative) rules out one of the key pressure-group resources. That is, decision makers are more likely to listen to a pressure group if it can offer solutions to problems, and offering alternatives is a useful negotiating position. In the case of animals, of course, it is correct to say that this will mean that the exploitation continues, but it is hard to deny that animals can benefit from such a strategy.

A Defense of the Unnecessary Suffering Principle

An account of the current state of animal protection should not stop at a mere description of animal welfare measures. Of crucial importance is identification of the rationale behind the changes that have occurred and that must form the basis of the strategy of the animal protection movement. This rationale, it seems to me, is encapsulated by the concept of unnecessary suffering. The animal protection movement has focused on campaigning to end unnecessary suffering. Surprisingly little mention has been made of animal rights. Thus, the focus has been on showing not that the use of animals is morally wrong irrespective of the benefits to humans, but rather that most, if not all, of the ways in which animals are currently treated are unnecessary in the sense that they do not produce human benefits or that such benefits can be achieved in other ways. Indeed, Francione (2000, xxiii–xxiv) himself adopts this approach in his book-length text on animal rights. We can all accept, he suggests, what he calls the "humane treatment principle," which prohibits the infliction of unnecessary suffering on animals. But, he continues, we do not practice what we preach because "the overwhelming portion of our animal use can be justified *only* by habit, convention, amusement, convenience or pleasure." As a result, "most of the suffering that we impose on animals is completely unnecessary *however* we interpret that notion." It is correct that Francione does think that all uses of animals are unacceptable according to this principle, whereas many would not. But he, like I, can agree on the fact that much can be done for animals by adopting this principle.

The political advantage of focusing on what is unnecessary has the crucial strategic utility of maximizing public and movement support. There is a consensus in most developed countries at least that our uses of animals are too often unnecessary, that they serve trivial ends, or that these ends can be achieved in alternative ways that do not involve their exploitation. A classic example of this was the campaign to ban the live exports of animals from Britain in the 1990s, which was based not on promoting vegetarianism or veganism but on banning a practice that was thought to be unnecessary. Likewise, the discourse of the anti-fox-hunting campaign was centered not on the rights of foxes but on ending a practice that was thought to be unnecessary.

Crucially, what is regarded as unnecessary is not static, nor is it objective. Indeed, over the past few decades what is regarded as unnecessary suffering has expanded to reflect a growing awareness of the different ways animals can suffer, changes in cultural norms, and technological developments that have made it possible to use alternatives. Thirty years ago or so, for example, the wearing of fur and the testing of cosmetics on animals was regarded as acceptable. Now, many people in the Western world frown upon both practices. In Britain, fur farming, as we saw, has been prohibited, and no licenses are now given for cosmetic testing on animals. Similarly, many aspects of factory farming—such as the debeaking of poultry and the use of veal crates, pig stalls and tethers, and the battery cage—were regarded as morally acceptable thirty years ago but are now being seriously challenged throughout Europe.

At the federal level in the United States, it is true that very little effective legislation protecting farm animals exists, although there have been some welfare measures such as the decision by the USDA in May 2008 to ban the slaughter for human consumption of so-called downer cattle, those unable to stand and walk unassisted. However, just as individual states are beginning to take action on climate change, the same seems to be happening with animal protection. Of most note here was the Californian ballot proposition that passed by 63 percent of the vote in November 2008 (amounting to over eight million people), with a turnout of 77 percent. This initiative—targeted at veal crates, battery cages, and sow gestation crates—prohibits the confinement of certain farm animals in a manner that does not allow them to turn around freely, lie down, stand up, and fully extend their limbs. Those exploiting animals in this way on farms have until 2015 to implement the initiative. The passing of Proposition 2 in California follows similar reforms in Florida and Oregon (banning of sow gestation crates) and Arizona and Colorado (veal crates and sow gestation crates). Also in the 2008 election, Massachusetts voters decided to ban greyhound racing.

Clearly, there are a number of weaknesses with Proposition 2, although this does not include the counterproductive argument, rejected previously, which Francione (2008) has applied to it. The proposition is far from ideal, and I would not want to claim otherwise. In particular, without a federal ban on confinement, there is an incentive for producers to move to other states where confinement remains legal. In addition, it does not necessarily mean the end of cages. It is, in other words, a moderate step forward. But a step forward it nevertheless is. There will be enormous pressure on other states to follow suit, not least from producers in California who will otherwise be at a competitive disadvantage. Through the reform, hens will be given more space, and the veal crate and sow gestation crate will likely go. In addition, smaller and more humane farms will have an increased competitive edge over factory farms. Finally, the issue of farm animal welfare was put on the political agenda.

The Consistent Application of Animal Welfare

There are at least two alternatives to the strategy, described earlier, that focuses on the unnecessary nature of much animal exploitation. One, of course, is the animal rights abolitionism that is the major target of this section of the book. Another focuses on what is perceived to be an inconsistent application of animal welfare, which, when corrected, offers a much stronger principle that can be used as a battering ram for reform in the way animals are currently treated. I have argued that the goals of the animal rights movement are unrealistic at present. This is largely because the underlying principle—that animals ought to have a moral status close if not identical to humans—is not accepted by the vast majority of society. Because of this, it is argued by O'Sullivan (2007), among others, that instead of focusing on this "external" inconsistency, there is a compelling case for focusing instead on an "internal" inconsistency.

This internal inconsistency, it is alleged, comes about because animals are treated in different ways according to the purpose for which they are being used. The laws protecting companion animals are generally much more stringent than those protecting farm and laboratory animals. To treat companion animals in the same way as farm and laboratory animals would invite prosecution. Thus, in Britain, it would be illegal for a member of the public to cage birds in such a way that they were unable to spread their wings, and yet this is exactly how factory farms, quite legally (for the present at least), treat laying hens.

This internal inconsistency, it is suggested, is invalid because the basis on which animal welfare is justified is the principle that animals, like human, are sentient. To treat equally sentient animals differently, therefore, is illegitimate. Indeed, it transgresses the equality principle that is a basic principle of liberal theories of justice. Once the inconsistency is recognized, the correction of this internal inconsistency is likely to result in fundamental reform in the way animals are treated, and all of this could be done without needing to demonstrate a higher moral status for animals than the moral orthodoxy allows.

A number of responses can be made to this consistency approach. In the first place, a recognition of the inconsistency might lead to the opposite conclusion—that companion animals are too well protected and ought to be subject to the same limitations as animals used on farms and in laboratories. Second, and more importantly, I would suggest that asserting the notion of equitable treatment, as a key feature of liberal thought, as a weapon against internal inconsistencies in the way animals are treated, is problematic. This is because, as we have seen, animal welfare is based on the principle that only unnecessary suffering ought to be prohibited. This means that the way animals are treated is not dependent on their level of sentience, but on the *purpose* for which they are being used. Now, the purpose of all animal utilization is the same in the sense that it is designed to benefit humans. Companion animals serve human purposes as much as food and laboratory animals do. However, in another sense, the purposes are very different. In particular, companion animals are better protected because inflicting suffering on them is not part of the purpose for which they are used. This is not the case with farm and laboratory animals, where the suffering inflicted is justified because it is deemed to be necessary.

It seems to me, therefore, that the equitable treatment of animals requires one of two possible moves. In the first place, we can invoke at least some aspects of the external inconsistency critique. In other words, we can claim that the moral status of animals is such that animal interests (for example, in not suffering) ought to be considered equally with those of humans. In this case, the unnecessary suffering principle is undermined. That is, in order for farm and laboratory animals to be treated in the same way as companion animals, we have to conclude that it is morally illegitimate to inflict suffering on the former in order to benefit humans (or at least it is if we are not prepared to consider sacrificing the interests of humans for the benefit of humans and other animals).

O'Sullivan (2007) suggests that the inconsistency she observes in the way animals are treated is at least partly a product of the lack of visibility that some animals have. Thus, some more visible animals—most notably companion animals—are treated in a much more favorable way than other less visible ones, locked away in farms and laboratories. For a variety of reasons, I am skeptical about this. For one thing, the animal protection movement has, for decades, spent its time publicizing what is done to animals in order to provide us with cheap meat and new drugs. A more valid explanation is that the public are well aware that animals are treated in different ways and are willing to accept that human benefits must sometimes be put before the interests of animals.

The problem with the first option is that it brings us back to the problem that the internal inconsistency argument is designed to alleviate: that it is unrealistic to expect humans to forgo the advantages that animal welfare provides for them. Another option, and the one this author prefers, is not so much to publicize the alleged inconsistency in animal welfare law, but to change public perceptions as to what should be regarded as *necessary* suffering.

Morals and Politics

As pointed out earlier, because it is difficult to think of abolitionist measures that will satisfy the requirement that the use of animals not be condoned, even implicitly, the strategy of animal rights abolitionism is based primarily on the vegan education campaign. This is encapsulated in the well-known animal rights slogan "go vegan." This is an example of a moral crusade, an attempt to change individual behavior. Such a strategy is popular with the animal protection movement in general, whether it is based on campaigns to encourage veganism, vegetarianism, the consumption of free-range animal products, or the purchase of cosmetics not tested on animals.

Why a Moral Crusade Will Not Work

Insofar as the moral crusade strategy is not accompanied by alternative political campaigns that aim at legislative change, it is deeply flawed. To see that this is so, it is necessary to consider the nature of the moral and political environment in which the animal rights movement operates. The moral crusade approach involves the assumption that all the animal rights movement has to do is to convince enough people of the merits of leading a vegan lifestyle, and it will eventually happen. In other words, it prioritizes the importance of ideas over interests, given that no animal rights activist stands to gain materially from the end of animal exploitation. Regan (2004, 181–96) provides one example of this approach. He suggests that the future success of animal rights depends on the conversion of what he calls the "Muddlers," those who are open to the animal rights message but who, for a variety of reasons, are reluctant to take the final step. Muddlers are resistant to animal rights, Regan argues, because the animal rights movement is seen as negative, outlandish, too conservative, or too unrealistic, or because it courts too many celebrity endorsements, or because its campaigns are sometimes tasteless, self-righteous, or violent, or because Muddlers themselves do not feel they can contribute anything worthwhile.

There is little doubt that all of the factors Regan raises as obstacles to someone somewhere becoming an animal rights advocate are important ones. However, this moral crusade, focusing on the conversion of individuals, can take the movement only so far. Consider one alternative. Imagine the state enforces veganism, prohibiting the eating of meat and the consumption of dairy products. We know this will work because the state has the authority and the power to enforce its will. By contrast, the battle of ideas in liberal civil societies is conducted within a pluralistic universe where the rationale is not for one set of ideas, or version of the good society, to prevail but for a plurality of views to coexist. In other words, by suggesting that our treatment of animals belongs to the sphere of morality is to inadvertently subject animals to the liberal principle of moral pluralism, whereby the way in which they are treated becomes a matter of personal preference rather than moral obligation.

The principle of moral pluralism has been described by Bellamy (1992, 219) as "the defining political characteristic of liberalism" in theory and practice. It is a principle that suggests that the liberal state should observe a neutral stance when faced with competing conceptions of the good. This is the idea, derived from a wider theory of liberty, that it is no business of the state to interfere in individual moral codes or individual conceptions of the good life. By contrast, a perfectionist theory holds that "the purpose of the state is to affirm and aid its citizens in seeking the realization of some idea of the good" (Neal 1997, 4).

The liberal principle of the neutral state has been the guiding force behind what many would regard as some of the most enlightened postwar legislation, most notably the reform of the law on homosexuality. Liberal, pro-choice abortion policy too is based on the principle "that where issues turn on controversial moral or religious conceptions they can justly be disposed of only in one way: by allowing people to follow their own judgment or conscience" (Barry 1995, 88). What is more, the assumption is that, for liberals, individual choice in the area of morality cannot be obstructed by majoritarianism. It is for this reason, of course, that liberal polities such as in the United States have constitutional devices specifically designed to constrain majority decisions.

Moral pluralism is anathema to a principle of justice because the latter imposes obligations whereas the former deals only with preferences. As Rawls writes (1991, 164), it is crucial that different conceptions of the good life "respect the limits specified by the appropriate principles of justice." In other words, the principles of justice "limit the conceptions of the good which are permissible" (Rawls 1991, 165), and as a consequence, some moral and political questions can be "removed from the political agenda" (Rawls 1993, 151). From the perspective of animals, focusing on individual lifestyle choices associates the treatment of animals with a moral preference rather than a principle of justice that would have to be enforced by the state.

Within a liberal realm of moral pluralism, competing moral outlooks are permitted, provided of course that they do not harm humans or seek to deny others their own different moral outlooks. In other words, MacIntyre (1988, 336) points out,

> Every individual is to be equally free to propose and to live by whatever conception of the good he or she pleases ... unless that conception of the good involves reshaping the life of the rest of the community in accordance with it.

In this liberal realm, treating animals with respect becomes merely a preference rather than a fundamental principle of justice. In other words, for example, *you* may choose to cook lobsters by throwing them alive into pans of boiling water, but my moral sensibilities are such that I am not prepared to do this. According to Clark (1987, 121) this means "Third parties have no right to come between the whaler and her prey, or the farmer and her veal calves, since none of us have a right to impose our 'merely' moral standards on other autonomous agents." The state, in addition, is not encouraged to intervene in order to impose my morality on you.

The practical implications for animals of the principle of moral pluralism have been profound. This is because the moral pluralism argument has been utilized, quite successfully, in practice by those who seek to exploit animals. There are two classic examples whereby those who seek to continue exploiting animals explicitly use the language of liberal moral pluralism to justify and preserve their activities. The first of these is hunting with hounds in general and fox hunting in particular in Britain. The hunting community has increasingly used the language of liberalism to defend its activity (Scruton 2000, 116–22), and the transformation of the hunting community's case—from being based on arguments that hunting is a form of pest control or that it serves an environmental function to one centring on liberty—has undoubtedly strengthened its position, not least because it has won it some allies in the liberal press and academic community. Thus, the late British journalist Hugo Young (1999) could write in the impeccably liberal *Guardian* that

> hunting is an issue about the toleration of choice. The ban, if it happens, will ask a serious question about Labour's reliability as a defender of minorities. It will show New Labour as a party of new illiberalism ... At the bottom of the rage to ban hunting is the sense that here is a sport engaged in only by a minority ... The defining progressive precept, however, should be toleration.

The second example of the conflict between moral pluralism and animal welfare concerns the issue of ritual slaughter. In many countries, including Britain and the United States (but not Switzerland, Norway, Sweden, or Ireland), ritual slaughter practiced by Jewish and Muslim communities—which involves killing the animals without pre-stunning—is permitted. In Britain, stunning has been required—for cattle, sheep, goats, swine, and horses—by national legislation since the 1933 Slaughter of Animals Act, updated by the 1974 Slaughterhouses Act, and for poultry by the 1967 Slaughter of

Poultry Act. All of these pieces of legislation contain exemptions for the Jewish practice of Shechita and the similar Muslim practice of Dhabh, whereby, on religious grounds, animals and birds killed for food must not have suffered any injury before slaughter if the meat produced is to be kosher (for Jews) and halal (for Muslims). Similarly, EU law excludes ritual slaughter from the general stunning requirement (Radford 2001, 117).

There is significant evidence that ritual slaughter represents a severe welfare problem, and over the years in Britain, ritual slaughter has been opposed by a variety of official committees. Yet ritual slaughter has survived, and it has survived because of the employment of liberal notions of moral pluralism and religious toleration. Thus, the British government has refused to ban the exemption on the grounds that it "recognizes a fundamental matter of religious belief to communities that are an important part of our national life" (HC Debs, 2 February 1997, col. 659). Significantly, Article 9 of the European Convention on Human Rights, now incorporated into British law in the 1998 Human Rights Act, recognizes religious freedom, and any future attempt at an EU or British government level to end ritual slaughter is likely to conflict with this provision (Radford 2001, 117). It is difficult to think of a scenario more in keeping with key liberal principles than this.

There is no doubt that moral crusades on behalf of animals have produced some desirable results. There are more vegetarians and vegans than there used to be, and as a result, more options are made available for vegetarian and vegan consumers. Moreover, the liberal emphasis on choice might seem a civilized way of dealing with inevitable differences of moral opinion. However, the moral crusade approach has severe disadvantages in comparison with a political campaign designed to achieve legislative change. In the first place, as I have emphasized, participating in the moral arena associates the cause with a moral choice and not a compulsion. The assumption underlying such participation is the principle that one moral view or set of moral views must not predominate. Certainly, the state in a liberal society cannot be seen to intervene to promote one moral stance over another. As Frey (1983, 15) points out, "for moral vegetarians, the very essence of whose position is choosing to abstain from meat for moral reasons, coercion of others seems precluded as a possible policy option'.

Second, although it cannot be proven that there is a link between the choices available for those who are morally committed to end animal suffering and the relative paucity of animal welfare statute law, the existence of the former undoubtedly makes the animal suffering that is still permitted more palatable. When challenged about the paucity of animal welfare legislation, or its weak content, state actors can simply respond by saying it is a matter for individual preferences. Thus, if a big majority choose not to be vegans, then the state does not feel obliged to act. So as long as the treatment of animals is regarded primarily as a moral, rather than a political, issue, only when the exploitation of animals causes harm to other humans can such activity be prohibited. Indeed, this helps to explain why defending animal interests as an indirect consequence of protecting human interests is a fertile strategy for the animal protection movement. Seeking to protect animals by engaging exclusively in a moral crusade thus has the effect of removing animals from the political arena and from the possibility of enforceable legislation applying to all. Indeed, it has the effect, unintended though it might be, of turning back the clock to a time when the state and the legal system did not recognize its direct duties to protect the interests of animals and was only willing to take action once the ill-treatment of animals led to human harms.

The prevalence of the principle of moral pluralism in practice varies from society to society and from one historical era to another. Here, it is perhaps not insignificant that in the United States, where liberal ideology plays a much more prominent societal and political role, animals are less well-treated than in many

European countries. The importance attached to individual autonomy and self-reliance against the interference of the state and society is reflected, first, in stringent property laws. As Vincent asserts, "property is the precondition to the development of the person. To interfere with property is a gross infringement of rights and liberties" (Vincent 1995, 43). In this context, it is not surprising, as Francione has pointed out, that attempts to enforce anticruelty statutes, which exist in most American states, are hindered significantly by the weight attached to property rights, and the general assumption that there has to be good reason for interference in property rights makes general legislative improvements in animal welfare difficult. By contrast, in Britain and other European countries, it might be suggested, the ideology of individual autonomy and self-reliance has been much less powerful. For example, despite the attempt by the hunting community to utilize liberal notions of moral choice, British politicians, backed by a majority of public opinion, chose to ignore it and press ahead with a ban.

The impact of moral pluralism on the well-being of animals is clear. I might decide to desist from activities which exploit animals, and my moral choice will be respected or at least tolerated. I might "go vegan," but the majority have not and are unlikely, unless forced by the state, to take the same option. Since this is about moral choice, other individuals are entitled to hold contrary preferences, and I am expected to respect these preferences and not obstruct their pursuit of them, even if I fundamentally disagree with them. In this context, contrast vegetarianism with the modern attitude most have to smoking. Whereas a group of vegetarians or vegans in a restaurant cannot expect that meat-eating be prohibited within their eye-range, smoking will be prevented where people are eating. This distinction comes about, of course, as a result of the fact that smoking in a populated environment is defined, in terms first developed by John Stuart Mill, as an other-regarding activity because of the alleged effects of passive smoking, whereas my moral repugnance at your meat-eating is not similarly regarded. The interests of the animals being eaten are disregarded completely in this scenario.

Because of the weaknesses of the moral crusade, the animal rights movement has no option but, as Stallwood (2008) has commented, to make

> society's treatment of animals the responsibility of society, not just the individual responsibility of some. The challenge is to bring animal rights into the political mainstream and make it a legitimate public policy issue. The present emphasis on individual action ("Go vegan!") must be expanded to include a political agenda for institutional change. Yes, individually, we're all responsible for what happens to animals in our personal and professional lives but collectively the commercial exploitation of animals is the responsibility of society and government.

Agency, Interests, and Politics

I have argued that a moral crusade for animal rights is not going to work by itself and has to be accompanied by a political strategy. Here, it is crucial to note that in the political arena it tends to be interests rather than ideas that are the main determinant of public policy outcomes. This is certainly the dominant model within political science. Insofar as ideas have an impact on public policy, it is argued, they are associated with important interests. Despite attempts to show that ideas can act as an independent variable, there has been little "convincing empirical evidence to support the claim that ideas affect policy outcomes in ways that are truly independent from the effects of interests" (Campbell 1998, 377).

Thus, the history of social reform movements suggests that it is not enough to hope that ideas will attract public support and, somehow miraculously, be converted into legislative goals and social conventions. Rather, the ideas that tend to predominant are those that are associated with important social groupings. For example, liberalism and socialism emerged as important nineteenth-century ideologies precisely because they were associated with the middle and working classes created by the industrial revolution. Feminism, likewise, is a hugely important social movement for the obvious reason that it appealed to a new female consciousness produced by wider social forces.

Emphasizing agency, therefore, requires us to focus on interests. As a result, animal advocates should abandon the view that everyone can be persuaded of the case for animal rights if only they understand the issues and are converted morally. Rather, animal advocates should look for social groupings, interests and corresponding ideological tradition that can justify or, even better, require the incorporation of animal interests. This is a difficult task for the animal rights movement because, as pointed out earlier, it seeks to promote the interests of nonhumans, and sometimes this will involve conflict with human interests.

It is traditional to divide pressure groups into interest and promotional groups, and the animal protection movement is an example of the latter type (usually described in the United States as public interest groups). A promotional group is defined as such because of its advocacy of a cause that is not in the direct economic interests of its members. By contrast, interest groups are those that exist to serve the mainly economic interests of their members. Most of the animal protection movement's opponents are formed into interest groups, representing agribusiness or pharmaceutical or academic interests. Promotional, or public interest, groups face a disadvantage not suffered by economic groups. In particular, the animal protection movement does not have the common geographical or occupational location associated with economic interest groups. This means that it is harder to recruit members for the animal protection movement, and as a result, interest groups defending the use of animals have a more assured source of income.

It is crucial to note that the animal protection movement, particularly the rights strand, has an additional disadvantage. Groups promoting human causes may not have members who stand to gain directly from the achievements of group objectives. It is uncommon, for instance, for the membership of a group campaigning on, say, housing issues to consist of the homeless. However, the constituency it seeks to represent is human and can be mobilized in pursuit of a group's objectives. The animal protection movement is very different. It cannot mobilize animals in support of its objectives, nor can it elicit the sympathy of other humans for the plight of members of their own species.

This, of course, is why campaigns designed to show that the exploitation of animals is unnecessary are attractive. If it can be shown that animal experimentation does not work, or is trivial, and that we do not need to eat meat and that meat has negative implications for consumers, the environment, and those working within the industry, then the conflict between human and animal interests disappears. Those reforms improving the well-being of animals that are beneficial to humans as a by-product are, clearly, more likely to succeed in that by associating animal protection with human interests, they identify an agency for change. If, on the other hand, we persist in saying that animal interests ought to be protected, irrespective of the cost to humans, then whatever the moral merits of so doing, persuading humans to accept these protections is clearly going to be more difficult.

Here, the notion of the "political opportunity structure" is important. Political opportunity theory argues that the degree to which social movements are successful in achieving their aims is dependent on a broader context (in other words, on the existence—or absence—of a specific political opportunity) (Meyer 2004). These political opportunities, for the animal protection movement, are likely to occur as a result of taking advantage of existing cultural cleavages. Thus, Evans (2008) has shown how animal protection was included in the national constitutions of Switzerland and Germany as a result of the animal protection movement tapping into existing salient issues. In the former case, the animal protection movement was able to exploit public concern about genetically modified organisms in general to achieve the inclusion of animal protection in a constitutional provision insisting on limits to gene technology research. In the latter case, the animal protection movement exploited the political saliency of ritual slaughter as a means of raising the issue of an animal protection constitutional amendment. In the case of Switzerland, the existing cultural cleavage exploited originated in a concern for human health. In the German case, the ritual slaughter issue had received its impetus from existing racial divisions (Christians against Muslims).[5]

In the pursuit of human allies, the animal protection movement has got to be flexible, recognizing that different allies and different ideological traditions may be appropriate in particular circumstances. In Britain, for instance, the campaign to legislate against the hunting of foxes with hounds and hare coursing was successful largely because it attracted the support of Labour Party MPs and the wider labor movement. This, in turn, is because hunting is perceived, however accurately, to be a class issue, a pursuit undertaken by members of the landed aristocracy and the wealthy. This is very different from other animal issues and illustrates that animal issues in practice tend to be confused ideologically. Thus, although much of the animal ethics literature draws from the liberal tradition—in terms of rights, utilitarianism, and contractarianism—the hunting community in Britain, as we saw previously, utilized liberal arguments to defend its position. Indeed, it elicited a good deal of sympathy by painting the opponents of hunting as an illiberal mob intent on an attack on a defenseless minority.

Continuing the theme of links with the left, there is some scope—as recognized by the late American animal rights campaigner Henry Spira—in seeking to mobilize those working in the animal industry, notably slaughterhouses and factory farms, because they are undoubtedly an exploited part of the labor force. As Spira himself pointed out, "we identify with the powerless and the vulnerable—the victims, all of those dominated, oppressed and exploited" (1983, 373). Spira had begun his political life on the left, being a union activist and a member of the American Socialist Workers Party in the 1950s.

In a similar vein, the campaign against the export of live animals from Britain in the 1990s mobilized a substantial proportion of the population, many of whom had never participated in any political campaigns before, let alone an issue involving the welfare of animals. This occurred for a variety of reasons. In the first place, it was an issue that could appeal to the whole animal protection movement and not just animal rights advocates. It was not an issue about abolishing animal agriculture or about stopping eating meat. Thus, all sections of the animal protection movement were able to participate. As Benton and Redfearn (1996, 51) pointed out,

> the limiting of the protests to identifiable "welfare" targets has been crucial in maintaining the breadth of public support which the campaign continues to enjoy. A large poster draped from a Colchester pub read "You Don't Have to Stop Eating Meat to Care—Ban Live Exports."

Furthermore, it is significant that Benton and Redfearn's study of the campaign against live exports revealed that some of the participants did not see animal protection as the main issue at stake, and very few saw it as the only one. As a result, the animal protection movement was able to draw in those concerned about local democracy, civil liberties, and police powers, thereby creating a powerful constituency (57).

The second possibility here is for the animal rights movement to embrace individuals with a *personal interest* in animal rights, in the sense that their lives would be materially or physically better if the interests of animals were protected. There is some scope for this. Those living with the pollution, noise, and stench of factory farms and abattoirs would have better lives if the factory farms and abattoirs did not exist. Similarly, intensive animal agriculture harms the interests of small farmers, and the food produced from factory farms is generally of a lower quality than free-range produce and is associated with human health problems. Likewise, those who have been the victims of a drug previously tested on animals but still found to be dangerous for humans to consume might be another group whom animal advocates could attempt to mobilize. In this context, it is significant that Proposition 2 in California was supported by a broad coalition of organizations, including some—such as the United Farm Workers, the Center for Food Safety, and the Consumer Federation of America—that focus on human interests.

Of course, there are some limitations to this strategy. Focusing on the environmental and health consequences of factory farming does not justify the abolition of all animal agriculture. In addition, many would argue that factory farming has had some positive impact on humans. Indeed, it has largely achieved its original function, which was to ensure a plentiful, cost-effective, and regular supply of food. Therefore, in some—probably the majority of—cases, the direct interests of humans are not necessarily served by an end to animal exploitation. Nevertheless, provided that the counterproductive argument can be defeated, as I think it can, there is no harm in, and a lot to be gained by, pursuing an unnecessary-suffering strategy.

A strategy focused on human interests will have greater utility if it is broadened. We can do this if, as well as identifying those human interests that are directly furthered by the protection of animals, we can also identify those interests that humans have in common with animals. To do this, we have to ask, to what degree can social groupings and the ideologies that bind them together identify with the interests of animals? Of greatest importance here is to ask whether a campaign for greater equality between humans and animals can be successful when great inequalities still exist between different humans. Those who are at present primarily concerned with issues relating to human exploitation and inequality are unlikely to want to embrace animal rights if animal rights advocates shun their concerns. They can be the agents of animal rights, but equally, animal rights advocates have to be prepared to be the agents for a transformation of the lives of other humans in need. In short, the animal rights movement cannot remain in principled isolation but should see itself as part of a broader progressive movement for the betterment of humans as well as animals.

Identifying shared human and animal interests is one thing. It is quite another for the animal protection movement to seek the tacit consent, or even the approval, of those directly involved in the exploitation of animals. The fact that some animal welfare reforms have been achieved in this context, however, is not necessarily a measure of their weakness. Insofar as animal protection organizations link animal welfare reforms with producer benefits, it is because they recognize that they have more chance of success by doing so. It is true that such a strategy invites accusations of selling out, and it is true too that animal protection organizations have to be careful to get the balance right. There is no conspiracy going on here, though, just a recognition of the political realities of the situation.

It should be pointed out, too, that some animal welfare reforms have been achieved despite the opposition of industry groups.

For example, the successful British campaign, led by Compassion in World Farming, to abolish sow stalls and tethers in the early 1990s was fought vigorously by agricultural interests as economically damaging to their industry. In addition, the poultry industry was certainly opposed violently to Proposition 2 in California (see earlier discussion), and opponents spent $8.5 million campaigning against it (Hall and Hirsch 2008). The final point to make here is that, in some instances at least, it is undoubtedly the case that the apparent compliance of industry groups is a product of their recognition that they cannot be seen to be obstructing the welfare demands of the animal protection movement. The role of three sets of actors—the animal movement, the producers, and the consumers—has to be taken into account in such situations.

We should perhaps see the use of animal welfare language by animal exploiters as a mark of the animal protection movement's progress in legitimizing the term. Here, too, it would be a mistake for animal advocates to evacuate the animal welfare territory and provide animal exploiters with the capacity to mold it to their own purposes unchallenged. Research has indicated, for instance, that those involved in animal experimentation in Britain, though paying lip service to animal welfare, operate with an ideological position that might be more accurately described as "animal use." Lyons (2006, 378) explains the difference as follows:

The "animal use" ideology encapsulates the core policy position of animal research interest groups, and is defined by a belief in the routine ethical acceptability of causing pain to non-human animals in order to serve what are perceived to be valuable goals such as the advancement of knowledge and the development and testing of various products for human use, ranging from cosmetics and household products. Self-regulation by animal researchers is another important facet of this position. In contrast, the "animal welfare" position does not automatically assume that animals' interests may be sacrificed for human interests, and instead requires an *independent* utilitarian cost-benefit assessment of animal research proposals where the interests of animals are given significant weight in a balancing exercise against predicted benefits for humans.

Further empirical research is needed to ascertain the degree to which political and social actors involved in animal exploitation still operate with an animal use ideology. To the extent that they do, it presents an opportunity for the animal protection movement to open up an ideological gap as well as a benchmark against which to judge public policy relating to animals.

A Moral Discourse of Animal Protection

A number of objections might be made to the new welfarism or animal protectionism that I have sought to argue for in this book. I have tried to deal with the criticism that it is strategically bound to fail by challenging the view that animal welfare is counterproductive and unlikely to provide genuine improvements in the way animals are treated. I have also pointed out that there is considerable support for the animal protectionism strategy within the animal protection movement. It is still open to the charge, however, that it is unprincipled because of the failure to recommend following, without qualification, the radical outcomes that follow from a set of ethical principles.

The problem with adopting such an approach is that the pragmatism it entails has received bad press, particularly, of course, within sections of the animal rights movement itself. It moves us away from a moral explanation and toward a political explanation for our actions. Arguments that are based on moral considerations, however, tend to have a higher status than those based on what is seen as the grubby world of politics. An important question to ask, therefore, is whether there is a moral, rather than a purely pragmatic, reason for preferring animal welfare over its rivals. In other words, can this preference, for working with what is rather than seeking to advocate a radical change, be theorized in a way that overrides the traditional rationalistic ethics that, as we saw earlier, do not appear to support animal welfare?

A number of lines of inquiry here are worth exploring. One is to adopt a conservative position associated, in particular, with Michael Oakeshott, the British political philosopher. In an article titled "The Concept of a Philosophy of Politics," written in the 1940s and posthumously published, Oakeshott recognizes the conflict between what he calls the "facts of political life" and the "rationalization of political life and activity." When this conflict occurs, Oakeshott argues that the latter must, "at all costs," conform to the former. That is, "A philosophy of politics must be a rationalization of political life and activity . . . it has to conform to the so-called 'facts of political life.' And by the 'facts of political life' is meant the character of political life as it is conceived by the ordinary, commonsense observer, the observer whose mind is yet uncloaked by philosophical speculation" (Oakeshott 1993, 122).

Oakeshott's justification for preferring the reality of political life to the rationalizations of moral philosophers seems to be that political philosophy, if it is to remain philosophical, must avoid making moral judgments "about which of many ends is preferable." All it can hope to do is examine and describe the concepts current in any particular society. Thus, a philosophy of politics can be described as "an explanation or view of political life and activity from the standpoint of the totality of experience" (126). In other words, "philosophy begins with the concepts of ordinary, everyday knowledge, and consists in an extended, detailed and complete exposition of those concepts" (128). Again, a philosophy of politics "is the attempt to think out to the end the body of concepts which together seem to comprise the world of political activity."

The problem with Oakeshott's aversion to normative political philosophy is that, at least in the article I am referring to, it is stated and not really (intelligibly at least) argued for. The objections to Oakeshott's position are pretty obvious. A moral position that appears to rationalize the status quo is profoundly conservative and may instead seek to disguise arrangements that benefit the self-interest of a powerful group. In the case of animals, the powerful group consists of humans, or at least those humans with certain interests (agribusiness, scientists) who particularly stand to gain from the exploitation of animals.

One way around this is to offer an account that suggests that, although rationalistic ethics is important, it is only one form of moral discourse, and a valid moral position must contain more than mere ethics. Support for this is leant by the argument put forward by the American theologian and ethicist James Gustafson (1996, 35–53), who identifies four modes of moral discourse— ethical, narrative, policy, and prophetic. For him, none of these discourses by themselves is sufficient to encompass the full range of moral discourse.

Gustafson's model of moral discourse has been applied to the ethics of climate change by the Dutch political theorist Menno Kamminga (2008). Here, it is argued that ethical discourse, which employs rationally rigorous modes of moral reasoning developed in the discipline of moral philosophy, has focused on developing cosmopolitan principles of justice. More specifically, it is argued that the industrialized nations must bear the cost of climate change, in the process aiding those in the developing world who are most unable to cope with its impact. From the perspective of other types of moral discourse, however, these cosmopolitan ethical principles appear to be inadequate. In particular, they fail to take into account the ways in which a moral identity is created and shaped by narratives within particular communities. And in these narratives, global principles of climate justice demand a sense of world community that does not exist and that cannot be a part of a policy discourse.

These different modes of moral discourse would seem to be equally relevant to the animals debate. The difference between an ethical and a narrative discourse are particularly pertinent here. Thus, much of the animal ethics discourse—the kind of discourse pursued by Regan, Singer, and Francione—does not take into account the ways in which a moral identity is created and shaped by narratives within particular communities. This narrative, I would argue, has shifted over the past fifty years or so, but only from an animal use narrative to an animal welfare narrative. In other words, although it is now recognized that animal interests are significant and ought to be taken into account by decision makers, it still remains the case that an animal rights discourse is alien to most Western public opinion. To put it another way, the ethical discourse of animal rights clashes with the narrative discourse present in much of the developed world. Kamminga (2008, 688) writes in the context of climate change that to focus moral discourse "too exclusively on ethical discourse would mean losing sight of spheres of choice and activity that appear to be of serious moral importance" for people. The same applies in the case of the moral debate about animals.

A distinction between political philosophy and moral philosophy might be helpful here. It might be argued that a *political* philosophy differs from moral philosophy in general by its need to take into account the realities of political life if it is to be regarded as politically relevant. This is probably closest to Oakeshott's meaning. So, unlike pure philosophy, which is not bound by the same degree of tangibility and relevance, "any adequate theorising about politics must primarily be about the lived, human experiences of the realm" (Ferguson 2004, 379). This interpretation of Oakeshott is from an article by the American philosopher Kennan Ferguson (2004). He notes the inconsistency between the preeminence of human beings in political thought and the attachment that human beings have to their dogs and, by implication, other companion animals.

I think that the apparent inconsistency noted by Ferguson is easily explained. That is, the way that humans treat companion animals is quite consistent with the moral superiority of humans and also quite consistent with the other ways that humans treat animals—as sources of food or clothes or as experimental subjects. It is just that, as with the inconsistency argument discussed previously, animals utilized as a source of companionship, or even love, serve a different function for humans than farm or laboratory animals. The former are utilized for human benefit in the same way as the latter, although the consequences for the latter are, of course, much more severe. As Richard Girling (1989) points out, "we feed emotionally on dog, cat or budgerigar, just as assuredly as we feed bodily on chicken, pig and bullock."

My target, though, is different. I am concerned with noting the real, and not apparent, disparity between the place of animals in some modern ethical thinking about animals, on the one hand, and the moral orthodoxy that dominates the way animals are thought about—and sometimes treated—in Western societies, on the other. One way of seeing the importance of this kind of narrative discourse is to focus on the importance of moral intuitions in constructing moral theory. This has been a common approach adopted by political philosophers such as Rawls (1972, 20), who refers to the practice as "reflexive equilibrium." Thus, despite the apparent objectivity of the principles of justice deriving from his social contract device, he does admit that these principles of justice are checked for consistency with our moral intuition. Here, it is instructive to note the countless examples where the impeccable logic entailed in moral theory-building results in conclusions that many find intuitively doubtful. One can think of Rawls's dismissal of desert as a valuable principle of justice, which many find deeply troublesome because it denies the importance of effort and incentives in the distribution of goods. Likewise, the utilitarian stipulation that our duties to all children are the same as the ones to our own is inconsistent with most people's gut feeling (Ferguson 2004, 380).

An instructive example of this dichotomy between rationalistic ethical principles and intuition from within animal ethics is the "argument from marginal cases," which has been a staple part of the case for animal rights. As discussed earlier, this argument asks, if we persist in justifying the exploitation of animals on the grounds that they are cognitively less able than humans, then what should we do with those humans—the seriously mentally disabled in particular—who do not themselves have the characteristics of personhood? Consistency would seem to demand either that we exploit human mental defectives as well as animals or that we exploit neither animals nor marginal humans.

As we saw, the argument from marginal cases has produced an extensive literature, with by no means a majority supportive of the position, and the debate continues with little to suggest a clinching argument either way. The conclusions drawn by Singer and others from the argument from marginal cases, however, are logically valid and very difficult to challenge. It therefore represents, perhaps, the nearest thing to a conclusive argument possessed by pro-animal philosophers. But this argument has not had the impact one might have expected. It is worth speculating why this is so. One answer might be that its conclusions are not consistent with the moral intuitions of most people; what matters to most people is the general differences between "normal" humans and animals. This in turn is a product of a narrative discourse that draws attention to the limits of rationalistic ethical enquiry.

The problem with accepting the intuitions that form part of a community's narrative discourse is that it results in a defense of the status quo. Gustafson's approach helps us to avoid this charge of conservatism in the sense that he is suggesting that a narrative discourse is by itself insufficient and needs the help of ethical discourse in order to avoid a mere defense of the status quo. Thus, a valid moral discourse about animals must take into account *both* ethical principles and the dominant narrative about their status. This narrative is at present dominated by welfare principles, but of course this may change in the future. It remains the case, however, that in the animals debate, there is a need for the ethics to be checked by the narrative if it is to speak effectively to an important contemporary concern.

Conclusion

This chapter has sought to argue that, although the philosophical case for granting animals at least some rights is strong, the achievement of animal rights goals are unrealistic at present. This would be problematic, and possibly fatal, for the animal rights movement if there were not a valid alternative. This valid alternative exists in the form of the political possibilities offered by the principle of animal welfare and the associated idea of unnecessary suffering. I have argued that these possibilities are not diminished by the fact that animal welfare does not challenge the property status of animals. In addition, despite the argument's innovative character, it is doubtful if drawing attention to an inconsistency in the way animal welfare is applied offers much advantage. Rather, much can still be made of the unnecessary suffering principle that is central to animal welfare. What is more, the animal protection movement, including those parts of it with an animal rights focus, has recognized this and has achieved its major successes through this principle's utilization.

This strategy is particularly sensible if one recognizes the peculiar difficulty faced by the animal rights movement. Animals cannot achieve their own liberation, and because of the reliance on human agency, it is hugely problematic to achieve reforms to the way animals are treated that will deny significant human interests. In this climate, the pursuit of abolitionist incremental steps, which are justified only if they are not to be seen as condoning the use of animals, are clearly unrealistic. Likewise, the retreat toward a moral crusade aimed at persuading people to desist from activities that cause animals to suffer is no alternative, given that framing animal rights as a moral crusade has the effect of reinforcing the view that the treatment of animals is a matter for individual moral choice and not a societal issue that has to be resolved politically by legislative means.

There is a useful parallel here in the environmental debate, where advocates of a limits-to-growth approach—in which the choice is postulated between economic growth and environmental protection—have been challenged by advocates of so-called ecological modernization (Garner 2000, 35–44). Advocates of this latter position suggest, correctly it seems to me, not only that a strategy based on limits to growth would be politically unacceptable but also that it is possible to reconcile economic growth with environmental protection. In a similar vein, animal protectionists, equally correctly, recognize that a fundamentalist animal rights position, centering on the abolition of the use of animals for human gain, is unacceptable for now. But they also recognize that there are benefits to be had for animals in seeking reforms that have the agreement or acquiescence of enough humans, whether these humans use animals themselves, work with them in some capacity, or are members of the general public. It can be conceded that animal welfare reform has been a gradual process, that sometimes the reforms fall short of what the animal protection movement wants, and that much more needs to be done. No one can surely claim, though, that progress has not been made.

Notes

1. This is a position that I have developed in a number of publications, but most notably in *Animals, Politics and Morality* (2004).
2. Here I am distinguishing between moral standing on the one hand and moral status or significance on the other. The former represents a position whereby at least some moral worth is attached to an entity, however small. The latter refers to the amount of moral worth. It is therefore possible to say, as the animal welfare position does, that animals possess moral standing but that their moral status or significance is less than humans.
3. It has been argued by the American historian Sheri Berman (1998) that the subservience of the German Social Democratic Party to this Marxist ideological position in the 1920s and 1930s explains why it did little to counter the economic crisis and the rise of the Nazis.
4. As Cochrane recognizes, the same applies to young children in the sense that it is not considered a harm that their activities are restricted by their parents because they are not regarded as fully autonomous agents.
5. It is not being argued here that the animal protection movement colluded in racist attacks on those practicing ritual slaughter. Indeed, the animal protection movement sought to defend the Muslim religion against attacks by arguing that there were religiously accepted alternatives to Kosher slaughter.

References

Barry, B. 1995. *Justice as impartiality*. Oxford: Clarendon Press.
BBC News. 1993. Hunting: How did your MP vote? June 30, 1993. http://news.bbc.co.uk/2/hi/uk_news/politics/3033846.stm/.
Bellamy, R. 1992. *Liberalism and modern society: An historical argument*. Cambridge, UK: Polity.

Bentham, J. 1948. *An introduction to the principles of morals and legislation*. New York: Hafner Press.

Benton, T., and R. Redfearn. 1996. The politics of animal rights: Where is the left? *New Left Review* 215.

Berman, S. 1998. *The social democratic moment: Ideas and politics in the making of interwar Europe*. Cambridge, MA: Harvard University Press.

Campbell, J. 1998. Institutional analysis and the role of ideas in political economy. *Theory and Society* 27:377–409.

Carruthers, P. 1989. Brute experience. *The Journal of Philosophy* 86(5):258–69.

———. 1992. *The Animals Issue*. Cambridge, UK: Cambridge University Press.

Cavalieri, P., and P. Singer, eds. 1993. *The great ape project*. London: Fourth Estate.

Clark, S. 1987. Animals, ecosystems and the liberal ethic. *The Monist* 79(3): 114–33.

Clarke, P., and A. Linzey. 1990. *Political theory and animal rights*. London: Pluto Press.

Cochrane, A. 2009a. Do animals have an interest in liberty? *Political Studies* 57(3):660–79.

———. 2009b. Ownership and justice for animals. *Utilitas* 21(4):424–42.

Cohen, C. 1986. The case for the use of animals in biomedical research. *New England Journal of Medicine* 315(14):865–70.

DeGrazia, D. 2002. *Animal rights: A very short introduction*. Oxford: Oxford University Press.

Descartes, R. 1912. Discourse. In *Rene Descartes: A discourse on method*, ed. J. Veitch, 90–97. London: Dent.

Dombrowski, D. 1997. *Babies and beasts: The argument from marginal cases*. Chicago: University of Illinois Press.

Dunayer, J. 2004. *Speciesism*. New York: Lantern Books.

———. 2007. Advancing animal rights. *Journal of Animal Law* 3:17–43. http://www.animallaw.info/journals/jo_pdf/jouranimallawDunayer2007.pdf.

Evans, E. 2008. Political opportunity structures and constitutional inclusion of animal rights in Germany and Switzerland. Paper presented at the annual meeting of the Western Political Science Association, Manchester Hyatt, San Diego, California. http://www.allacademic.com/meta/p237881_index.html.

Ferguson, K. 2004. I love my dog. *Political Theory* 32(3):373–95.

Francione, G. 1995. *Animals, property and the law*. Philadelphia: Temple University Press.

———. 1996. *Rain without thunder: The ideology of the animal rights movement*. Philadelphia: Temple University Press.

———. 2000. *Introduction to animal rights: Your child or the dog*. Philadelphia: Temple University Press.

———. 2008. A losing proposition. About.com: Animal Rights. http://animal-rights.about.com/od/proposition2ca2008/a/FrancioneProp2.htm.

Frey, R. 1983. *Rights, killing and suffering*. Oxford: Clarendon Press.

———. 1987. Autonomy and the value of animal life. *Monist* 70(1):50–63.

Garner, R. 1998. *Political animals: Animal protection politics in Britain and the United States*. Basingstoke, UK: Macmillan.

———. 2000. *Environmental politics*. Basingstoke, UK: Macmillan.

———. 2004. *Animals, politics and morality*. 2nd ed. Manchester: Manchester University Press (second edition).

———. 2005. *Animal ethics*. Cambridge, UK: Polity.

Girling, Richard. *Sunday Times Magazine*, November 12, 1989, 59.

Gray, J. 1997. *Endgames: Questions in late modern political thought*. Cambridge, UK: Polity.

Gustafson, J. 1996. *Intersections: Science, theology and ethics*. Cleveland, OH: Pilgrim Press.

Hall, C., and J. Hirsch. 2008. Prop. 2 unlikely to hike egg prices. *Los Angeles Times*, November 6, 2008. http://articles.latimes.com/2008/nov/06/business/fi-farm6.

Heywood, A. 2007. *Political ideologies: An introduction*. Basingstoke, UK: Palgrave Macmillan.

HMSO. 1997–2007. *Statistics of scientific procedures on living animals*. http://scienceandresearch.homeoffice.gov.uk/animal-research/.

House of Lords. 2002. Select Committee on Animals in Scientific Procedures. *Minutes of evidence, 17 July 2001*.

Hume, D. 1739/1978. *A treatise on human nature*. 2nd ed. Ed. L.A. Selby-Bigge and P.H. Nidditch. Oxford: Clarendon Press.

Jones, P. 1994. *Rights*. Basingstoke, UK: Macmillan.

Kamminga, M. 2008. The ethics of climate politics: Four modes of moral discourse. *Environmental Politics* 47(4):673–92.

Kant, I. 1965. *Metaphysics of morals*. New York: Bobbs Merrill.

Kelch, T. 1998. Toward a non-property status for animals. *N.Y.U. Environmental Law Journal* 6(3):531–85.

Lyons, D. 2006. Evolution of British animal research policy. PhD diss., University of Sheffield.

MacIntyre, A. 1988. *Whose justice? Which rationality?* London: Duckworth.

Mason, J., and P. Singer. 1990. *Animal factories*. New York: Harmony Books.

Meyer, D. 2004. Protest and political opportunities. *Annual Review of Sociology* 30:125–45.

Midgley, M. 1983. *Animals and why they matter*. Harmondsworth, UK: Penguin.

Mill, J. S. 1969. Three essays on religion. In *John Stuart Mill: Essays on ethics, religion and society*, ed. J. M. Robson. London: Routledge and Kegan Paul.

————. 1972. *Utilitarianism, on liberty, and considerations on representative government.* London: Dent.

Narveson, J. 1987. On a case for animal rights. *Monist* 70:30–47.

Neal, P. 1997. *Liberalism and its discontents.* London: Macmillan.

Nozick, R. 1974. *Anarchy, state and utopia.* Oxford: Blackwell.

Oakeshott, M. 1993. The concept of a philosophy of politics. *Religion, politics and the moral life*, ed. T. Fuller, 119–37. New Haven: Yale University Press.

Olson, M. 1965. *The logic of collective action.* Cambridge, MA: Harvard University Press.

Opotow, S. 1993. Animals and the scope of justice. *Journal of Social Issues* 49(1):71–85.

O'Sullivan, S. 2007. *Animal visibility and equality in liberal Democratic states.* PhD diss., University of Sydney.

Poulantzas, N. 1968. *Political power and social class.* New York: Routledge Chapman & Hall.

Radford, M. 2001. *Animal welfare law in Britain.* Oxford: Oxford University Press.

Rawls, J. 1972. *A theory of justice.* Oxford, UK: Oxford University Press.

————. 1991. Justice as fairness: Political not metaphysical. In *Equality and liberty: Analysing Rawls and Nozick*, ed. J. Angelo Corlett, 145–73. Basingstoke, UK: Macmillan.

————. 1993. *Political liberalism.* New York: Columbia University Press.

Regan, T. 1984. *The case for animal rights.* London: Routledge.

————. 2004. *Empty cages: Facing the challenge of animal rights.* Lanham, MD: Rowman and Littlefield.

Rollin, B. 1981. *Animal rights and human morality.* New York: Prometheus.

Rowlands, M. 2002. *Animals like us.* London: Verso.

Sabatier, P. 1992. Interest group membership and organization. In *The politics of interests: Interest groups transformed*, ed. M. Petracca. Boulder, CO: Westview.

Sapontzis, S. 1987. *Morals, reason, and animals.* Philadelphia: Temple University Press.

Scruton, R. 2000. *Animal rights and wrongs.* London: Metro.

Singer, P. 1990. *Animal liberation.* 2nd ed. London: Cape.

————. 1993. *Practical ethics.* Cambridge: Cambridge University Press.

Spira, H. 1983. Fighting for animal rights. In *Ethics and animals*, ed. H. Miller and W. Williams. Clifton, NJ: Humana Press.

Stallwood, K. 2008. The animal rights challenge. Paper presented at the Minding Animals Conference, London, December 5, 2008.

Tannenbaum, J. 1995. Animals and the law: Property, cruelty, rights. *Social Research* 539:125–93.

Townsend, A. 1976. Radical vegetarians. *Australasian Journal of Philosophy* 57:85–93.

Vincent, A. 1995. *Modern political ideologies.* Oxford: Blackwell.

Wise, S. 2000. *Rattling the cage: Towards legal rights to animals.* Cambridge, MA: Perseus.

Young, H. 1999. The intolerant in pursuit of political correctness. *Guardian*, July 13, 1999.

3

A Discussion Between Francione and Garner

I n this section, we discuss some of the issues raised by our respective essays. The discussion is divided to reflect the three major areas of disagreement between us.

First, Francione maintains that animals have an interest in continued existence and a right not to be treated as property and that we cannot justify animal use, however "humanely" we treat animals. According to Francione, although there may be differences between humans and nonhumans, just as there are differences among humans, all sentient beings are equal for the purpose of not being treated exclusively as a means to the ends of others. Garner recognizes that animals have an interest in not suffering, but he disagrees that they have an interest in continuing to live that is relevantly similar to that of humans. He maintains that the lives of animals have less moral value than those of humans and that although we ought not make animals suffer in unacceptable ways, our use of animals does not inherently violate their right not to suffer. So the first part focuses on issues concerning the personhood and moral status of animals.

Second, Francione maintains that animal welfare regulation is problematic as a matter of moral theory. If animals have a right not to be used, we should not be advocating for more "humane" animal exploitation any more than we should be advocating for "humane" rape given that we accept that women have a right not to be raped. He also argues that welfare reform is, as a practical matter, problematic because the property status of animals results in a very low level of protection, and welfare reform actually makes people feel more comfortable about animal exploitation, which perpetuates animal use. Garner rejects the notion that animals have a right not to be used, and, although he is critical of welfare reform, he maintains it can be improved. He sees reform as moving incrementally toward the recognition of the right of animals not to suffer in unacceptable ways. Therefore, the second part focuses on the pros and cons of welfare reform.

Third, Francione proposes as a matter of strategy that animal advocates engage in creative, nonviolent vegan education as the primary means of achieving the abolition of animal exploitation. Although Garner sees vegan education as important, he also believes that legislation that implements welfare reform is crucial. The third section, which overlaps with the second to some degree because it involves a discussion of welfare reform, explores several matters of movement strategy.

We also address one preliminary matter concerning the use of the word "fundamentalist" to characterize the abolitionist approach.

Preliminary Issue: Is Abolition "Fundamentalist"?

GLF: As a preliminary matter, I note that throughout your essay, you characterize the abolitionist position as "fundamentalist." I think that is unfortunate for at least two reasons. First, this term has come to have a particularly pejorative meaning in the post-9/11 world, and I think that it tends to interfere with discussion and not to promote it. Second, you regard the abolitionist position as fundamentalist because it maintains that we cannot morally justify any animal use. Do you regard the position that we cannot justify any rape or pedophilia as similarly fundamentalist? If not, and if you regard it as permissible or even obligatory to take the position that any rape or pedophilia is to be regarded as morally impermissible, are you not merely begging the question about the abolitionist approach as applied to nonhumans and assuming that animal exploitation is less morally problematic than human exploitation?

RG: I recognize the pejorative label often attached to the concept of fundamentalism, and that is why I have used the term abolitionism more often to describe your position. Nevertheless, I think that the term "fundamentalism" does have some explanatory utility and should not be regarded necessarily in a negative light. Indeed, in the context of animal rights, I suggested that it is a style of argumentation that has had enormous benefits in mobilizing activists around a distinct and absolutist set of views. In this context, I don't expect my own position to gain as much grassroots support as yours because it is a much more nuanced argument, couched in caveats and qualifications. Hardly the stuff of clarion calls to action!

I think when using the term, we need to distinguish between moral principles and strategy. Used in the former sense, your position is no more fundamentalist than mine. I would hold fundamentally to the view that animals have a right not to suffer, just as you would hold fundamentally to the view that animal use ought to be abolished. Both of us, in addition, would hold fundamentally to the view that it is not possible to justify any form of rape or pedophilia. Neither of the first two objectives is widely accepted whereas the latter are. It is in the strategic sense that your argument is more fundamentalist than mine. Thus, even if I accepted the case for abolition of the principal ways in which animals are used (and, incidentally, I do think that some uses of animals ought to be abolished either because their use is unnecessary or because the suffering inflicted cannot be reduced or eliminated), then I would recommend the adoption of any strategy that improved the condition of animals, irrespective of whether a particular use was abolished in the process. You think that strategy will not work, not least because it will make using animals more acceptable. As I explained in my essay, I disagree with this for a variety of reasons.

GLF: But why is my position fundamentalist even in the strategic sense? We are both proposing incremental strategies. My proposal is to put our time and resources into nonviolent vegan education, which can take a variety of forms. This incremental strategy is, for the reasons I argue, not only sound as a pragmatic matter but also more consistent with the principle that animal use, however "humane," is not morally justifiable. Your proposal is to pursue welfare reform that I regard as largely useless and counterproductive. Your incremental strategy reflects the moral principle that you defend, which is that we may use animals as long as we respect their right not to suffer. We both have moral principles that you agree are "absolutist," and we both have incremental strategies to implement those principles. I fail to understand why my incremental strategy is fundamentalist and yours is not. Indeed, to call my incremental strategy fundamentalist is merely to beg the question.

In addition, you say that my position is fundamentalist because it is not "nuanced" like yours. I am actually confused by your position that animals have a right not to suffer but do not have a right not to be used. I do not understand how your position provides any concrete normative guidance either as a matter of individual moral choice or as a matter of general movement strategy, given that virtually *all* animal use will involve suffering, and you provide no way to identify what you consider morally acceptable levels of suffering. My approach recognizes that we cannot justify using and killing animals however "humanely" we treat them and has veganism and creative, nonviolent vegan education as its strategic focus. Maybe that lacks nuance, but I am not sure how the greater normative clarity of my position makes it fundamentalist. Finally, even if *you* do not regard the fundamentalist label as necessarily pejorative, the label is usually used by new welfarists in its most negative sense to characterize the abolitionist perspective.

RG: I am, of course, begging the question. I was using the label fundamentalism in a neutral sense to refer to a style of strategic argumentation. In this sense, your strategic fundamentalism is valid *if* no reforms short of abolition are feasible and *if* supporting such an approach is counterproductive. I reject both arguments, and so I do not think that, on this occasion, a fundamentalist strategy is the correct one.

GLF: I have never said that no reforms short of abolition are feasible. I have said that reforms will generally be limited given the status of animals as chattel property and that welfare reforms make consumers feel more comfortable about animal use and do very little (if anything) to reduce animal suffering. In any event, given that "fundamentalist" is generally applied in contexts involving religious fanaticism (often coupled with extreme racist, sexist, and hetero-sexist views), I am afraid that we really cannot get back to it being used in any neutral sense. We need to put that term on the shelf.

RG: As a last point, I said that your approach (whether we describe it as "fundamentalist" or not) is more likely to be popular among those who are already committed to animal rights, but less likely (for reasons I explore in more detail later in this section) to be accepted by the public in general.

GLF: I note that although the abolitionist movement is certainly growing, most activists who regard themselves as "already committed to animal rights" are still involved with mainstream animal organizations, all of which accept some version of your protectionist approach. To the extent that the public does not embrace the abolitionist approach as readily, that may have a great deal to do with the fact that what is perceived as the mainstream "animal rights movement" is not promoting it and, indeed, is hostile to it, labeling it as "fundamentalist."

The Personhood and Moral Status of Animals

GLF: You describe the traditional welfarist position as maintaining that we can use animals exclusively as means to human ends if we derive a benefit in so doing but that we cannot similarly use humans even if there is a benefit for other humans. That is, welfarism recognizes the moral value of human life and the existence of moral rights that render impermissible certain forms of human exploitation but does not recognize that animal life has any inherent moral value or that animals have any moral rights.

You claim that I incorrectly characterize Peter Singer's theory as welfarist because, as a utilitarian, Singer does not recognize moral rights for nonhumans or humans.

I disagree that I mischaracterize Singer as a welfarist. Being a utilitarian is not inconsistent with being a welfarist. Indeed, the theory of animal welfare was formulated in large part by nineteenth-century utilitarians, such as Jeremy Bentham and John Stuart Mill. Like Bentham and Mill, Singer maintains that the *use* of animals as human resources does not as a general matter raise a moral question and that it is the *treatment* of nonhumans that is the primary focus of concern. Also like Bentham and Mill, Singer has a presumption against the use of humans as replaceable resources. Whether that presumption against the use of humans reflects some unarticulated rights notion or represents a form of rule utilitarianism (as a rule our using humans as replaceable resources will not maximize moral good even if such use would do so in an individual case), the presumption has the practical effect of acknowledging the moral value of human life and recognizing rights-type protection for humans. In any event, I regard Singer's view that we can use animals as long as we accord moral significance to their interest in not suffering as a form of welfarism. It may be more progressive than classical welfarism (although, as you acknowledge, Singer does promote traditional welfare reform as an advocacy matter) because Singer claims to accord greater weight to animal interests, but it is, for all intents and purposes, welfarism all the same even given your own description of welfarism. Do you disagree?

RG: I would want to clarify, first, what I think is meant by animal welfare. You are correct to say that it recognizes the moral value of human life and the existence of moral rights for humans and correct too that it denies that animals have moral rights. It does not, however, deny that animals have moral value in the sense that it recognizes that animals can be wronged directly. Wronging an animal comes about, according to the animal welfare position, when the suffering inflicted does not serve any significant benefit for humans or other animals.

I can also give my interpretation of Singer here, although, of course, this is only my interpretation and not necessarily the one that he would accept. I maintain that Singer cannot be classified as a welfarist. In the first place, he is not committed to focusing only on the treatment, rather than the use, of animals. As an act utilitarian, he could (and indeed does) argue that an analysis of preference satisfactions results in the moral validity of abolishing the principal ways in which animals are exploited, in the laboratory and on the farm. Whether he is right on this will depend on an empirical examination of the evidence. I am uncomfortable with this contingent conclusion, preferring the greater individual protection afforded by rights theory. Nevertheless, his assumption—that we ought to consider the interests of animals and humans equally—puts him at odds with animal welfare, which assumes from the outset that the moral superiority of humans justifies according rights to them.

You are right to suggest that, all things being equal (which, of course, they are often not), he regards human life as more valuable than animal life. This does not mean, however, that he thinks that humans have a right to life whereas animals do not, as the animal welfare position holds. It simply means that when we are faced with choosing between saving a human life and saving an animal life then, all things being equal, we ought to choose the former. But this would not always be the case. It would depend on the value of that particular life. Thus, if we had to choose between a human who was seriously impaired and a healthy animal, then the choice would not be as easy. In other words, the choice is not based on species membership but on the value of continued life, whether human or nonhuman. Indeed, Singer has courted more controversy by challenging the sanctity of human life than he has by defending the interests of animals.

Following this, it is right to say that Singer has a presumption against sacrificing the lives of normal humans. But he cannot, as an act utilitarian, have a presumption against the use of normal humans as replaceable resources. Utilitarians do have the problem that their logical conclusion (that it may be justifiable to exploit humans in order to maximize happiness or preference satisfaction) is counter-intuitive. Bentham failed to draw this logical conclusion, and Singer likewise is reluctant to do so. The animal welfare response here is to say that we should not use humans as part of a cost-benefit calculation because this is to infringe their rights. This, however, is not Singer's response. Instead, he would, I think, employ the logic of the argument from marginal cases and suggest that if we are not prepared to treat humans as part of a utilitarian cost-benefit calculation, then we should not be prepared to use animals in the same way. The result is that animal interests are treated in the same way as those of humans, a very different outcome from the animal welfare position.

GLF: When I say that the welfarist position does not accord moral value to animal life, what I mean is that welfarists regard the use and killing of animals as not raising a moral issue per se. That is, welfarists maintain that it is morally acceptable to use animals even for unnecessary human purposes but that we have a moral obligation that we owe directly to animals not to impose unnecessary harm on them in the process. Moreover, I maintain that although the welfare position supposedly recognizes animal interests in not suffering as morally significant, because animals are property, these interests are generally protected only when there is a resulting economic benefit.

Although I accept (and have always acknowledged) that Singer's version of welfare is more progressive than classical welfare (at least in theory because, in practice, he supports traditional welfare reform), he maintains, just as did Bentham, that because most nonhumans do not have the sort of self-awareness that we associate with normal humans, they do not have an interest in continued existence, and we do not harm them by using them for our purposes and taking their lives as long as we treat them reasonably well. Singer thinks that we have to give more weight to animal interests, but, like the classical welfarists, he maintains that animal use per se is not morally problematic.

As I said previously, Singer's presumption against using normal humans as replaceable resources must be based either on some notion of moral right or on rule utilitarianism. In either case, Singer's views on the use of humans as replaceable resources are inconsistent with his being an act utilitarian and different from his analysis of the use of nonhumans as replaceable resources. That is, it is not just that he thinks we ought to prefer humans over nonhumans in situations of conflict; he regards it as acceptable to use animals as replaceable resources (as long as we treat them well), whereas he presumes against such use in the case of humans. Singer very clearly regards humans as morally superior to nonhumans.

Finally, it is wrong to say that Singer advocates the abolition of the use of animals in vivisection and for food. As an act utilitarian, I am not sure how he could do this, but in any event, he does not. He advocates that these institutions be reformed to provide for the greater consideration of animal interests, but he certainly does not advocate abolition of these institutions.

RG: I think we can agree that Singer adopts a more progressive ethical position than classical welfarism. Whether we want to describe that as a version of welfare or not is a matter of semantics. I prefer not to use that term because Singer wants to go much further in protecting animals' interests in not suffering. You are right to say that he does regard humans as morally superior to animals. However, unlike classical welfarism, he is not prepared to sanction the view that, because humans are autonomous or are persons and animals are not, we should treat *all* human interests (including an interest in not suffering) as more important morally than *all* animal interests. This is the basis of his principle of equal consideration of interests. As a result, he does not think that we should always prioritize humans' interest in not suffering.

The question about his attitude to abolition is a complex one. As a utilitarian, Singer is committed to engaging in a cost-benefit analysis whereby the preferences of animals (in not suffering) must be balanced against the preferences of those who gain from inflicting suffering on animals. Singer has argued that this alone can justify the ending of animal agriculture and all but the most benign forms of animal experimentation. His critics (including you) are correct to cast doubt on the validity of his conclusion that his non-speciesist version of utilitarianism does justify abolitionist conclusions. There are two elements to this doubt. One is the possibility, outlined in my essay, that the costs to humans of abolition might outweigh the costs to animals. At the very least, this is a contingent matter. Second, Singer's claims to be putting forward an abolitionist position are dependent on his showing that the use of animals for food and experimental purposes must involve an unacceptable level of suffering. I think his case here is greater for animal experimentation than it is for animal agriculture.

So I do not think we differ that much on our interpretation of Singer's position. I agree that basing an animal ethic on their sentience, as Singer does, means that it is not, without additional arguments, a wrong to kill animals painlessly, nor is it wrong to deprive them of their liberty, provided this does not result in their suffering. In addition, I am uncomfortable with utilitarianism, preferring instead to suggest that animals have a right not to have suffering inflicted on them. The question to ask then is what this means in terms of how animals ought to be treated, and my essay explores this dimension of the debate.

There is a second way in which Singer could, and has, argued for abolition. This is the argument that distinguishing between the treatment of humans and animals, on the grounds that the former are persons and the latter are not, falls foul of the fact that not all humans are persons. According to the argument from marginal cases, therefore, if we are not prepared to treat marginal humans in the same way that we treat animals, then we should not be using and killing animals for human benefit. It is in this sense that Singer is able to argue that we should not use animals *or* humans as replaceable resources. As I said in my essay, I have doubts about the efficacy of the argument from marginal cases, and my own position is built on what follows if we dismiss it from our ethical armory.

GLF: We agree that Singer, as a utilitarian, has certain theoretical problems with abolition. But I continue to be mystified as to why you say that Singer advocates the abolition of the use of animals for food or experiments based on a cost-benefit analysis. For example, with respect to eating animals, he says (and this is cited in my essay), "There might be some people who say, 'You can't be compassionate if you end up killing the animals.' I just think that's wrong.... I think as long as the standards really are compassionate ones, that do as much as they can to give the animals decent lives before they're killed, I don't have a problem with it." Singer may think that a cost-benefit analysis militates against intensive agriculture, but he certainly does not advocate ending all animal agriculture. As for an abolitionist argument based on marginal cases, Singer certainly seems prepared to treat at least some marginal humans as resources.

As I discussed in *Introduction to Animal Rights: Your Child or the Dog?* if Singer (or any other utilitarian) recognized that animal interests will never be given equal consideration because of their property status, he might be compelled to conclude that the property status of animals cannot be morally justified and support at least a limited version of abolition. But Singer does not accept that property status is structurally defective as far as assessing animal interests is concerned. Neither do you. I think that you are both wrong, but we will get to that issue below.

—◄►◄►◄►—

GLF: You seem to agree with Singer, Regan, and others that the lives of nonhuman animals have a lesser moral value than do the lives of humans because animals do not have an interest in continued existence (Singer) or because animals have fewer opportunities for satisfaction than do humans (Regan). I do not see how you (or Singer or Regan) can maintain these positions without accepting very species-based accounts of self-awareness and opportunity satisfaction. That is, are you not simply accepting the view that an animal does not have an interest in her life because she does not have the same sort of self-awareness that we associate with normal, adult humans? And who are we to say that our enjoyment of fine art or moral philosophy has any greater moral significance than, say, the enjoyment that my rescued border collie, Katie, experiences when we play with a ball in the back garden?

RG: I am accepting the view that, all things being equal, nonhuman animal life (of most nonhuman species at least) is of less moral value than human life. In doing so, I am following the lead of many (if not most) pro-animal philosophers. This is not, of course, an exact science, and I am aware of the philosophical doubts here, particularly when it comes to the cognitively more able species such as the great apes. In the first place, even if we accept that animal experiences are less sophisticated than those of humans, there is still the possibility that they may be more intense than ours. Second, animals have experiences humans do not, and these may be extremely enriching. At the very least, therefore, I recognize we should exercise caution before claiming that the subjective experiences of animals are somehow inferior to human experiences.

Nevertheless, we also need to try to avoid making claims that are open to challenge, particularly if there is an alternative position that is stronger intellectually and that still offers a strong ethical case for the better treatment of animals. And this is exactly the case here. In other words, exercising caution about the value of animal lives does not, as my essay tried to show, prevent us from adopting an ethic that accords significant moral value to animals, thereby justifying radical reforms to the way they are currently treated. Thus, faced with those who argue that humans are morally superior to animals because we have greater cognitive capacities than they do, we can respond, as I wrote in my essay, in two main ways. First, we can invoke the argument from marginal cases and argue that not all humans are autonomous. Second, we can adopt the position that animals have an interest in avoiding suffering that is equivalent to humans' interest in not suffering. Therefore, if humans have a right not to suffer, then so do nonhuman animals.

GLF: Your response highlights a fundamental difference between us (and between me and most "pro-animal philosophers"). I reject the notion that humans have more opportunities for satisfaction and that, therefore, our lives are worth more because death is a greater harm to us. I do not think that, as an empirical matter, it is at all clear that humans have more opportunities for satisfaction than do nonhumans, and I think that the view that Regan, Singer, and you support is based on nothing more than species bias. Moreover, I do not think that we can draw any normative conclusions about the value of life based on those considerations in any event. Indeed, if that were the case, the life of a severely depressed person would necessarily have less moral value than the life of a person who was not depressed. The life of a less intelligent person would have less moral value than the life of a more intelligent person.

We cannot avoid the issue of the moral value of animal life, particularly when the default position is that animal life has lesser moral value. It is precisely that thinking that leads us to the view that it is acceptable to use animals for human purposes as long as we mitigate their suffering. You are proposing that we do not need to address the matter of the relative moral value of life because we can rely on the less controversial notion that animals have a right not to suffer. But *all* use will involve suffering or distress of some degree. Therefore, in the end, your position requires that we determine some *acceptable* level of suffering. Even if, as a matter of theory, your position would require that we make significant changes in animal welfare, animal interests are, as a practical matter, almost always going to be given less weight because the judgments about "acceptable" levels of suffering are going to be made by humans whose lives matter more as a moral matter and whose suffering is almost always given greater weight precisely because of these views about moral superiority.

RG: Here, the ethical difference between us is clear. I would reject the argument that my ethical position reflects a species bias, precisely because I am distinguishing between the moral status of most humans and most animals not just on species membership, but on what I take to be a morally important characteristic possessed by most humans but not by most nonhuman animals. My claim is that, in general terms, the package of cognitive abilities possessed by normal adult humans (including the most and least intelligent and the most and least depressed) is greater than those possessed by most adult nonhumans.

I accept that philosophical work is required on the nature and degree of animal suffering that ought to be deemed acceptable, and our judgment will also need to be informed by empirical research on animal suffering. As a practical matter, I think it is clear that some uses of animals cause more suffering than others. I think the fundamental difference between us is that you regard the use of animals as illegitimate because you regard what you see as the enslavement of animals as a form of suffering irrespective of what is done to animals during their "enslavement." As I have argued, I do not accept that view. Rather, captivity becomes problematic ethically when it involves suffering. Of course, too, I accept that it is humans who will make judgments about what is acceptable, but then that is a merely empirical matter that amounts to saying that might equals right. Both of our ethical positions seek to challenge that assertion.

GLF: First, your position is very much like Mill's notion that humans "have faculties more elevated than the animal appetites." In any event, I disagree that differences in cognitive abilities mean that human abilities are "greater" for the purpose of making normative judgments about the moral value of animal life that would justify animal use. You deny a species bias, but the characteristics to which you attach moral significance *are* linked to species in that you arbitrarily attribute moral significance to human-like cognition.

Second, I do think that captivity itself causes distress to many animals, but that was not the point that I am making here. My point is that you think we can avoid the issue of the moral value of animal life by focusing on the right not to suffer. I disagree in that I think that all use will invariably involve suffering apart from the suffering that results from captivity. For example, the most "humane" family farm involves considerable animal suffering. Therefore, your position is reduced to determining what degree of suffering is "acceptable."

Third, it is not clear to me how you can even say as an empirical matter that animals have an equivalent interest in not suffering when you maintain that there is such a sharp divide in cognitive abilities based on species.

Fourth, I do not see how such a view would not commit you to making normative judgments among humans who have different levels of cognitive abilities.

RG: I would maintain that the capacity of animals to suffer can be regarded as separate from their lack of autonomy. I do think that there comes a point when different levels of cognitive abilities among humans become morally significant. The key question is the capacity to be autonomous. In my view, most humans are and most animals are not autonomous.

●●●

GLF: Following from the previous question, you claim that humans are autonomous, and so liberty is inherently or intrinsically valuable to us, whereas for animals liberty is only a means to an end of achieving other goals. What is the basis of this position? That is, why do you believe that only humans are autonomous or that animals are not autonomous? Again, is this not a matter of species bias in your analysis?

RG: There are two distinct parts to your question. The first relates to the claim that humans are autonomous whereas animals are not, and the second relates to what follows if we accept that is the case. I share with most pro-animal philosophers the view that the cognitive ability of normal adult humans is greater than that of normal, adult nonhuman animals. I do not think there is anything really controversial in that statement, although what follows from it is morally significant. Claiming that normal adult humans are autonomous, or are persons, whereas animals are not, is a shorthand way of making this point.

The validity of the claim depends a great deal, of course, on how autonomy and personhood is defined. As I wrote in my essay, Regan, for one, wants to argue that at least some nonhuman mammals possess enough mental complexity to be morally considerable and that this, in particular, justifies the claim that death is a serious harm to animals. Now, I do not dispute Regan's description of the mental capacities possessed by mammals. Indeed, few would dispute that many species of nonhuman animals have capabilities that go way beyond their ability to experience pain and basic pleasures. Most nonhuman animals—including mammals and birds—are capable of having beliefs and desires, however simplistic these beliefs and desires may be, and acting on them. But this does not mean that any nonhuman animals have the characteristics, exhibited by normal adult humans, that are necessary for personhood or autonomy. This would include self-consciousness and a high degree of rationality enabling them to devise long-term life plans based on beliefs and desires.

The philosopher Raymond Frey (1987) comes closest to articulating the distinction I am trying to make here. He distinguishes between what he calls "control" autonomy (possessed by human persons) and "preference" autonomy (possessed by some species of nonhuman animals and human nonpersons). The former, for Frey, involves a much higher quality of life involving a rational assessment of desires and a willingness to shed or moderate some, particularly first-order (more base) desires if they are not consistent with an individual's conception of the good life. The latter, which he equates with Regan's "subject-of-a-life" criterion, on the other hand, involves the satisfaction of "first order" desires, which only requires that beings be able to have desires, or preferences, and have the ability to initiate actions with a view to satisfying them. For Frey, Regan's preference autonomy is an "impoverished" form of the concept, lacking all of the features of his "control" sense of the term.

Two final points here. First, it is an open question whether some species of nonhumans—the great apes and cetaceans in particular—do exhibit the characteristics of the "control" version of autonomy or personhood. As I pointed out, however, the effect of granting them personhood is to create another moral boundary, one containing humans and the more cognitively able nonhumans and the other containing all other nonhuman animals. Given this, it is better, it seems to me, to dispense with this attempt to show how like us nonhuman animals are, in favor of establishing the significant moral worth that I believe can be established for nonhuman animals by virtue of characteristics we know they possess.

The second point is that my position is not "species biased" in the important sense of the term. A genuine species bias would use species alone to justify differential moral entitlements. My starting point is to identify morally significant characteristics independently of species.

GLF: You maintain that full personhood requires humanlike self-awareness and the ability to make long-term life plans and so on. I regard that as arbitrary. Human and nonhuman cognition may be different in many respects, including with respect to autonomy, but I would not say that this has any normative significance whatsoever (beyond ascertaining whether a particular animal has a particular interest solely as an empirical matter). That is, I do not think that these cognitive differences support any justification for using animals in situations in which we would not use any humans as long as we respect what you view as the right of animals not to suffer. I fail to understand why personhood depends on animals having minds that are similar to those of humans. Any sentient being has an interest in her life and in continued existence, and you cannot deny that interest protection, and view as justifiable the use of an animal as a resource, without assuming that human interests are morally more important. This is a major point of disagreement between us.

Also, you claim that your analysis is not speciesist in this regard. Does this mean that you think that the life of a human who is cognitively impaired has a lesser moral importance than one who is not? There are clearly humans who lack the attributes of personhood as you have described it or who have them to a lesser degree than most others. Do we just stipulate that they are persons because they are human? Is it acceptable to use cognitively impaired humans in situations in which we would not use normal humans if the right of the former not to suffer were respected?

RG: I think that we have articulated accurately the differences between us here. The question of the moral status of cognitively impaired humans, of course, has been an important debate within the animal ethics literature, and bioethics more broadly. Without going into detail here, I *do* think that there is an ethical case for treating so-called marginal humans differently from "normal" adult humans, and to some degree, this does happen in practice. The problem here is that as soon as we start getting involved in the debate over the argument from marginal cases, the moral inferiority of animals in relation to "normal" adult humans is assumed.

I also think that the use of the words "inferior" and "superior" in the debate about the moral status of humans and animals is unfortunate. A preferable way of describing the aims of the exercise is to talk in terms of attaching moral entitlements to those who can benefit from them. Thus, arguing, as I have, that animals have less of an interest in liberty and continued life than humans is not some kind of punishment meted out because animals are '"inferior" to us. Rather, it is to say that animals will benefit less than humans from liberty and continued life. This is the basis, of course, for the conclusion that—because animals can benefit in the same ways as humans from the avoidance of suffering—their interests in so doing should be treated equally.

GLF: I have never denied that differences between and among humans may justify differential treatment for some purposes. It may be justifiable to give a greater level of economic compensation to a skilled brain surgeon than to a janitor. I am talking about treatment exclusively as a resource. That is, I do not think that we, for example, distinguish between a more intelligent human and a less intelligent human for the purpose of determining who can justifiably be used as an unwilling subject in a painful experiment.

As for language, I quite agree that we should not use "inferior" and "superior" (or similar expressions) in the debate; the use of these terms begs the question by constructing a hierarchy that already involves normative notions. I do not think that we can say that, based on cognitive sophistication, a human benefits more from an entitlement to life than a sentient nonhuman any more than we can say that one human benefits more than another from such an entitlement based on that ground. I really do not understand how you (or Singer or anyone else) can say that animals benefit less from continued existence or liberty than do humans without making all sorts of speciesist assumptions. But, as you acknowledge, our differences here are clear.

●●●

GLF: Singer and others claim that some nonhumans, such as the great apes, have cognition that is more abstract and similar to ours, but that, for the most part, animals live in a sort of "eternal present" that makes their lives worth less than the lives of humans as a moral matter. You appear to share that view.

Putting aside whether animal minds are really qualitatively different from human minds and also putting aside what flows as a moral matter from any such empirical fact, how would you apply this to a human who had transient global amnesia and had a sense of self only in the present? Is the life of a person with this condition worth less than the life of someone without it? If so, how do you avoid making normative distinctions about the relative value of life of humans based on characteristics such as intelligence, imagination, intellectual sophistication, and so on? Although we may pay a more conventionally intelligent person more than a person who is judged to be less intelligent, for purposes of whether we use either as a forced organ donor or as a non-consenting subject in a biomedical experiment, are they not equal as a moral matter?

RG: For reasons that I explored previously, I don't think I would share the view that animals live in an "eternal present." In answer to your question about the severely disabled human, I would make two points. The first would be that I think our moral obligations to such an individual *would* be different in some ways from those we owe to normal adult humans. For one thing, their capacity to suffer would be qualitatively different, as would the quality of their life. Secondly, I do not think it is possible to equate an individual with transient global amnesia with differing levels of intelligence among normal adult humans. I still insist on the view that the cognitive capacities of normal adult humans are greater than those of the cognitively most able nonhuman animals.

GLF: I got a strong sense from your essay that you were very much inclined toward the view that animals exist in the "eternal present," but in any event, I understand your answer to my question to be that the life of someone with transient global amnesia is worth less than the life of a person without that condition. I would disagree with that position. It would certainly be justifiable to treat a person with this condition differently for certain purposes; I would not, however, say that there was a difference in the value of life for purposes of use as a resource (even if the right not to suffer were respected).

But you have not answered my further question. I was not asking about the relative characteristics of human and nonhuman cognition; I was asking about why you would not apply your views about the moral value of cognitive characteristics to humans based on intelligence, sophistication, and so on. The fact that you think that most normal humans have greater cognitive capacities than nonhuman animals does not address why significant differences in cognitive capacity among humans would not be morally significant and why it would not, for instance, be morally justified to use a person with mental disabilities as a forced organ donor if her right not to suffer were respected.

RG: The extent to which it would be justified to treat "marginal" humans differently from "normal" adult humans, even to the point of justifying ending their lives, would depend on what was meant by "significant differences" and what loss or harm is likely to occur as a result of death. At the extreme, I think it is true that in some severe cases (the brain dead, the severely cognitively impaired), we do regard a marginal human's interest in continued life as minimal if not nonexistent, precisely because the loss of their lives is not a significant harm to them (although, of course, it may be of great concern for their friends and family, an additional ethical complexity). I recognize, too, that our treatment of even the most "marginal" humans is different from our treatment of animals, and the argument from marginal cases is effective in drawing attention to this. By this, I mean that even in these severe cases, we agonize over the right thing to do, and sometimes the courts are required to adjudicate in life and death decisions. Human life, of all qualities, is regarded with respect. This, of course, is very different from the throwaway attitude we have toward animal lives, where animals are killed for every conceivable human purpose.

Where we draw the line, here, is problematic of course, and I am not, for one moment, suggesting that those with relatively minor mental disabilities, and those who are less intelligent than other humans, should be treated as if their lives were of less value. I think, though, that if one could picture a human with the characteristics of most animals, excluding the more cognitively able species, then it would be morally justifiable to regard them as beings who have less to lose by death. Of course, this does not mean that we can treat the lives of either with disrespect. Applying a principle that I explore in more detail later in this discussion, their lives should be sacrificed only when to do so is to save the lives of normal adult humans. After this explanatory detour, I would then confirm that I think it would be morally acceptable to use a marginal human, in the sense that I have tried to define such an individual, as an organ donor. I would add, too, that if forcing such an individual caused suffering, it would not be legitimate morally.

GLF: We simply disagree on whether death is a greater harm for humans than for nonhumans. I have no confidence that we can say that, and I am not even sure what you, Singer, or Regan mean when you say that this is so. That is, it seems that what is meant is that death deprives humans of more of the things that humans value; that is true, but trivially so. If I follow your thought experiment and imagine a human who has the cognitive ability of my border collie, I see a human who, like my border collie, probably has greater joy and less anxiety than I do. In any event, I completely reject this notion that we can make judgments about the moral value of life—human or nonhuman—based on cognitive sophistication. I understand that in some cases, such as permanent brain death, a being may stop having interests altogether. But as long as a being has interests, then our judgments about the harm that death constitutes for her and our notions about opportunity satisfaction involve moral judgments that beg the question at issue. And again, it is still not clear to me why, given your views, you would not be committed to giving more weight to the interests of a more intelligent person than to the interests of a less intelligent one.

You do, however, again make a comment with which I think I agree but that leads you very strongly to the abolitionist position and that creates a serious tension with your overall protectionist/ new welfarist position. You seem to say that in a conflict between a normal human and an animal, we cannot sacrifice the animal unless it is to save the life of the human. I have argued in my work— most particularly in *Introduction to Animal Rights: Your Child or the Dog?*—that even if we can be excused or even justified in prefer- ring humans over animals in situations of true conflict (and I reject preference on the grounds of species), we cannot be justified in creating these conflicts in the first place. We cannot say that it is "necessary" to prefer a human over an animal when that preference is based on our pleasure, amusement, or convenience. Therefore, we cannot justify using animals *at all* for food or for any sort of entertainment purpose, such as hunting, circuses, zoos, and so on. To the extent that you agree with that, you would have to accept that sentient nonhumans have a right not to be used at all for these purposes and not merely that they have a right not to be exposed to levels of suffering that are not "acceptable."

●●●

GLF: You distinguish between a right to life for nonhumans, which you do not think can be morally justified, and a right not to suffer, which you support. But what does this mean? How are you using "right"? I understand a right to be a way of protecting an interest; the interest cannot be ignored or abrogated merely because it will result in beneficial consequences for others. You seem to agree with this because you say that your position would rule out (at least as a matter of moral theory, if not practical politics) imposing suffering on animals just to benefit humans. You then use two examples that confuse me.

First, you say that we could use animals in experiments if this would contribute significantly to saving human lives, which you think have greater moral value than nonhuman lives, as long as we did not cause the animals to suffer. If there were no suffering or harm involved in experiments, we would be using humans solicited as paid volunteers, would we not? In any event, how can animals ever be used without causing them to suffer in some way? For example, even if an animal does not suffer pain as part of a medical experiment, the animal has been bred and raised and transported and confined and prepared for the experiment. Surely, this involves suffering. Are you saying that the right you support would allow for inflicting distress and other deprivations on nonhumans?

Second, although you claim that a right not to suffer would rule out using animals for food, you also claim that using animals for food would be acceptable if we abandoned intensive agriculture in favor of a system that minimizes animal suffering. There is an inconsistency here. If you accept any use of animals for food, then you compromise your belief in the right not to suffer because *all* systems of agriculture, including the most "humane," will cause some level of suffering. Moreover, how is your position any different from Singer's position that it is morally acceptable to eat animal products if we take care to eat animals that have had a relatively pleasant life and a relatively painless death?

RG: On the first point, I am saying that I do not think that nonhuman animals have an interest in life, or at least not as great an interest as normal adult humans. As I have said, this qualification is important because I am not saying that killing animals is of no moral concern. Rather, I am arguing that there is a moral case for saying that the lives of humans matter more than those of nonhuman animals and that therefore if it was a choice, then we should choose the human. By contrast, nonhuman animals do have an interest in not suffering that is equivalent to a human's, and should this be translated into a right not to suffer, this interest in not suffering cannot be sacrificed ordinarily for the goal of achieving a greater good.

In terms of the examples cited, I think it is important to recognize the nuances of my argument. In particular, it is necessary to distinguish between two slightly different ethical positions. The first is the argument (what might be called the sentience position) that even though humans are autonomous and nonhumans are not, as explained previously, it does not follow that we ought to similarly downgrade an animal's interest in not suffering. In other words, whereas animals do not have a right to life (because they lack autonomy), they do clearly have an interest in not suffering. The second (what might be called the enhanced sentience position) might go further than this by suggesting that although humans have a greater interest in life, this does not mean that animals have *no* interest in life.

The qualification in the enhanced sentience position is clearly significant. The sentience position would allow for scientific experimentation and the raising and killing of animals for food *provided* that no suffering on animals was inflicted. The enhanced sentience position, however, would be much more restrictive. It would rule out scientific experimentation on animals and the raising and killing of animals for food unless human life were at stake, *irrespective* of the level of suffering inflicted. It might be claimed that some uses of animals in the laboratory do serve the purpose of saving or protecting human lives. It is much more difficult, however, to justify the killing of animals for food. It would be justified only if human starvation were likely to otherwise result. In the developed world at least, this is clearly not the case.

I think the enhanced sentience position is probably ethically more desirable. Politically or strategically, however, I would probably opt for the sentience position. This is because it is not necessary to engage in interminable, and probably indeterminable, debates about the respective quality of human and animal lives. In further defense of the sentience position I have articulated in this book, it is important to remember that using animals may fall foul of the principle that it is wrong to inflict suffering on them, irrespective of its purpose. For example, in the laboratory, procedures that caused animals to suffer would be illegitimate if we held that animals had a right not to suffer, and this principle would be applied *before* we got to the issue of the value of animal lives. For radical changes to our treatment of animals to be justified, therefore, only requires us to show that animals can suffer in similar ways to humans. Deciding at what point the suffering inflicted on animals becomes illegitimate is, as you imply, a difficult question. If it is defined stringently enough, it would probably rule out any uses of animals, which I know you would support. However, what we do know is that the suffering inflicted in many (if not most) laboratory procedures is high enough to be clearly unacceptable. Likewise, the sentience position would clearly rule out the current industrialized system of animal agriculture. Whether or not an extensive system of animal agriculture could ever be created that minimized suffering to an acceptable level is an open question. I personally doubt it.

GLF: I have two responses here. First, although throughout your essay you characterize the abolitionist position as unrealistic and as too idealistic, what I think is unrealistic is your notion that it is possible as a practical matter to use animals without causing them to suffer. What are you talking about? How *could* this be the case? Yes, I understand that in theory it might be possible to raise and kill an animal without there being any pain or distress or harm. I use "might" deliberately because I think that domestication itself involves harms to nonhumans apart from any other distress or pain. But even if we put that consideration aside, I do not understand how we can, as a matter of practical reality, use animals for food or for other purposes without there being pain, suffering, distress, and so on.

Perhaps this is why you seem to equivocate about the content of the right not to suffer. In your essay, you appear to propose what you are distinguishing here as the sentience position, and that fits with your view about the difference between human and nonhuman autonomy and the lesser moral value of nonhuman life. Your right not to suffer does not rule out any suffering but only unacceptable levels of suffering, and you have not proposed any way to determine when suffering is not acceptable. That is, although you seem inclined to regard much suffering as not acceptable, you do not propose any principled basis for identifying such suffering. This is one of the very great weaknesses of the animal protection or new welfarist position.

Second, as a general matter, I do not understand how you derive a right not to suffer given that you do not recognize a right not to be used. I maintain that humans do not have (and, as a practical matter, cannot have) a right not to suffer at all, but have a right not to suffer at all from being used as the replaceable resources of others. Therefore, we cannot protect humans from all suffering, but we recognize that humans can and should be protected from any suffering incidental to their being deprived of their fundamental interests by being used as chattel slaves, forced organ donors, and so on. This right not to suffer incidental to being used exclusively as a resource is derived from our recognition that humans, if they are going to be members of the moral community, must have a basic right not to be the property of others. I argue that we cannot justify denying this fundamental right to nonhumans if they are going to be members of the moral community. But I conclude that recognition of this right requires that we abolish animal use and not merely regulate it. You do not recognize such a right for animals because you allow for use as long as the right not to suffer is respected. I am bewildered as to the source of the animal's right not to suffer if the animal does not have a right not to be used as a resource.

RG: As I have said, a great deal would depend on what degree of suffering is regarded as acceptable. You are right to identify the lack of a precise guide as a weakness of my position, and advocates of a position such as mine need to work this out with greater clarity. That does not mean, however, it cannot be done. I do insist that we can talk sensibly about degrees of suffering. Remember, too, that I am not arguing, as a welfarist would, that we must balance the suffering inflicted on animals against the likely benefits to humans. All suffering (at levels beyond what we deem to be acceptable) must stop, even if benefits to humans are lost in the process.

I also take your point that it is difficult to envisage the use of animals as sources of food and as experimental subjects happening without the infliction of some suffering. If we adopted a stringent approach to the level of suffering deemed acceptable, then an abolitionist goal becomes justified morally. Likewise, even though I agree with you that all domestication of animals involves some suffering, we can distinguish between, say, the keeping of animals as companions (provided they are treated well) and the use of animals as sources of food and as experimental subjects. The former is less of an issue for animal advocates. Indeed, many have companion animals themselves.

Your second point highlights the key ethical differences between us, and to avoid repetition, I will not reprise my justification for denying to animals a right not to be used. The source of an animal's right not to suffer at the hands of humans is the interest they have in not suffering. According to a strict interpretation of the sentience position, which I have qualified in this discussion, animals do not have an interest in not being used or an interest in life. Of course, suffering is an inevitable feature of human and animal life. The suffering I am referring to is that which is deliberately inflicted on animals in order to further some human goal.

GLF: Putting aside the difficulty of determining in any morally satisfying way what constitutes an acceptable level of suffering, I fail to understand how, as a matter of process alone, acceptable suffering can be determined without bringing in the notion of human benefit. That is, although you claim to reject the traditional welfarist position that purports to balance human interests against animal interests, you have merely substituted "unacceptable" suffering for "unnecessary" suffering. The traditional welfarist claims to recognize that animals have a right not to suffer "unnecessarily"; you maintain that animals have a right not to suffer "unacceptably." You acknowledge that you have not provided a way to determine what constitutes acceptable suffering, and I suggest that however you do so (short of accepting the notion that no suffering as a result of use for humans is acceptable), you need to rely on some sort of balancing involving human interests.

As far as your derivation of the right not to suffer is concerned, you are again assuming that animals can be property without there being suffering, or at least without there being suffering that exceeds whatever it is that you regard as acceptable. I reject that both as a matter of moral theory, because I reject your notion about the moral value of nonhuman life, and as a matter of the real world of facts, because animals who are chattel property will always be treated terribly, however you determine the level of acceptable suffering. (I will discuss the issue of companion animals later in the discussion.) Moreover, I continue to be somewhat perplexed as to how you derive a right not to suffer from an interest in not suffering when we recognize not that humans have a right not to suffer at all but, rather, that they have a right not to suffer at all from being used exclusively as resources.

Finally, concerning what constitutes acceptable suffering, it would seem to me that your view that animals do not have an interest in continued existence, autonomy, and so on would necessarily shift things in favor of humans. Mill and others held the view that because nonhumans are cognitively different from humans, human suffering should be assigned greater weight. It would seem that similar thinking would influence your determination of what constitutes acceptable suffering because balancing human and animal interests would necessarily be involved.

⌖⌖⌖

GLF: You seem to think that ethical principles cannot be defeated by empirical arguments. I find that curious. Does not "ought" imply "can"? If your moral theory is completely unworkable as a practical matter, is it a plausible moral theory? For example, if we cannot use animals without causing them to suffer, which I maintain is the case, then is the moral theory that you promote—that we can use animals as long as we do not make them suffer—plausible?

RG: There are two distinct questions here. I was simply saying that it is the conventional view that the correctness of normative statements cannot logically be decided definitively by the use of empirical statements. It was for this reason that the logical positivists concluded that normative statements were meaningless. I do not, obviously, share their view. On the second question, I am not sure, as I discussed in the answer to the previous question, whether suffering can be minimized to a satisfactory degree. If not, all well and good. We have arrived at the same end point, albeit by different routes!

GLF: Well, I have for years been urging animal protectionists (including you!) to recognize that apart from the theoretical objections to animal use based on the moral value of nonhuman life, the practical realities of animal use are such that the goal of progressive welfare regulation *cannot* be achieved or even identified. *All* animal use involves pain, suffering, and harm, and there is *no* principled way to determine what levels of pain are "acceptable."

The Critique of Animal Welfare Regulation

GLF: As a general matter, you have an interesting way of structuring the argument on the value of welfarist regulation. You appear to think that a heavy burden rests on the opponent of welfarism to demonstrate that it is ineffective and that the abolitionist approach, which focuses on nonviolent vegan education, would be better. You *assume* that welfarist reform is effective and that the abolitionist approach would not work.

You appear to believe that because most animal organizations pursue welfare reform, there is a presumption that welfare reform is effective in both the short and long term. Does that not beg the question on several levels? For example, the fact that most animal groups pursue welfare reform has to be considered in light of the empirical fact that the big fundraising dollars are in welfare reform. That is, as I have argued at length here and elsewhere, animal organizations need a steady stream of winnable campaigns on which to raise money. The economics of these groups virtually ensures that they will pursue welfare reform and that they will focus for the most part on economically inefficient industry practices that are vulnerable anyway because they are more likely to achieve "victories" in these cases.

Given that you acknowledge that animal welfare reforms have met with little success, why not say that the burden rests on the promoters of animal welfare to show that welfare reform is an effective use of resources?

RG: The fact that most animal organizations focus on achieving welfarist reforms is, of course, not evidence that such a pursuit is valid. They might be wrong, as I know you think they are! Likewise, your argument about the need for such organizations to raise finances is well made. On the other hand, the fact that animal organizations choose to focus on winnable goals suggests that other goals, and particularly the abolitionist goals you have advocated, are not winnable, at least at present. It also suggests that some goals are winnable. What did you have in mind here? Why are these "wins" not worthwhile?

I do think that welfare-type regulations are more effective than you do, but I do not assume it as such. I begin by making the point that if it can be shown that it is not counterproductive to pursue welfarist or regulatory goals, then the burden of proof rests on those who would challenge the utility of doing so. In other words, in order to maintain your insistence that we should focus entirely on a vegan education campaign, you would have to show that absolutely no benefits for animals derive from regulatory reforms. This, I think, would be a difficult task. After all, I am not saying that a vegan education campaign is wrong. In fact, I think it is entirely appropriate provided that it is part of a broader strategy.

GLF: For the reasons I explain in my essay (and in much of my other work), I think that most supposed welfarist victories do nothing more than ensure that animals are exploited in an economically efficient manner. Although I accept that making exploitation more efficient may incidentally involve some welfare benefits, these benefits are not significant, and such an approach does nothing whatsoever to change the moral status of animals or to move toward the abolition of animal use or even the significant reduction of animal use.

In any event, I would say that the history of the animal welfare movement is all the proof that was needed to justify the conclusion that it is a miserable failure. In the past thirty years, that effort has been particularly well funded and focused, and it has failed. There has been *very* little return on the effort expended. The fact that animal welfare groups continue to promote animal welfare is neither surprising nor any evidence whatsoever that welfare regulation has any benefit for animals. I do accept that the welfarist campaigns have economic value for these organizations. But that, of course, is a different matter.

●●●

GLF: You do not address the argument that in many cases, welfare reform reinforces the property status of animals by making animal exploitation more efficient. If that argument is valid, then it would seem to present a *most* troubling problem for the new welfare/ animal protection approach. What is your take on this?

RG: I do not dispute the fact that welfare reforms may sometimes have this effect. One question to ask here, though, is whether these improvements to the welfare of animals are not then worth having. You provide the example of the stunning of large animals on the grounds that stunning protects carcasses and slaughterhouse workers. Does this mean that the animal protection movement should have opposed the introduction of stunning?

The other key question to ask here relates to intention. Is it in fact the case that only those reforms that increase the efficiency of animal exploitation will ever be considered and introduced? This is an empirical question. I would say that it is clearly the case that reforms improving the welfare of animals that also have the effect of making animal exploitation more efficient are inevitably easier to achieve. It is therefore strategically sensible (as in the campaign for more humane poultry slaughter) for the animal protection movement to make an efficiency argument if there is one to be made. In addition, though, there are also plenty of examples where, in the case of animal agriculture, producers have campaigned vigorously against suggested reforms on the grounds that it would mean the end of the road for them economically. But they have still lost.

Of course, I am not naïve enough to think that economic efficiency has little influence. Clearly, it is hugely important. One final question that might be asked here, though, is, what is meant by economic efficiency? One definition might be the production of a product in the quickest possible time at the cheapest possible price. Another, broader definition might be related to profitability. This latter definition would have to take into account consumer preferences. If we factor in consumer desire for quality together with their concern for ethics, then it is possible to equate economic efficiency with high standards of animal welfare. I am not saying that this happens now, although there is clearly a market for "free-range" products, but there is clearly the potential for making economic efficiency more compatible with animal welfare. This link has been made, for example, by the European Commission in the debate over the Laying Hens Directive, an issue to which we return later in this dialogue.

GLF: As I said previously, I accept that making exploitation more economically efficient *may* have welfare benefits, although I think that these benefits are generally not significant and are often never really provided. For example, there are major problems with getting slaughterhouses to stun animals properly. Moreover, such reforms do *nothing* to shift the paradigm in favor of recognizing the inherent value of animal interests. Indeed, they further enmesh animals in the property paradigm. And if these reforms result in increased production efficiency, as we both agree that at least some do, then it is not necessary for animal groups to advocate for those reforms because institutional users will implement them in any event in the ordinary course, or in response to more abolitionist demands.

You seem to be comfortable with the animal protection movement, at least at this stage of history, acting in the role of an advisor to institutionalized exploiters about how to be more efficient institutional exploiters. And that is clearly what the protectionist/ new welfarist movement has become. Organizations such as CIWF, PETA, and HSUS are actually promoting reforms that they characterize as strengthening institutional exploiters.

You note that in some cases, producers have made the argument that welfare reform will put them out of business but have lost anyway, and the reforms were passed or adopted. Putting aside that, for strategic reasons, producers almost always make the claim that reform will harm them economically whether that is the case or not, and accepting that some welfare reforms may impose slightly higher costs on particular producers, can you identify any industry that has met the "end of the road" as the result of welfare reform?

Finally, as for whether efficiency is related only to profitability or can factor in demand for high welfare, I agree that if consumers demanded higher welfare, producers would satisfy the demand. There is certainly a niche market for free-range products. But as you acknowledge, there is no evidence to suggest that economic efficiency is being coupled with high welfare standards or any welfare standards that do not amount to anything more than efficient exploitation as I use that notion. You seem to think that this can change, but you have not identified what new argument or approach is going to effect that change.

RG: I am certainly not "comfortable" with the animal protection movement merely existing as advisors to "institutionalized exploiters about how to be more efficient institutional exploiters." But I do think it should be part, albeit only a part, of a broader strategy involving both accommodation and opposition.   .

As we both know, animal agriculture, and indeed animal exploitation of all kinds, continues to prosper. The only exception in the UK is fur farming, which now no longer exists. Of greater importance, though, there is no doubt that reforms, and changing consumer demands, have had an impact on the way animals are raised, reducing suffering in the process. One can think here of decisions, in the UK, to ban the veal crate and sow stalls and tethers. There is a sense, too, that legislative reform follows, rather than leads, public opinion. We will discuss the issue of battery cages later. For now, though, it should be noted that consumer demand in this area, at least in the UK, has moved far ahead of what is being proposed at the European level.

This is confirmed by a recent survey by a market research company (*Guardian*, May 15, 2009), which reports that in 2008 expenditure on eggs produced in genuine free-range conditions (where hens must have continuous outdoor daytime access and where intensity levels must not exceed more than 1,000 birds per hectare) constituted almost half of the UK market in eggs (eggs produced by barn hens accounted for only 4% of the total expenditure). Caged eggs still account for the majority (just over 50%) of volume sales, but the gap with free-range alternatives is closing. Indeed, the proportion of free-range eggs sold is expected to rise further this year. This is partly a product of the fact that major British supermarkets, such as Waitrose, Marks & Spencer and Sainsbury's, no longer stock battery eggs, which is itself a sign that consumer demand for them is declining. Regulation has played a part here too, given that packaging of eggs produced in battery conditions cannot use descriptions or pictures of hens roaming freely.

GLF: Although there have been some ostensibly more progressive reforms in the UK, they really do not amount to very much as an overall matter. I see it as no different from a regulation that limits the torture of human beings to four hours a day rather than four and a half hours. That is an 11 percent reduction of torture time, but we are still left with people being tortured for four hours daily. If you look at the life and death of a veal calf, pig, or laying hen, I would say that even in the UK, all three are routinely treated in ways that would constitute torture if humans were involved. These animals may be tortured slightly less in the UK than they are in France or Spain, but in all three countries, they are tortured, and the difference in treatment between the UK and other countries certainly cannot be said to be comparable to the reduction in my example of human torture. So yes, there may be differences, but the differences are minor. I agree with your statement in *Animals, Politics and Morality* that in Britain, despite any changes, the "fundamentals remain" (Garner 2004, 118) concerning factory farming.

I should add that gestation crates and veal crates increase animal stress and lower productivity; providing animals more space increases productivity and is economically efficient. With respect to the eggs, I am not sure that it is correct to say that all free-range eggs in the UK are produced with the stocking density of no more than 1,000 birds per hectare, but even if that is the case, the increase in production cost of free-range eggs at that stocking density is about 18 pence per dozen; we really are not talking about anything particularly dramatic here. Finally, you seem to ignore that a good part of the motivation for purchasing "higher-welfare" products is that they are perceived as more wholesome and healthy. This is particularly the case with eggs. In any event, none of these examples represents a reform that constitutes the "end of the road" for industry.

●●●

GLF: You claim that it is "intuitively odd" that I should be promoting abolition when there has not been much success in regulating animal exploitation. Putting aside that you acknowledge that animal welfare efforts, which have involved an enormous amount of resources, have met with limited success, your comment ignores the argument that the property status of animals structurally limits the scope of welfare reform and that we really need to put those resources into effecting a paradigm shift through educational efforts focused on veganism and abolition. That is, we need to move the discussion to the issue of animal use rather than animal treatment. What is "intuitively odd" about that? You may not (and clearly do not) agree with my views on abolition, but I do not think that the failure of animal welfare reforms means that advocacy of abolition is remarkable or odd in any way; indeed, what I find odd is that welfarists continue to promote regulation despite its very clear failure to do much in the 200 years that it has been part of moral and legal thinking about animals.

RG: Your position is "intuitively odd" at first sight because it appears to be saying something like this: "We haven't been very successful in achieving reforms to the way animals are treated because humans insist on causing them to suffer for the variety of benefits they get from so doing. So let's instead try to persuade them that they should not exploit them at all despite the fact that they would then lose all of those benefits." Intuitively, my initial response to this argument is to say, If we can't persuade enough humans to accept moderate reforms to the way animals are treated, how on earth are we going to persuade them to go much further and accept abolitionist objectives?

The fact that something is "intuitively" odd does not mean, of course, that it is wrong. Intuitions are there to be challenged, and that is exactly what you do in a very effective way. What I try to do then is to examine critically your substantive arguments, which, although I disagree with some of them, I do not find odd. My disagreements with your position, which I explore in detail in my essay and in responses to other questions in this section, focus on my doubts about the arguments that animal welfare is counterproductive, has failed to make any substantive improvement to the lives of animals, and is structurally constrained by the legal construct of property.

As a result, I do not see the need to focus exclusively on a vegan education effort, although I do accept that it should be a part of an effective strategy. Indeed, I think it is essential to focus on such a campaign if we are to achieve the paradigm shift that we both would like to see. And here, in ethical terms at least, I do not think that the distinction between regulation and use is particularly useful. Despite the fact that I have doubts about the claim that animals have a right to life, I do think that the suffering inflicted on them by humans is wrong. That proposition alone, I would suggest, represents a paradigmatic shift in thinking.

GLF: The modern animal movement has *never* promoted a clear and unequivocal abolitionist/vegan message. On the contrary. Almost all of the large groups in the United States, UK, and elsewhere promote a welfarist approach, and to the extent that they even talk about the abolitionist/vegan approach, they present it as some sort of distant and utopian goal. They often pejoratively label veganism as "absolutist," "fundamentalist," or "purist" and, following Singer, promote being a "conscientious omnivore" as a morally defensible position.

Please understand that I am not saying that if all of the animal groups shifted focus and promoted a clear and unequivocal abolitionist/vegan campaign, we would abolish exploitation overnight or anytime soon. But we would at least start the required paradigm shift by focusing discussion on the right issues. The welfarist model has failed and will continue to fail because it focuses discussion on the wrong set of issues. And I very much disagree that the right not to suffer, without a discussion about the morality of use per se, is going to lead anywhere other than to more of the same welfare regulation.

As for whether the welfarist approach has gotten us anywhere or whether the property status of animals involves a structural constraint on welfare reform, we will have to agree to disagree. Frankly, I think the empirical evidence is about as clear as it can be on these points.

RG: I do agree, of course, that the animal protection movement (including the rights faction) has focused to some degree on achievable welfare-based reforms. Despite this, I do also think that the distinction between the reformist character of animal welfare and the abolitionist goals of animal rights is well-known. The debate about vegetarianism versus free-range versus factory-farmed, which is well ensconced in popular culture, is ample testimony to this. There is clearly a huge difference between saying that being a "conscientious omnivore" is ethically preferable to not caring at all how our food is produced and saying that it is a an acceptable moral position. From my perspective, much would depend on what a "conscientious omnivore" is, given that it is a vague term that could be consistent with a variety of ethical positions.

GLF: I disagree that most people understand the issues; indeed, from my perspective, most "animal people" do not understand the issues. Singer is not saying that being a "conscientious omnivore" is morally preferable to having no concern about animals or that one product may be preferable because it involves less harm than another, but that being a "conscientious omnivore" is an ethically defensible position. That is, Singer and other new welfarists are arguing that eating "happy" animals and animal products *is* ethically acceptable and not just that it's better than consuming conventional products. That message is seriously confusing animal advocates.

●●●

GLF: I am rather surprised that you regard the evidence about the counterproductive effects of animal welfare as "anecdotal." There has been what can fairly be called a substantial amount of evidence that, in the United States and Britain, many people are returning to eating meat and animal products, or are not inclined to give up eating meat and animal products, because their concerns about the treatment of animals have been met or at least ameliorated by supposedly improved welfare regulations. The number of vegetarians in Britain fell in 2008, and this has been attributed to the perception that animals are being treated better. I would welcome your comments on why you regard this evidence as anecdotal. Is it any less anecdotal than the evidence that welfare measures provide significant benefits to nonhumans?

Moreover, animal welfare reforms are almost always marketed to the public by the very animal advocates who promote them as assuring higher welfare. These campaigns deliberately encourage the consumption of these supposedly "happy" meat/animal products. For example, the RSPCA Freedom Food campaign is explicitly aimed at portraying the foods that have this label as being produced in a "humane" way. Putting aside that there have already been many cases in the UK in which producers who have the RSPCA Freedom Food stamp of approval have been exposed as engaging in heinous animal abuse, these schemes are, on their face, intended to encourage the public to believe that certified products have been "humanely" produced. Another example (among many) is PETA's campaign to promote the gassing of poultry. Putting aside whether this method of slaughter has significant welfare benefits, PETA has promoted boycotts of restaurant chains until they implement gassing. In the case of KFC in Canada, which agreed to phase in gassing, PETA praised KFC for being concerned about animal welfare and called off the boycott. It is simply impossible not to interpret that campaign as sending out a very clear moral message about the consumption of gassed poultry.

Given that the prevailing paradigm, which is explicitly endorsed by people such as Singer and by just about all animal organizations, is that we can use nonhumans as long as we treat them better, why are you skeptical that the claims of animal advocates that treatment is improved have had their intended affect—making people feel better about animal treatment?

RG: I would certainly welcome the opportunity to examine major survey research on the reasons why people cease to be vegetarians. This kind of quantitative research is very different from the evidence that would be required to demonstrate that the welfare of animals has been improved by regulatory efforts. I must confess that I have not seen any convincing large-scale evidence demonstrating that a belief that animals are more humanely treated is the most important reason why people revert to consuming animal products. An additional reservation is whether this kind of response is genuine or merely a product of respondents giving an answer that they feel is acceptable ethically. This is important because your argument relies on a link between a genuine belief that the welfare of animals has improved and a decision to consume them; otherwise there is no meaningful correlation between the two things.

Of course, too, we are talking about a mere belief here that animals are treated in a more humane way, irrespective of whether it is right or wrong in fact. If you are claiming it is factually true that the welfare of animals has improved, then you are accepting a central point of mine that animal welfare does, at least sometimes, work. I would also repeat the point that there is a case for saying that it *is* ethically more desirable to consume genuine "free-range" animal products than to continue to gorge on factory-farmed animals, although not as acceptable as refraining from eating them at all. I do not think that it is beyond the intelligence of average human beings to recognize these moral distinctions. If it is not a fact that the welfare of animals has improved, as I assume you would contend, then surely the point is for the animal protection movement to go out and redouble its efforts to reveal this. If this means challenging the validity of some of the Freedom Food–type schemes, as it probably does, then all well and good. Presumably, if this was done effectively, fewer people would cease to be vegetarians. I do not see how proclaiming that it is wrong to use animals at all is going to persuade, at least in the short term, those people who are prepared to revert to consuming animals if they think they have been treated more humanely.

GLF: Although I am not aware of any formal studies of the reasons that people are reverting to eating animal products or generally feeling better about consuming animal products, there certainly is a great deal of evidence that this is the case in the form of the emerging "happy" meat/animal products movement. Indeed, the assumption that people will feel better about consuming "happy" animal products is the motivation for the RSPCA Freedom Food label and similar efforts. These groups would not be promoting such efforts if they did not believe that these labels were reassuring the public.

Is there a case for saying that it is better to consume a product that involves less suffering than more suffering? Yes, of course. There is also a case for saying that it is better not to torture someone you are going to kill. But in both cases, we do not address the fundamental moral issue. The problem is that the animal movement is promoting the more "humane" exploitation as normatively desirable in an affirmative way. That is disturbing in my view.

You say, "I would also add that there is a case for saying that it *is* ethically more desirable to consume genuine 'free-range' animal products than to continue to gorge on factory-farmed animals, although not as acceptable as refraining from eating them at all." Change the verbs around so that it reads, "I would also add that there is a case for saying that it *is* ethically more desirable to gorge on genuine 'free-range' animal products than to continue to consume factory-farmed animals, although not as acceptable as refraining from eating them at all." This shows the same point albeit in a different light!

As for the movement "redoubl[ing] its efforts to reveal" that welfare reforms do not amount to much or that labeling schemes are not effective, may I ask *who* is going to do this? The *entire* corporate welfarist movement—virtually *every* large animal group in the United States, UK, and elsewhere—supports these welfarist reforms and labeling schemes and bases significant fundraising efforts on them. These reforms and labeling schemes *are* the campaigns of these groups, and therefore, it is unrealistic to expect that the groups that promote these reforms and schemes are going to criticize them! I know from personal experience that to challenge or criticize these labeling schemes or welfare reform generally, or even to seek to discuss whether these efforts are effective or worthwhile, is to invite being labeled as "divisive," "fundamentalist," "purist," "elitist," and so on. Although there is a grassroots critique of welfare reform that is emerging as the result of the Internet, which has facilitated communication among advocates outside the traditional organizational structure, this critique is still limited because the large organizations have a great deal of money, and they still can influence media to a greater degree and to a great extent control the shape of the public discussion.

RG: It *is* more desirable ethically not to torture someone before killing him than to both torture and kill him. Of course, the reason that your parallel sounds disturbing is because we think of the person being tortured and killed as human. But to extrapolate from humans to animals in this way presupposes that animals are persons and can be harmed by death in the same way that humans can. This is precisely what my ethical argument has sought to deny. Much depends here, of course, on what is meant by "humane exploitation." My position is that we can set the bar on this at a very high level, one that would be very disturbing for the agribusiness industry.

In answer to your second response, those in the animal movement who feel uncomfortable with the claims being made by some groups and individuals about labeling schemes and so on should be the ones challenging them. This would be preferable to focusing exclusively on a vegan education campaign. Indeed, it would help that campaign. I would not describe such an exercise as "divisive," provided that credit is given when significant welfare benefits have been achieved.

GLF: We have to agree to disagree on whether death per se is a harm to nonhumans. But we have the same problem even if we stick with your right not to suffer. It is better to torture a human less rather than more, but we would not campaign for more "humane" torture. We also have to agree to disagree that your notion about what constitutes "acceptable" suffering is in any qualitative way different from the traditional welfarist notion of "unnecessary" suffering. Like Singer, you are more progressive as far as where you would set the bar, but, in the end, what we are talking about is some version of "humane" exploitation.

As far as a critique coming from within the movement, the opportunity costs are high in that the organized movement aggressively portrays such critics in the most pejorative light possible and never engages the substantive issues anyway. For example, the critic of welfare reform is often denounced as "not caring about the animals suffering now," and there is never any substantive discussion of the different perspectives.

●●●

GLF: You claim that even if there were empirical non-anecdotal evidence that welfare measures reassured the public and encouraged continued consumption of animals, that evidence would not be decisive because it would be as or more likely that welfare measures were mobilizing public concern about animal treatment and creating support for further reform. But does that not beg the question as to whether welfarist measures actually improve the treatment of animals in significant ways? Is that not precisely what you are assuming throughout your defense of welfarism?

RG: It is credible to suggest that continually keeping the issue of animal welfare in the public eye will have the effect of making the public more aware of animal issues. This is true whether or not animal welfare issues are ultimately successful. It is true, I concede, that this would also occur as a result of a vegan education campaign, and that is one reason why I support such a campaign, provided it is part of a broader strategy. Another argument to bear in mind here is that such a vegan campaign might also have the effect of promoting a form of defeatism in the sense that the goals are so far in advance of the current state of public opinion that the mountain to climb will seem formidable. I know that animal rights activists get extremely frustrated at the lack of progress.

GLF: I would suggest that if, despite 200 years of animal welfare, we are where we are, we have pretty good reason to believe that a focus on animal welfare is not having much practical effect. Indeed, if anything is—and should be—defeatist, it is the absolutely miserable failure of animal welfare reform.

Moreover, I would also argue (as I do in my essay) that it is a zero-sum game in that resources allocated to welfare reform are resources that are not directed to abolitionist/vegan education. So pursuing both approaches comes at a cost, and the issue is whether the extraordinary amount of resources that have been invested in animal welfare has paid anything remotely approaching a commensurate dividend. I think not.

It is my view that if the considerable resources of the animal movement were devoted primarily to abolitionist/vegan education in the 1980s, when the movement first started debating the rights/welfare matter seriously, we would now have a more effective movement in at least three respects. First, we would have many more vegans and a significant vegan movement. Second, we would have a political base united around abolition that could achieve meaningful prohibitions and not merely regulationist reform. Third, we would have succeeded in moving the moral paradigm further in the direction of abolishing use.

RG: It is a little misleading to talk in terms of 200 years of welfare reform. Much of the nineteenth-century efforts were very small-scale, and most of the regulation relating, for instance, to farm animal welfare has occurred in the last thirty or forty years. Your latter point here involves a counterfactual, whereby we are asked to think about a past that did not occur. These "what if"–type questions are notoriously difficult to confirm, or indeed deny.

GLF: There was actually a pretty active and ambitious animal welfare movement throughout much of the nineteenth and twentieth centuries in Britain, and an active one in the United States during the twentieth century. In any event, in my view, however you look at it, the animal welfare approach has been a miserable failure.

GLF: You maintain that the argument that welfare reform is counterproductive fails because those already firmly committed to abolition are unlikely to start eating animal products again because of supposedly better regulation. I agree, but your comment misses the point. There are clearly many people who are concerned about the morality of animal use and the treatment of nonhuman animals but who are not quite sure of how that moral concern translates into practical action.

If we tell those people that there is a solution to these problems—animal welfare regulation—that allows them to continue to eat animal products, then is it not clear that the overwhelming number of people will simply consume "happy" animal products? My point is that many people will give up animal products altogether if they are educated about why animal use cannot be morally justified as a general matter and about the reality that all animal consumption (including of supposedly "humanely" raised and killed animals) involves horrendous suffering. I think many, many people really do care about this issue. Do you disagree?

RG: In answer to your question about the impact of reforms to the way animals are treated, I would reiterate the points I made previously. I think it *is* more desirably ethically to eat animals who have been raised and slaughtered humanely. The key point for me is, what do we mean by "humane"? The animal protection movement ought to be stretching the definition of "cruelty-free" to the point where the conditions of farm, and other, animals are significantly improved. I do not think it is beyond the whit of an increasingly highly educated public to recognize that some improvements in animal welfare are better than none, but that more can be achieved.

In any case, I honestly do not think we have much of a choice but to accept the need to campaign for more effective animal welfare. I would regard as unlikely the assumption that "many people" will give up eating animals if they are made aware of the horrendous suffering they endure. Even if we accept the argument that some former vegetarians are reverting to meat-eating because they have been persuaded that farm animal welfare has improved, the fact remains that most (the vast majority) of humans are not vegetarians or vegans. Indeed, some (the majority?) of humans seem oblivious to the plight of other humans. The fact that millions of humans in the developing world go without the basics of a decent life does not persuade enough people in the developed world to really help them in a way that would make a substantial difference. If humans will not help other humans, why do you think they are likely to help members of different species?

GLF: My point is that the animal movement—including Singer, the so-called father of the animal rights movement—is telling the public that it is a morally defensible position to be a "conscientious omnivore." The animal movement is characterizing veganism as "absolutist," while uniformly sponsoring these "humane" labeling schemes as normatively desirable and as helping us to identify products that can be consumed consistently with our moral obligations to animals. This sends out a very clear normative message—animal exploitation can be morally acceptable if it is done correctly and with an acceptable level of suffering.

I am aware that most people are not vegetarians or vegans. But I think that we would have *many* more vegans if we educated people not just about the horrendous suffering of animals but also about the general moral problems involved in using sentient nonhumans as food sources or for other purposes. People do not think clearly about this point, and for many—not all—the light really does go on when you present the moral argument in an accessible way. That has certainly been my experience, and I can also say that I have heard from a number of grassroots groups in the United States and elsewhere that they have had great success promoting the abolitionist/vegan approach. It is ironic that the main opposition to the abolitionist/vegan approach comes from the large animal welfare organizations, which go out of their way to downplay veganism and portray it as absolutist, extreme, and unnecessary.

I have no doubt that money and time invested in clear and unequivocal vegan education will pay a better dividend than will the same resources invested in welfare reform. Indeed, if you take all the many millions of dollars that have been spent and all the labor that has been expended over the past twenty years on welfare reform, I think we end up with virtually no dividend, and we may even have exacerbated the problem by making animal consumption more acceptable. I realize that your assessment is different, but I am still at a loss to understand why you think that there has been significant progress.

There is a problem analogizing helping humans and helping nonhumans in that the latter—or at least the billions that we bring into existence to eat—would not exist if we did not generate the demand. So it's not a matter of helping animals; it's a matter of not using them. Having said that, however, I certainly do not disagree that we need to be doing a better job with respect to both nonhumans *and* humans, and I think that the plight of both have to do with the way the issues have been conceptualized and how the discourse has been shaped. These elements have to change. I am not willing to give up and conclude that most people do not care about these issues. I believe that people do care but that we have done a completely inadequate job of educating people about matters of human *and* nonhuman rights. We have presented normative options that preserve and facilitate the exploitation of humans and nonhumans instead of seeking to shift the moral paradigm. Part of the problem is that institutions such as academia and the media have vested interests in the status quo.

Finally, you suggest that protectionists stretch "the definition of 'cruelty-free' to the point where the conditions of farm, and other, animals are significantly improved." But that would require a substantial education campaign to create public demand for significantly higher welfare products that would be much, much more expensive. If that is a realistic scenario, then a situation in which there is a substantial vegan population is also possible. In other words, your scenario is no more realistic in a practical sense than mine.

●●●

GLF: You claim that decades of abolitionist campaigns have not resulted in support for abolition. Maybe I missed those decades, but I do not think that this characterization is accurate. Although some advocacy organizations maintain that we should not exploit animals at all, all of those groups also support welfare reform, and in the majority of cases, the welfarist message is what has been front and center. This sends a most confused message to the public. Again, if people are told that they can satisfy their moral obligations by doing less rather than more, that is what they will do. In any event, there has *never* been a sustained, movement-wide campaign maintaining that veganism is the nonnegotiable bottom line. It is bewildering to me that you can just declare that such an approach will not work when it has not even been tried and where there is some empirical evidence that ethical veganism is a very compelling approach that has resulted in an emerging vegan movement.

RG: You are right, of course, that abolitionism has not been center-stage politically, but then I think you have to ask why this is the case. At a societal level, however, the picture is slightly different. As you know, the modern animal protection movement (from the 1970s in the UK and the 1980s in the United States) has been marked by its greater radicalism. In fact, most of the media attention, in the UK at least, has focused on the demands of the radicals who have called for the end of animal agriculture and animal experimentation. I am also not sure why you think the public are getting a confused message. It is quite understandable to say "We would like to see the end of these practices, but we realize that is a big step to take. In the meantime, if animals are to be used, we would like to see them treated as well as possible." This allows for a vegan education campaign to coexist with a reformist one. I do not know for sure whether a campaign based on ethical veganism will work. I suspect not for the reasons I have stated. But I would not want to stop anyone from adopting such an approach.

There are parallels here, as I wrote in my essay, with the socialist movement. The socialist movement, particularly in Europe, has always been a broad church, and it has also faced the dilemmas of squaring short-term reformism (of capitalism) with a long-term abolitionist objective. There have always been some in the socialist movement who have argued, following classical Marxism, that the transformation of capitalism is more likely if it remains unreformed and its inequities allowed to remain. There is little evidence that an unreformed capitalism will lead the working class to the socialist paradise. But perhaps the most interesting development has been the claim that the reformed capitalism that has developed, particularly in western Europe (involving the creation of a welfare state, the use of Keynesian demand-management techniques, and so on), has actually transformed capitalism. A genuine animal protectionism, I think, should aim for this kind of objective. As with social democracy, it is crucial that the state play a crucial role in achieving this goal.

GLF: Abolition has not taken center stage because the welfarist organizations do not want it as center stage. It is easier to fundraise when you promote welfare reforms and do not seek to persuade people to make changes in their lives. As for the confused message, I see the movement as representing to the public that welfare reforms actually result in significant improvements in animal welfare and as promoting the idea that being a "conscientious omnivore" is a morally defensible position. The message that is getting across is not that we should eventually stop eating or otherwise exploiting animals but that we should treat them better in the meantime. The message is instead that consuming "happy" meat and animal products is perfectly acceptable.

I also want to note that some of the more radical demands have been made by those who support violence, and for the reasons I describe in my essay, I reject violence, and I am not surprised that views expressed in that context have not been taken seriously.

Finally, I reject the notion that there is a parallel here with the reform of the socialist movement. Animals are not similar to workers. The latter are participants in a capitalist or modified capitalist economy. They derive certain benefits from that participation, and, to some degree, they can move from the working class into the capitalist class. However exploited workers are in the modern capitalist state, they are not treated exclusively as economic commodities; there are some interests that humans have that cannot be traded away. Changes in the capitalist economy may actually (and many do) provide significant improvements for workers. Animals do not benefit from participation in the economy; all animal interests are ignored except for those interests necessary to achieve the economically efficient exploitation of animals. Animal welfare reforms do not benefit animals in the way that reforms of capitalism benefit workers; animal welfare reforms benefit "conscientious omnivores," who feel better about animal exploitation.

The more pertinent parallel is with the antislavery movement. Even if you disagree with me (as you do) about the autonomy interests of animals, the analogy still holds because in both systems, all of the fundamental interests of sentient beings are commodified and treated as tradable depending on economic consequences.

RG: I accept totally that there is not a direct analogy between animals and workers in a capitalist society. It is true that the latter, unlike the former, are not treated exclusively as economic commodities. Having said that, in the nineteenth century, prior to the advent of universal suffrage, workers had very little claim to "participation" in capitalist society, and their economic condition was much worse than it is now. Sociologists would also challenge your claim that, even now, there is a great deal of social mobility enabling people to "move from the working class into the capitalist class."

Nevertheless, there is an analogy between the strategic argument you put forward and that provided by sections of the socialist movement. This is the position that significant improvements in the treatment of animals (workers) cannot occur within the existing speciesist (capitalist) system and that, moreover, attempts in this area will or may have the effect of making the transformation of that system more difficult to achieve. My disagreement with both those contentions forms the centerpiece of the case I have put forward in this book.

•••

GLF: You claim that the argument that welfare reforms are counterproductive is internally inconsistent because on one hand, if animal welfare reforms do not significantly improve animal treatment, then the public would not be persuaded that the continued consumption of animals is acceptable because animals are being treated more "humanely," but on the other hand, if these reforms do improve animal treatment in significant ways, then they are inherently desirable because they reduce suffering.

Welfare reforms do reassure the public that animals are being treated "humanely" and encourage continued consumption, but this effect does not depend on these reforms actually providing for better treatment; these welfare reforms are aggressively characterized in that way by the animal organizations that promote them. The argument that animal welfare reforms are counterproductive in no way rests on those reforms being effective.

RG: Yes, I agree. As I said earlier, the perception is as important as the reality. And I agree too that animal organizations need to be careful when they make claims about the welfare "improvements" they are backing.

GLF: But how can this be achieved when it is in the economic interests of these organizations to do the exact opposite and to portray these reforms as resulting in significant improvements in animal welfare?

RG: But this can work both ways. If the public are convinced that the reforms have achieved the goal of the "more humane" treatment of animals, then they might take the view that there is no need to support these organizations anymore because they have achieved what they set out to do. According to this logic, it is in the interests of animal organizations to continue to criticize animal exploiters. Indeed, this is the argument that opponents of animal welfare often use—that a campaign for one particular reform will be followed by others demanding more and more.

GLF: In order for these large welfare organizations to function, they have to have a steady stream of supposed successes, and this militates in favor of portraying just about anything as a "victory" but following up with another moderate campaign. The bottom line is that there are many organizations with a large donor base and a great deal of money, and the state of animal welfare is still appallingly low. Yes, I know what opponents of animal welfare say publicly in terms of fearing the efforts of protectionist reformers, but I (and they) also know that they do not have a great deal about which to be frightened.

‑●●●‑

GLF: You accept the welfarist argument that the abolitionist approach as I have developed it maintains that more animal suffering is better because it will lead to abolition. There are at least three problems with this. First, I have been very careful in all of my writing to make clear that less suffering is always better than more suffering but that the fundamental moral question is whether we have the right to use animals at all, however "humanely" we treat them. That is, it is better to beat slaves nine times a week rather than ten times, but that ignores the fundamental question about the morality of slavery. Second, I have also been very clear that, as an empirical matter, animal welfare regulation does little more than ensure that animal users and owners act rationally and exploit animals in an economically efficient manner. That is, welfare regulation does not significantly decrease suffering. Third, if welfare regulation makes people feel more comfortable about continuing to exploit nonhumans and consume animal products, then net suffering may actually increase.

RG: I respect and accept totally your condemnation of suffering. I also accept that your position does not depend on the suffering of animals getting worse, although if the logic of your argument is followed, it might help. The problem, though, is that if we also accept your view that to support welfare reforms is to make abolitionist objectives more difficult to achieve, then you must logically resist those reforms that might reduce suffering. You repeated such a position in an earlier exchange in this section when you said that "many people will give up animal products altogether if they are educated about why animal use cannot be morally justified as a general matter and about the reality that all animal consumption (including of supposedly 'humanely' raised and killed animals) involves horrendous suffering." The logic of this position is that if this horrendous suffering were reduced, then these people would not give up animal products altogether. Of course, I accept that you do not think that welfare reforms reduce suffering significantly. Much depends on what we both regard as "significant" here. But do welfare reforms never reduce suffering, however small? And if they do, are you saying we should reject these improvements in animal welfare, however small they might be?

GLF: I am not resisting "reforms that might reduce suffering." I am offering what I argue is an effective alternative to welfarist reform—non-use of animals. I maintain that most welfare reforms do absolutely nothing to help animals. The public is told—falsely—that reforms have ameliorated the "worst abuses." The public is told—wrongly—that we can act morally by eating "happy" meat/animal products. If welfare significantly improved animal welfare and moved public consciousness in the direction of recognizing the inherent value of nonhuman animals, I would still find it difficult to advocate for regulatory reform rather than abolition because I would be reluctant to advocate means (regulation of use) that were inconsistent with the end (no use); I would, however, at least understand the appeal and practical utility of the welfarist approach. But animal welfare does not work, and I am quite frankly mystified as to why anyone promotes it. Campaigns for welfare reform express an almost religious faith. There is certainly no empirical evidence to justify this continued focus on welfare reform. Changes, "however small," as you put it, do not cause any shift whatsoever in the moral paradigm. It is also necessary to assess whether small changes are worth the resources required to achieve them.

Moreover, I note that you do not address my concern about an increase in net suffering. If, as I maintain, animal welfare reform makes the public feel comfortable about animal exploitation, it may well increase net suffering, and this seems to be reflected in the overall increase of the numbers of animals used for food. If there are people out there who have given up certain animal products because of a concern about treatment, and if their concerns are addressed by animal organizations that label animal products with a seal of approval, those consumers start consuming again. So any improvement in welfare (and I maintain that this is minimal) is offset by a net increase in animal use, suffering, and death.

RG: I take on board what you say about not resisting reform, but I am still not entirely clear. Your position would seem to be that even if an effective welfare reform were introduced (and I know you think that is very unlikely), you still would be reluctant to support it because it would make your long-term goal (the abolition of the use of animals) less likely. In order to try to clarify this, imagine a hypothetical situation whereby a reform—say, to abolish battery cages and replace them with a genuine free-range alternative—was made. Would you oppose such a measure?

I suspect that you would be reluctant to support such a reform with any great enthusiasm and that this reluctance would be based on the argument that improvements in farm animal welfare will lead to a decline in the number of vegetarians, therefore resulting in a net increase in suffering. I should deal with this point here. My answer is that even if we accept that some current vegetarians will revert to meat eating—and I'm not totally convinced by this—it is questionable whether net animal suffering will increase as a result. Interestingly enough, Singer is one of the best-known exponents of the view that vegetarianism is justified on the grounds that it is the best way of reducing animal suffering. Clearly, if we all desisted from consuming animal products, then net animal suffering would be reduced radically. However, universal vegetarianism is not the issue at hand here. Rather, we are being asked to consider whether a small number (in relation to the entire human population) of lapsed vegetarians will make a difference to the amount of animal suffering.

It is doubtful that such a small reduction in vegetarians and vegans would make a difference to net animal suffering. In fact, it is extremely questionable whether, even at the highest levels that have so far existed, vegetarianism and veganism have made a discernable difference in the number of animals raised and killed for food. Indeed, as you have often pointed out, the number of animals raised and killed for food has increased massively in the past twenty or thirty years *despite* an increase in vegetarians and vegans during the same period. Therefore, any real reduction in the number of animals raised and killed for food depends on the proposition that considerably more vegetarian and vegan converts than have ever existed previously will materialize as a result of removing the complacency that allegedly follows from improved animal welfare. As a result of this, the proposition continues, a threshold is reached whereby the animal agriculture industry begins to be harmed seriously. Whether we can ever reach such a threshold position is one question. More to the point is this question: why should we expect this to happen merely as a result of the perception that animal welfare has not improved? After all, if the proposition is correct, then why were there not many more vegetarians and vegans at a time when factory farming was first being criticized, and no reforms to it had yet been proposed or accepted?

The reality is that because, as I pointed out in my essay, a change in diet is a voluntary act conducted in a climate in which abstention is regarded as a moral choice, and not a compulsion, the vegetarian and vegan route to the reduction of animal suffering is, at the very least, a long-term ambition. I have argued that, in the meantime, we should do all that we can to reduce animal suffering through legislative means. I am confident that the long-term goal of both of us is not compromised by this.

GLF: Concerning your question about how I would react to a hypothetical welfare reform that really did make a significant difference in reducing suffering, I would respond as I do whenever I am asked about *any* welfare reform. I would say that less suffering is always better than more suffering, just as not torturing a human before murdering him is better than torturing and murdering him, but that we need to confront the more fundamental moral matter that we cannot justify animal use at all. Moreover, given that one's advocacy efforts are a zero-sum matter—the time that we spend advocating for reform is time that we do not devote to abolition—I would say that our time is better spent educating others about why they should not be consuming animals at all. I would never say that to consume the "humanely" produced product is ethically defensible.

With respect to your observations about the effects of animal welfare, I am not saying that the primary harm of what is presented as successful reform and improvement is the reversion of vegetarians and vegans to eating more animal products. I am saying that, as a general matter, I think that many if not most people are concerned about the moral issues implicated by animal exploitation. Some of these people have already made changes in their lives; some are considering what to do. To the extent that the animal movement is sending out a message that people who are concerned about the issue can address the moral issue and make a real difference by supporting welfare reform, this message is problematic because it does not address the moral issue of use, incorrectly represents these welfare reforms as making a significant difference in animal welfare, and makes the concerned members of the public more comfortable about continuing to consume animal products.

As for your observations about the legal compulsion and moral choice, it is my view that legal compulsion is going to be useless unless there is a larger base of people who really have accepted a shift in the moral paradigm. To put it in other words, you cannot reasonably expect to get laws that impose regulations that reflect the inherent value of animal interests and reject the property paradigm until a larger segment of society shifts its moral vision away from the property paradigm.

●─●─●

GLF: You argue that if we do not recognize that animals have a morally significant interest in their lives and continue to use them as our property, we can have equality between human and animal interests as long as we respect the right not to suffer. Putting aside the problem I raised before that some animal suffering is always incidental to any animal use, are you not being naïve here at best? How can it be possible in any way for animal interests in not suffering to be accorded equal consideration with human interests as long as nonhumans have the status of chattel property?

RG: I was putting forward an ethical principle that an animal's interest in not suffering ought to be regarded as equal to a human's interest in not suffering. I further argued, following the British political theorist Alasdair Cochrane, that ownership is not inconsistent with protecting an animal's interest in not suffering. This is because although *possession* clearly restricts the freedom of most species of nonhuman animals, it does not necessarily infringe their interest in not suffering. Likewise, the *use* of animals does not necessarily infringe an animal's interest in not suffering. If this is right, your critique of the ownership of animals only follows if we add the claim that animals possess an interest in not being used against their will. I reject this claim on the grounds that most species of nonhuman animals do not have the capabilities that would enable them to be harmed by being used in this way. This is why I also reject equating the ownership of animals with slavery.

Of course, as we both agree, animals do suffer, but I do not accept the primary explanatory role you attach to property and ownership as a cause of this suffering. Put simplistically, the fact that animals suffer is not a product of ownership but a product of society's attitudes toward animals and the political dominance of economic interests who gain from inflicting suffering on animals. So I am saying that I do not accept that the ownership of animals acts as a structural constraint on their better treatment. But I am not naïve enough to suggest that the political, economic, and ideological obstacles that do exist will be easy to dismantle. And this, of course, is why I think the abolitionist agenda is unrealistic at present.

GLF: I understand your position, but I still do not understand how you can, as a practical matter, think that an animal's interest in not suffering can be accorded equal consideration (or even significant consideration) if animals are chattel property. It did not work with chattel slavery, and it certainly is not going to work with animals. I fail to understand how your proposal is any more realistic than you think mine is. Is my proposal of veganism any less realistic than your fantasy situation that someone who has purchased a herd of cattle (or any other animals) for the purpose of fattening and slaughtering them is going to treat those animals as beloved nonhuman companions? I really do think that this scenario is completely unrealistic and, as a matter of basic economics, impossible. Any animal use will involve suffering, and the scenario that you present—animal property that does not suffer—is wildly unrealistic.

I accept that abolition will be difficult to achieve because it will involve shifting the moral paradigm, but that is the only way that things will change. And as difficult as that will be to do, it will, I submit, be less difficult than achieving recognition of a right not to suffer that will provide significantly greater protection to animal interests than welfare regulation, which does little more than make humans feel better about animal exploitation.

RG: I hold the position that the ownership of animals is logically separate from the issue of suffering; that it is possible to own something and treat it in a variety of ways. The way we treat companion animals, for instance, is very different from the way that we treat domesticated animals on farms and in laboratories, yet both are regarded as property. Your position is that the ownership of animals is, in practice, inseparable from the issue of suffering because at least some animals are owned precisely because of the economic benefits that derive from them, and for this economic benefit to be realized, the infliction of suffering is necessary.

I have three main responses to this. The first is to say it is not ownership that is the issue here but the purposes for which animals are used once they are owned. For example, animals used in agriculture are treated in the way they are for a variety of reasons, including the perceived need for a cheap source of protein and the political influence of those who exploit animals in this way. The second response is that ownership of something does not necessarily entitle the owner to do what he likes with his property. There are plenty of examples where the state regulates what can be done with our property. We are not permitted, for instance, to treat companion animals in any way we see fit. I may be naïve and unrealistic to think that the economic influence of agribusiness can be tamed, and I may be naïve and unrealistic to think that humans can be persuaded that treating animals in this way is wrong. This, however, has nothing to do with the ownership of animals as such. The third response is that I think it is possible to continue to use animals for food while reducing the level of suffering that we inflict on them. Whether suffering can be reduced to the point where my ethical principle is satisfied is an open question. In this sense my *ethical* position is no more "realistic" than yours.

The key difference between us is that I do not think, as you do, that there is an inseparable link between property and suffering. The consequence of this is that I think it is possible for suffering to be reduced gradually while the existing property paradigm exists. No doubt you will respond to this by saying that there is no evidence that such a gradual decrease in animal suffering has occurred despite decades of animal welfare campaigns. Insofar as you are right about this, your target, in my view, should not be property but the influence of agribusiness and the unwillingness of most humans to accept that many of things we do to animals are wrong.

GLF: As far as companion animals are concerned, it is certainly the case that many—perhaps most—people treat these animals horribly. If you are referring to the relatively small portion of people who really do regard their nonhuman companions as family members, then I would suggest that these people do not think of their animals as property. But because these animals are property as far as the law is concerned, owners are free to value their interests at zero. We love the five rescued dogs with whom we share our home, but as far as the law is concerned, we have the right to provide a very low standard of care, and we can dump them at a kill shelter or have them killed by a veterinarian whenever we want.

Yes, we do regulate property use, but we regulate it for the benefit of other humans; we do not regulate property use for the benefit of the property. That is why the regulation of human slavery failed and why the regulation of animal exploitation also fails. The beneficiary of these regulations is always the exploiter and not the property.

In any event, the notion that we are ever going to be able to couple property status with some very high level of animal welfare is not an open question. As a matter of human psychology, we are never going to get that level as long as most people think it is acceptable to eat animals or use them for other frivolous purposes. As long as we are eating and consuming animals, we will not be able even to understand the notion that these animals should be treated like, or more like, the way some people treat their dogs and cats. We would not eat these animals if we thought of them as we do our dogs and cats. As a matter of economics, it cannot happen.

I do agree that we need to persuade people about the immoral and unjustifiable nature of animal exploitation, but that is simply another way of getting them to see that the property status of non-humans is morally objectionable and should be rejected.

$-\!\!\bullet\!\bullet\!\bullet\!-$

GLF: You maintain that I claim that because animals are property, the law regards them as inanimate objects. That is mistaken; I have never said that. What I have said is that because animals are property, we generally protect their interest in not suffering only to the extent that we derive an economic benefit. But I have never denied that classical welfarism recognizes that animals are different from other things we own.

RG: What I meant was that if an animal's interest in not suffering is recognized only when it increases economic efficiency so that we derive an economic benefit, then this is tantamount to saying that the benefits to animals are indirect. This would be like saying, for example, that my car benefits from my desire to treat it in a way that maintains as much of its value as possible. What distinguishes animal welfare law from this is the assertion that animals can be harmed directly and should be protected against suffering, irrespective of the benefit to us that might derive from so doing. Of course, what you are saying is that the property status of animals trumps this intention. As I said earlier, I reject this view.

GLF: I am not denying that animal welfare recognizes, at least in theory, both moral and legal obligations owed directly to animals. I am just saying that, for the most part, we recognize those direct obligations only when we get an economic benefit.

RG: And it is this last point that I deny. Sometimes an economic benefit does result, as I said earlier, but I maintain that it does not have to.

GLF: I have never said it has to. I have said that it does result in an economic benefit in most cases, and where it does not do so, the cost increase is low, and given the inelasticity of the demand for many of the products and the niche demand, the effect of reform is almost nonexistent and offset by the ability of industry and animal advocates to assure the public that something that troubles many people as a moral matter is really nothing about which to worry.

●●●

GLF: You often cite the ban on hunting foxes with hounds as an example of the success of new welfarism. Why? In my view, that legislation has been nothing short of a disaster. The supposed ban is ineffective; it is not enforced and is openly violated without reaction by the authorities, and it will probably be repealed.

RG: I regard the abolition of the hunting of foxes with hounds, and the coursing of hares, as important partly because it encapsulates the value of a strategy based on the unnecessary suffering principle. That is, the campaign against fox hunting was based on the principle not that foxes have rights but that the hunting of foxes for fun is unnecessary in a civilized society. The main problem with the legislation is not that it has been widely flouted and ignored by the police but that its wording has allowed for confusion as to what is and is not against the law. A number of successful prosecutions have been mounted. In addition, hare-coursing events (involving the setting of greyhounds on hares) have been banned successfully.

I would make three additional points in response to your critique of the anti-hunting measure. The first is that we ought to beware of believing some of the claims of the hunting community. It is, of course, in their interests to claim that it is business as usual. The evidence suggests this is not true. What has to be understood is that the killing of the fox is a relatively minor part of the whole paraphernalia of hunt meets. They serve many different purposes, ranging from a demonstration of horse-riding skills to a variety of social functions. Hunts have endeavored to keep these other functions alive, and a number have replaced the hunting of a live animal with drag hunting. And this brings me to my second point, which is that despite the cultural importance of hunting in Britain, and despite the political saliency of the claim that abolition would infringe longstanding liberties, an anti-hunting measure was still successful. Think of the cultural earthquake that would surround the banning of bullfighting in Spain, and you get a sense of the magnitude of the change.

The final point is that repealing the legislation will not be as easy as you suggest. At the very least, it would require a Conservative victory at the next general election, an outcome that is not by any means a foregone conclusion. Even with a Conservative victory, repeal is by no means certain. Without going into too much detail here, the easiest way for a bill to become law in Britain is for the government of the day to support it. Without government time, a so-called Private Member's Bill will almost certainly fail. Any future Conservative government will have to think long and hard before committing itself to the parliamentary time necessary for a repeal. Not only will a majority of the public oppose a repeal on ethical grounds, but spending a disproportionate amount of time on such an issue also may well be regarded in a negative light, particularly with the range of problems a future Conservative government is likely to face.

GLF: The supposed ban prohibits using hounds to hunt foxes but allows hunters to use hounds to follow a scent and to flush out a fox (or other wild mammal) and then shoot the animal or use a falcon to kill the animal. Supporters of hunting are flouting the law and encouraging exploitation of all loopholes with the result that more foxes are being killed than before the ban. Not a single hunt has gone out of business. There are twice as many registered hounds as there were three years ago, and the number of people hunting has increased.

RG: I would accept that the legislation is far from perfect. The act was never intended to ban the killing of foxes. It is the way they are killed that is crucial. It is illegal for hounds to tear a fox apart, and those hunts that break the law here can be, and have been, prosecuted successfully. As I said, the fact that hunts still exist is to some extent a product of the variety of functions—other than killing animals—that they perform.

◀●●▶

GLF: I regard the supposed ban of battery cages in Europe by 2012 as a classic case of the failure of welfare reform. The European Commission regulation allows for "enriched cages," which even some moderate welfarists have criticized as no better than conventional cages. But welfarists also proclaim this as a victory for animals and tell the public that the regulation demonstrates that the property status of animals is not a bar to meaningful reform. I am interested in your take on this EC regulation.

RG: There are some benefits of enriched cages. More space is mandated for birds, as is the provision of litter, perches, and clawing boards. I would agree, though, that these are minor improvements. A number of additional points need to be made here though. In the first place, if the "counterproductive" argument is rejected, then the improvements would seem to be worth having as a first step to the complete abolition of cages for laying hens. The second point is that the response to the EU directive by animal protection groups needs to be unraveled. In 2008, the European Commission announced that it would not extend the deadline for the abolition of conventional battery cages, despite industry pressure. The animal protection movement praised the commission for not giving in to these demands more than it offered praise for the measure itself. The attitude of key British animal protection organizations to the directive in general, however, has been hostile. In particular, both the RSPCA and Compassion in World Farming have openly criticized the British government for not going further and abolishing all cages for laying hens. Incidentally, as I said previously, some major British retail outlets will no longer stock battery eggs. And this brings me to the third point. The role of the European Union is to set minimum standards, and individual member states are entitled to go beyond them. In Germany, for instance, a decision has been made to ban all cages (barren and enriched) by 2012. Do you think that the animal rights movement should welcome this?

The problem with the EU, in animal welfare terms at least, is that it has to appeal to the lowest common denominator. These standards are pretty low, and with the accession of new member states, particularly from Eastern Europe, that have no tradition of animal welfare, they have gotten lower. In addition, the problem for member states seeking to go beyond minimum standards is the argument that they then have to operate at a competitive disadvantage. It is in this context that my earlier comment about using welfare standards as a selling point becomes relevant. Indeed, the European Commission has used this argument to justify the Laying Hens Directive in the face of a challenge from European producers that they would suffer economically as a result of the lower production costs in developing countries. Thus, the directive offers EU producers a competitive advantage over third-country producers by meeting a growing consumer demand for welfare-friendly eggs.

GLF: But some of the same organizations that have criticized the enriched cages have also praised them as an important step forward, so I disagree that their praise was directed only to the decision of the European Commission not to give in to demands for an extension of the deadline (that will not be met in any event). I think that the behavior of the animal movement concerning this issue is a textbook illustration of the inability of welfare groups to criticize welfare reforms in a coherent or useful way. I agree that the EU "has to appeal to the lowest common denominator," and that is precisely the problem with thinking that welfare reform will develop in any significant way. Finally, I do not think that the supposedly higher-welfare eggs result in any significant difference in the welfare of the hens. I have seen cage-free facilities, and they are terrible.

RG: All that I can say is that the literature I have seen from British groups such as the RSPCA and CIWF has been hostile to enriched cages, and these groups have made it quite clear they do not see it as the end of the road in terms of reform. We can both agree that the reform does not go far enough, but there is evidence that consumers are increasingly turning their back on battery eggs in favor of genuine free-range alternatives, and this, as in Germany, is likely to be reflected in legislation at some point.

GLF: I agree that some of the literature from the British groups does criticize the enriched cage. But other statements of these very same organizations are in conflict with their criticisms. This is the problem, and it is not confined to Britain. In the United States, we have groups such as PETA advocating that people ought to be vegan at the same time that they call off a boycott of KFC because KFC has agreed to gas hens, thus implying that patronizing KFC is now acceptable, at the same time that they are giving awards to supermarket chains such as Whole Foods in recognition of their "Animal Compassionate" program, and so on. This causes tremendous confusion.

—●●●—

GLF: In *Rain Without Thunder,* I stated clearly that animal rights advocates should avoid single-issue campaigns in favor of education and campaigns to promote ethical veganism. That is, I regard single-issue campaigns, even if they involved bans and not regulations intended merely to make exploitation more "humane," as problematic for a variety of theoretical and practical reasons.

I argued that *if* advocates wanted to promote single-issue campaigns, they ought to promote only those that represented substantial departures from the property paradigm; that is, that they pursue prohibitions that went beyond regulations that make exploitation more efficient and that explicitly recognized the inherent value of animals. I set out five conjunctive conditions for identifying such campaigns, and although I acknowledged that the success of any such campaign that satisfied all of these criteria was highly unlikely, I recognized that such campaigns might have educational and political value.

In any event, you claim that there have been some incremental abolitionist measures adopted that do not meet all the criteria that I developed in *Rain Without Thunder* but that qualify as abolitionist, which, you maintain, demonstrate that protectionist reform can be consistent with abolitionism. For example, you cite the ban in Britain on exports of live animals. Putting aside that as far as I understand, that ban is no longer in effect or, at least, has been significantly modified and weakened, a serious problem with that campaign is that it has always been confused, with many advocates suggesting that it was the transport, and not the use or eating, of animals that was the problem.

Moreover, you ask whether, by accepting incremental abolition as a viable objective for the animal rights movement, there is an implicit message that other forms of animal exploitation are morally acceptable. For example, if advocates pursue a ban on the leg-hold trap—or on fur generally—is that not an implicit endorsement of alternative methods of fur production or on the use of wool or leather? It is precisely because I think that single-issue campaigns—even bans—involve such an implicit endorsement that I find them problematic and urge advocates to concentrate instead on vegan education. But if a single-issue campaign were to satisfy the criteria that I set forth in *Rain Without Thunder*, the matter of the implicit endorsement would be resolved because such a campaign would have to make explicit that no exploitation was acceptable and that the particular ban was merely a step toward the acknowledged goal of complete abolition. That is, the problem of the implicit endorsement has to be addressed up front and explicitly.

I mentioned in my essay, and I want to reiterate here, that some of the examples that I used in my discussion of incremental change in *Rain Without Thunder* have caused confusion, and I would approach the issue differently if I were writing that book today.

RG: That is all very clear, although, for the reasons that we have discussed, I do not think we should restrict campaigns in the way you suggest.

●●●

GLF: Just as you do not address the problem that animal welfare regulation generally makes exploitation more efficient and limits protection for animal interests to what will provide economic benefits for humans, you similarly do not address the argument that it is more effective as a practical matter to devote resources to vegan education rather than to welfare reform. If my analysis is correct, then how can you plausibly maintain your view as to either the desirability of welfare reform or the relative value of vegan education?

RG: If your arguments about the impact of property on welfare measures stand up, it would be logically correct to divert resources to vegan education. Because I have doubts about their validity, however, I do not have to accept this conclusion. I will reiterate, though, that I am not opposed to vegan education, but only to the proposition that this should be the *only* strand in the strategy of the animal rights movement.

GLF: I remain unclear as to what anchors your faith in welfare given that you cannot cite examples that do not fit my analysis. But given that you do not oppose animal use per se, you can promote veganism only as a way of reducing suffering and not as any movement baseline. That is what leads to "flexible" veganism.

ooo

GLF: You do not address the fact that in the past decades, free trade agreements and arrangements such as the European Union have made any national welfare reform nothing more than symbolic—even if, contrary to my view, such reform resulted in significantly greater protection for animal interests—because if demand does not decrease, products made in lower-welfare economies can usually be imported even if reform causes an increase in price.

RG: I agree that globalization presents real challenges for animal welfare, some of which I dealt with in answer to a previous question. It is still possible (as with the cases of Germany in relation to battery cages and the UK in relation to sow stalls and tethers) for individual states to take independent decisions. Moreover, it is possible to tackle the question of economic competitiveness in two ways. The first, as previously stated, is to include higher welfare standards as a selling point. The second point is that once political will is exercised by governments to introduce improved animal welfare standards, the trading environment immediately changes. In this changed environment, producers can become allies in campaigning for welfare improvements to be introduced in the whole trading area. The emergence of a European dimension to environmental policy, for instance, owes much to the pressure exerted by business interests in countries such as Germany and Holland where more stringent environmental regulations had been adopted.

GLF: As I mentioned previously, I see no evidence that the higher welfare standards you contemplate as a selling point are likely to become part of the efficiency equation as long as our focus is treatment and not use as a general matter. As far as your second point is concerned, I also see no evidence either that governments are introducing significant welfare changes, given the "lowest common denominator" problem we discussed previously, or that changes by individual states have or will generate the sort of producer behavior you note in the environmental context where human interests are more directly implicated.

●●●

GLF: You seem to think that the widely accepted principle that it is morally wrong to inflict unnecessary suffering on animals can—in its present form and without a paradigm shift in our thinking about animals or acceptance of a morally significant interest in continued existence—be used to significantly improve the plight of animals. Is this a correct view of your position? If so, you and I understand that principle in very different ways. I maintain that the principle needs to be reinterpreted in light of our failure to justify animal use—however "humane"—and a rejection of the property status of animals. If my reading is correct, you are applying the principle to issues of treatment; I am applying it to issues of use. Those are two very different approaches.

RG: The two great advantages of the unnecessary suffering principle are its flexibility and its compatibility with widely accepted norms. It is flexible in the sense that it is not inconsistent with abolitionist objectives, but it also justifies reforms short of abolition. Should a particular use of animals be regarded as unnecessary, because it is trivial or because the objectives of the use can be achieved in other ways, then abolition is justified. It is compatible with widely accepted norms in the sense that it requires nothing more than an acceptance that animals have moral standing and that they can be harmed directly. In some ways I would argue that the ways in which the unnecessary principle has been used and interpreted have changed markedly in the post-1945 period, and much of this is due to the reinvigorated and radicalized animal protection movement.

This does not represent the paradigm shift you are referring to, but it is significant nevertheless. By this I mean that what is now included in the list of animal uses that might be regarded as unnecessary has been transformed as a result of a changing ethical climate as well as a greater knowledge of animal capabilities. It is now widely accepted, in Britain at least, that animals should not be used to test cosmetics or the effects of tobacco products. A majority (in most opinion polls) frown upon the wearing of fur, the hunting of foxes with hounds, the use of wild animals in circuses, and the use of great apes in scientific research. And even though animals are still reared and killed for food and for medical research, a sizable minority think this is wrong, and an even bigger number question whether it is really necessary to cause animals to suffer so appallingly in factory farms merely in order to make our food marginally cheaper.

Of course, translating these cultural shifts into workable public policy has been slower than we would like. But I do not think it is time yet to give up on the political process.

GLF: I disagree with you about some of the changes that you think have occurred. But we agree that significant changes are not likely to result until the unnecessary suffering principle is reinterpreted. My point is that you have on a number of occasions expressed surprise that I use the principle in my work, given that I criticize your reliance on it. My criticism was that your reliance on the principle to effect meaningful change in the treatment of animals was not realistic given the status of animals as chattel property. I have never doubted that the principle could be important if we focused on use. But that would require that we recognize that animals have a morally significant interest in not being used at all and not just an interest in not suffering. This is an important point of disagreement between us.

I note that you recognize that a significant portion of the population is concerned about the use of animals for food, in experiments, and so on. I agree. I just think we need to present a clear strategy to these people and not encourage them to think that the problem can be solved by "happy" meat and other "conscientious omnivore" solutions.

Finally, as for the political process not moving fast enough, I would say that the level of progress has made "glacial" look rapid. As for some of the supposed advances you identify, the fur industry is stronger than it ever has been, and fur is enjoying a resurgence even in Britain. Concern about the nonhuman great apes is, as I have argued, based on their being similar to humans, and that merely redefines a speciesist hierarchy and does not eliminate it.

●●●

GLF: As long as animals are chattel property, and as long as we are using animals in ways that cannot be regarded as "necessary" under any interpretation of that term, how do you understand the notion of "unnecessary" suffering? What sort of coherent meaning can be given to that notion in shaping campaigns?

RG: As I said previously, what is regarded as "unnecessary" suffering is flexible enough to be used as a battering ram for change. It has the effect of putting the defenders of animal use on the defensive because it is engaging with them on a moral terrain to which they cannot possibly object.

GLF: But again, as long as we focus on the necessity of treatment and not the necessity of use, and as long as animals are chattel property, we cannot expect significant change. The proof of this is that the principle of unnecessary suffering has been part of the moral and legal landscape for 200 years now, and the situation for animals is about as bad as it has ever been.

Movement Strategy: Moral Education versus Legislation

GLF: As a preliminary matter, let me say that I think that the expression "moral crusade" is, like "fundamentalism," normatively charged and unhelpfully so. But be that as it may, you argue that attempting to shift the paradigm through an educational campaign aimed at promoting veganism involves dealing with individual preferences in a context of liberal pluralism, whereas legislation compels behavioral changes. Your position here begs the question about the relationship between law and morality. It is my view that without a paradigm shift in our moral thinking, legislation will continue to do what it has done for the 200 years that we have had animal welfare as a central social value—very little. The ability of legislation to compel any significant changes in behavior in the absence of a prior significant shift in moral attitudes is severely limited.

If we had a political movement centered around the moral idea that animal use cannot be justified—if we had, in effect, a political movement similar to the abolitionist movement that existed concerning slavery—it would at least be possible that we could get legislation that would actually prohibit significant animal uses as part of a campaign aimed explicitly at total abolition. What evidence do you have that legislation can be a primary force here? After all, you acknowledge that legislation has done very little up until now.

RG: I certainly did not intend to use the label "moral crusade" in a pejorative sense. I regard it as an honorable pursuit, something that the animal protection movement ought to be proud of. I would agree further with you that changing the moral climate is important, and to a certain extent, as I mentioned previously, that has already happened in relation to societal attitudes about the use of animals. I have regularly argued in this book that a vegan education campaign is an important activity.

However, I have also pointed to the dangers of turning animal protection entirely into a matter of moral preferences. At least in the short term, this lets political actors off the hook because they can safely deflect calls for animal welfare legislation on the grounds that this is a matter for individual conscience. That is, for instance, they can say, "If you don't like battery cages, then buy free-range alternatives." This implies that in a pluralistic liberal society, it is an item of faith that if one set of moral preferences is allowed to exist, then individuals should be allowed to hold the opposing view and act on it. Only if we say that it is morally wrong to inflict suffering on animals because to do so harms living and sentient beings can we prevent this from happening. And this transforms the treatment of animals from a moral issue to a political one requiring state action.

I take your point that legislation will follow a changed moral climate. I also think, however, that you underestimate the extent to which political action can itself change the moral climate. One example I can think of here is the wearing of seat belts in cars. There was no clamor for this measure to be introduced in the UK, but once political elites had decided on it, a favorable moral climate, helped by a high-profile media campaign, was created. The role of political elites in helping to shape the moral climate, then, is important.

GLF: I am not saying that we do not need political and legal devices to enforce morality; my point is that in the absence of a shift in the moral paradigm, the state is not likely to do anything other than promote the same sort of welfarist regulation that has been promoted in the past. That is, the state is not going to enact legislation that will significantly affect the economics of animal exploitation; that would be impossible as a political matter. Even in the unlikely event that the regulation was not cost-effective and raised the price of animal products, this would not move the matter out of the realm of moral preferences. If there is a continued demand for the lower-welfare product, the reality in the era of free trade is that the lower-welfare product will continue to be sold. You cannot deal with the issue of animal exploitation as a political or legal matter in the first instance; if the moral paradigm does not shift, the political and legal processes can do little.

I do not think that the seat belt example is relevant in this context. That was a debate involving personal responsibility and prudence. Moreover, the seat belt requirement was a measure that was strongly supported by the insurance industry, so there was a powerful economic force behind the law.

RG: I do not accept that the state will necessarily always oppose measures that damage the economics of animal exploitation, but I do accept that economic interests are powerful. The key point for me, though, is that this debate will always be fought out in the *political* arena, and decision makers will have to reconcile competing interests, which include the demands of producers, consumers, animal activists, and political elites themselves. The moral climate is, of course, important, but in a pluralistic democracy there will always be some people who hold an opposing moral view, and if we make the treatment of animals a moral rather than a political issue, then the state will be reluctant to translate moral views into legislation. It is also possible for the state and political elites to help shape this moral climate. There are, you are right, significant differences between the seat belt example and the animals issue. The point I was making was a more general one—that legislative action, and the consequent political debate, is sometimes required to shape the moral climate.

꘎꘎꘎

GLF: Is it not the case that the welfare regulation that you support is itself the product of a competing "moral crusade"? That is, your position, which I think is shared by the modern new welfarist movement—that we cannot justify a moral right of nonhumans not to be used and can justify only a right not to be subjected to suffering incidental to human use—certainly represents a moral theory as much as does the abolitionist approach. Indeed, and rather ironically, it is precisely these new welfarists who consistently portray veganism and abolition as matters of personal preference and not as matters of baseline morality. The abolitionist approach focuses on education but makes very clear that animal exploitation may be a matter of choice in that we presently permit humans to exploit animals, but that exploitation cannot be morally justified, and veganism is the only rational response if one believes that animals are members of the moral community.

RG: You are conflating two separate arguments here. At the ethical level my approach certainly represents a moral crusade as does any other position that seeks to tell us how we ought to behave. It is at the strategic level that our views differ. If I were to say that we ought to engage in an education campaign to persuade others that they should not support animal research that causes suffering or eat animals who have suffered, I would be engaging in a moral crusade. If I were then to say that we should reject measures that do not conform to the anti-suffering ethic (because they eliminate some but not all suffering) on the grounds, say, that to support such measures might give the impression that it is acceptable to inflict some suffering on animals, then the education campaign would be our only strategy. What I have tried to demonstrate is that this strategy pursued on its own is inadequate. And I would still say that this strategy is inadequate *even if* I held exactly the same ethical principles as you.

GLF: This seems to be the same argument you made in response to my opening comment on fundamentalism—that because I advocate a campaign of education and do not support welfare reform, my approach is somehow qualitatively different from yours. But again, you assume that welfare reform results in significant welfare benefits for nonhumans and that I am willing to forego these. We disagree here. I do not think animal welfare reform does provide significant benefits for nonhumans. Moreover, the only way that you can move matters beyond the minimal level of welfare protection that presently exists is through an education campaign that gets people to demand much higher welfare. So we both have an educational strategy. Your strategy is to educate the public to demand animal products that are produced pursuant to significantly higher welfare standards, which would require persuading the public to accept much higher prices. My strategy is to educate them about not using animal products at all.

●●●

GLF: Let me ask you a question that may appear to be personal and may be so, but is relevant to our discussion. Are you a vegan? I realize that whether you are or not has no bearing on the validity of your arguments. But I am curious nonetheless. I find that most advocates of the welfarist position are, at best, what Singer calls "flexible vegans" who still consume animal products. I regard "flexible vegans" as proof of the failure of the welfarist approach; even animal advocates accept that animals have lesser moral value and that we really can produce animal products in a "humane" and morally acceptable way.

RG: I have been a vegetarian throughout my adult life, and I am currently a dietary vegan, and I do not wear leather. I would hope, though, that my ethical principles guide my personal behavior rather than the other way round. I am also continually aware of the need to avoid preaching too much about my ethics and hectoring others to adopt the same lifestyle choices as I have. I think this is a real problem with the animal rights movement. As I have argued elsewhere (Garner 1998:78–81), there is a danger that participation in the animal rights movement becomes an end in itself rather than a means to the end of improving the lot of animals.

At the risk of intellectualizing what was a personal question, it is worth invoking some of the social movement literature to explain the problem that I think the animal rights movement has. The starting point here is the attempt by political scientists to explain why people join and participate in pressure groups. It was once assumed that it was natural for individuals to join groups as a means of achieving collective goals. This optimism was altered fundamentally by the work of Mancur Olson (1965), who put forward a rational choice theory of interest group politics. To cut a long story short, Olson argued that because individuals are concerned only with maximizing their own utility, they will not see membership in groups as worthwhile because they can take a "free ride" and enjoy the benefits gained from collective action without paying the costs (time and money) of membership.

From then on, explaining the recruitment and mobilization of individuals by groups became a "problem" for political scientists. Why do individuals join groups? What do they get out of being in groups, particularly if they could take a "free ride" as Olson had suggested? One answer to this question is that individuals join groups because of the psychological benefits they get from membership itself, and one psychological benefit is a feeling of belonging. Moreover, one important way of enhancing belonging is to feel and be perceived as different from others. Note that it is being claimed here that the benefits of membership are not the achievement of public policy goals but membership itself.

Interest group scholars have commented on the importance of these psychological factors, which they have labeled as "solidaristic collectivism" (Sabatier 1992). Such an approach would seem to be applicable to the animal rights movement in the sense that animal rights, with its distinctive and clear-cut abolitionist ideology, provides a useful device for organizational recruitment and maintenance because it generates a collective identity that unites members and sets them apart from others. I think that the problem with this is that the need for exclusivity will conflict with the achievement of organizational goals, which, as I have argued it does, requires the dilution of abolitionism at least in the short term.

I recognize that this is not an argument that is going to endear me to many animal rights activists, but this, in part, reveals the truth of what I am saying. That is, an exclusive abolitionist agenda that refuses to accept the validity of measures to improve the treatment of animals is likely to appeal to animal rights activists not necessarily because they think it is going to succeed anytime soon, but because it preserves their moral purity and membership in an exclusive club. If we are really serious about improving the lives of animals, this attitude should be avoided at all costs. I am not, of course, saying that your position is an expression of this attitude because you do have serious and sophisticated intellectual reasons for advocating abolitionism. But it is easy to see why abolitionism appeals to some animal rights activists irrespective of its prospects of achieving the goals of the movement.

GLF: First of all, I reject the notion that, as an empirical matter, there is a movement with a "distinctive and clear-cut abolitionist ideology." On the contrary, the mainstream movement consisting of the large national organizations does not in any way advocate for abolition; they advocate for welfare reform. In any event, I have long maintained that there are problems with these advocacy groups as a general matter and that they may be more of an impediment to progress than a facilitator of it. The abolitionist movement is almost exclusively a matter of grassroots activism that does not fit the traditional models about pressure groups. Abolitionist activism is not aimed at creating political or legal pressure or concerned with building large, wealthy organizational structures; it is aimed at changing basic moral thinking through education.

Second, and I really do hate to say this yet again, but you are assuming—as you have done throughout—that animal welfare works. I disagree. Moreover, you also assume that there is not an independent basis for saying that a movement's ends should inform its means. On your reasoning, it would have made sense to claim that Gandhi was a "purist" because he stressed that violence should never be used as a means to achieve freedom, which he saw as itself involving nonviolence, and that, were he really concerned about the suffering of the people of India, he would have promoted violence.

Third, although I agree that "preaching" and "hectoring" are unhelpful, I would not see veganism as a "lifestyle choice." Deciding what sorts of sports you play or places to take vacations involves lifestyle choices. If you agree that the right not to suffer means that you personally cannot justify the consumption of animals, is that not more like your decision that you cannot morally justify consuming pornography or your decisions about other important human rights? Others may see veganism as a lifestyle choice, but I am surprised that you describe it in that way.

RG: You are right to say that abolitionism is a feature of the grass roots of the movement, and my argument was directed largely at this part of the movement. In addition, I was applying the group theory that I have described to those activists who do insist on an abolitionist ideology. All social movements, however formally organized they are, do face mobilization challenges. By an end in itself, I meant that if I am right that the separateness and exclusivity that comes from being in the animal rights movement is a key mobilizing factor, then there is a danger that this militates against expanding the number of those who are "in the animal rights club," a goal to which we both aspire. Of course, I recognize that your argument—that animal welfare does not work and that there is no point in having an objective short of abolition—trumps my point. I just do not agree with this argument. Finally, perhaps my use of the phrase "lifestyle choice" is unfortunate. I did mean it in the sense you suggest, as a moral imperative that I believe others should pursue as a matter of urgency. We share the view, though, that too much preaching and hectoring about this can be counterproductive.

GLF: The abolitionist movement, although growing, is still tiny relative to the new welfarist/protectionist movement that you support. I think that many of the characteristics of group identity that you have discussed here are relevant to that movement as well. I also think that the mainstream animal protection movement has a cult-like dimension that requires absolute loyalty to the organization's campaigns and goals, however incoherent, as a condition of membership. In any event, no abolitionist thinks that there will be success anytime soon; the idea is that continued pursuit of the welfarist agenda will lead only to continued failure and to the "happy" meat movement, which I regard as the most regressive thing that has occurred in the recent history of animal ethics. There must be a fundamental change in thinking, and that is not going to come from welfare reform.

☞☞☞

GLF: You take several positions concerning the relationship between new welfarists and institutional animal exploiters. First, you maintain that new welfarists link reforms with producer benefits for strategic reasons. Do you deny that these reforms have economic benefits for producers?

Second, you discuss reforms that have been achieved even though there was opposition from industry. Is it not the case that any regulated industry commonly fights further regulation as a routine matter, in order to impose an opportunity cost on opponents, even if industry is not particularly concerned about a proposed change or even if industry is in the process of transition away from a challenged practice? I believe that such strategic behavior is part of the literature on the sociology of reform movements.

I remember once being told by someone at the National Institutes of Health that the research establishment was publicly opposing the 1985 amendments to the U.S. federal Animal Welfare Act, which proposed, among other things, the establishment of animal care committees, even though researchers were not concerned about these committees and saw them as helping to take the steam out of the antivivisection movement, which in the 1980s was gaining strength. But the research community was concerned that if they did not oppose these amendments, the antivivisection movement might propose reforms that the researchers would find threatening and objectionable. The amendments passed, and the creation of animal care committees not only helped to weaken the antivivisection movement by giving researchers a mechanism to assure the public that supposedly thorough ethical reviews of research were being conducted, but also effectively resulted in a shutdown of information about research because members of animal care committees were threatened with criminal prosecution for revealing anything that might have a proprietary value to researchers or their institutions.

Third, you claim that in some cases, industry complies simply because it cannot be seen as resisting the demands of the welfarists. Can you give me an example of what you are referring to here?

RG: As I have said, producer benefits do sometimes, but not always, accrue from welfare reforms. I also accept that because of the economic and political clout exercised by industry interests, those reforms that do have a benefit to producers are more likely to succeed. You are right too that producers tend to fight reforms even if they are not particularly concerned about losing the particular battle. This might happen because of a calculation about opportunity costs. It also might happen because industry interests regard even minor reforms as the thin end of the wedge. Accept a minor reform now, and this sets a precedent from which more major reforms might occur in the future.

In answer to your third point on industry compliance, I meant two different but related things. First, there is the compliance that sometimes precedes legislative or regulatory initiatives. In Britain, for instance, the National Farmers' Union recognized, from the 1970s onward, that it needed to take animal welfare more seriously, and it did little to oppose the most indefensible aspects of factory farming such as the veal crate. Likewise, the Research Defence Society in Britain has always refused to take a position on the toxicity testing of non-therapeutic products because, particularly in the case of the most indefensible types, such as the testing of cosmetics, it perceives that explicit support would damage its own case for therapeutic research. Second, there is the compliance that often follows legislative or regulatory welfare initiatives, where industry will often use the improved welfare standards that result as a selling point for their products.

I would not want to claim that all of the preceding represents a sea change in the way that industry regards animal welfare. Far from it. But I would argue that the increasing incidence of state regulation of animal exploitation represents an important development. You are right to say that the ideology of animal welfare has been around a long time, but I suspect (and much more empirical research is needed to demonstrate this) that animal exploiters still hold to some extent an ideology that might be more accurately described as "animal use" rather than animal welfare. As I argue in my essay, the former regards it as acceptable to inflict suffering on nonhuman animals if a benefit to humans of virtually any kind results, and it also does not accept that it is the role of the state to intervene to protect animals using an independent cost-benefit calculation. This animal use ideology still lives on to varying degrees. What is important to recognize, though, is that a genuine animal welfare represents, in my judgment, a significantly different and improved ethical position.

GLF: Well, then we agree that welfare reforms are often beneficial for producers and that producers often resist reforms for strategic reasons. So when animal welfare groups are promoting reforms as advantageous for producers, they are not, as you suggest, doing so merely for strategic reasons in that producers actually do benefit from some of these reforms. Producer resistance to reform does not mean that the reform will not be in the interests of the producer but means only that producers may put up a show of token resistance as a means of imposing opportunity costs on animal advocates to avoid further, more significant reforms later on.

I am not sure that the examples you cite show that welfare demands resulted in industry compliance. For example, the veal crate was (and is being) phased out because it resulted in high veterinary costs, and alternatives were actually cost-efficient.

Finally, I continue to be puzzled by the notion that "an independent cost-benefit calculation" can be performed given that nonhumans are chattel property.

—◗◗◗—

GLF: You distinguish between interest groups and promotional groups, and you claim that the latter advocate on behalf of a cause that is not in the interest of its members. But is it not the case that animal welfare is in the interest of large organizations, most of whose members want to be reassured that it is morally acceptable to continue to use animals to a greater or lesser extent? Most wealthy organizations in the United States and Great Britain are those that promote welfare reform. Do you think that the reality of organizational finances plays a role here?

RG: As I said earlier, organizational finance is a factor here, but I do not hold the view, as you seem to, that animal organizations are more interested in their own financial positions than in the welfare of animals. They may be misguided (although I do not think they are), but I do not think they are engaged in a deliberate subterfuge. What I meant was the simple fact that the members of animal organizations are humans, and the beneficiaries are designed to be nonhumans.

GLF: I understood your point, and I am not saying that anyone is necessarily engaging in intentional subterfuge. My point is that in your essay, you argue that because the animal protection movement is a promotional group, it suffers a disadvantage relative to the interest groups that protect the financial interests of animal producers. I am saying that whatever their motivation for promoting reform, the reality is that the promotion of reform is in the financial interests of these organizations precisely because their members want to be reassured that it is acceptable to continue to use animal products. In that sense, animal welfare organizations are very much unlike other promotional organizations, such as organizations that promote the interests of the homeless and whose members want to see an end to homelessness. The beneficiaries of animal organizations *are* their members, who want to see animal suffering decreased but who want what is, in effect, an indulgence granted by these organizations concerning the continued use of "happy" animal products. Moreover, if I am right about animal welfare reform making animal use more efficient and encouraging the consumption of animal products, then institutional exploiters are also beneficiaries of the welfarist campaigns of these organizations.

RG: I take your point. It is, of course, an empirical matter whether the members of animal groups promoting reform do contribute because they want to be reassured that it is okay to continue benefiting from animal exploitation. Many may not have this attitude. Personally, for instance, I contribute to animal groups that promote reform to farm animal welfare even though I desist from using animal products, and I would be surprised if I was the only one.

◦◦◦

GLF: You claim that approaching animal ethics from the perspective of ethical theory is not adequate because it does not take dominant narratives about the moral status of animals into account. But what is the dominant narrative other than the competing ethical theory that it is acceptable to use animals?

RG: I would want to be more subtle here. It is true that the dominant narrative does accept that it is not unethical to use animals, but there are a number of ways in which "use" can be interpreted. As I explained, I do not regard ownership and use as necessarily inimical to a reduction, maybe substantial, in animal suffering. There is a parallel here in the debate within environmental ethics. Traditionally, environmental ethicists have been polarized between those who hold an anthropocentric (or human-centered) ethic and those who hold an ecocentric ethic that removes humans from the moral pedestal. Increasingly, though, it has been recognized that it is possible to distinguish between a hard-nosed exploitative anthropocentrism and a more environmentally benign version. I think the same applies to the issue of animal use. In other words, it is possible to distinguish between an interpretation of "use" that is deeply exploitative to animals and an interpretation that allows for the protection of many animal interests.

GLF: My point was simply that you cannot criticize ethical theory for not taking dominant narratives into account without recognizing that the dominant narrative is in favor of exploitation (whether deeply exploitative or not). That is, to say that ethical theory is inadequate because it excludes the dominant narrative is to say nothing more than that the ethical approach is inadequate because it does not take into account that the prevailing discourse is in favor of some form of continued exploitation. That begs the question about the legitimacy of the dominant discourse. To say that the abolitionist perspective is problematic because it does not take into account a dominant narrative that may (or may not) be moving in a direction of more benign use is merely to say that the abolitionist approach is problematic because it does not recognize the protectionist or new welfarist narrative, or the more exploitative narrative. Moreover, I disagree that we can distinguish between uses in the way you suggest because that is just another way of promoting welfare reform over abolition.

RG: Yes, I recognize that merely accepting the dominant narrative is a justification for maintaining an unacceptable status quo. All I was suggesting is that we should take account of Gustafson's point that any effective moral discourse must temper an oppositional ethical discourse when it is faced by a very different narrative discourse.

〰️〰️〰️

GLF: You claim that new welfarists have accepted that the abolition of animal exploitation is not acceptable at the present time, so they seek welfare reform as a way of moving in the abolitionist direction in the undefined future. But do they? For those who take the position advocated by you and Singer—that animals have a morally significant interest in not suffering but do not have a morally significant interest in not being used—the goal is not necessarily to abolish animal use but to improve animal treatment. Is that not the case?

RG: I cannot speak for others who might be, or wish to be, characterized as "new welfarist" in orientation, and as you know, I prefer not to use that term anyway. As far as my own position is concerned, I may be described as, for want of a better term, a "contingent abolitionist." That is, you hold that abolition follows automatically from the ethical principle that it is morally wrong for animals to be used because you equate ownership with slavery. My ethical position is that it is not intrinsically wrong to use animals and becomes an ethical problem only when use results in the infliction of suffering. I tend to think that the use of animals for, say, food production is unlikely to reduce their suffering enough to meet my ethical standard. As a result, I would argue that animal agriculture ought to be abolished. Any use of animals, therefore, is contingent on the degree of suffering involved. Sometimes it may be justified; at other times it may not.

GLF: But your contingent approach leaves open what constitutes an "acceptable" level of suffering. There is no principled position being put forward here; it is very idiosyncratic.

RG: It is contingent on the question of whether, in any particular case, abolition is justified, but this is based on the *principle* that inflicting suffering on animals for our benefit is wrong.

GLF: Yes, but as you acknowledged earlier, a principal weakness of your position is that you cannot provide any criteria by which to access whether suffering is "acceptable." That leaves you with engaging in the same sort of balancing involved when we try to determine what constitutes "unnecessary" suffering.

RG: I said that criteria for determining whether a particular level of suffering is acceptable have not been fully worked out. I also said, however, that such criteria *could* be developed. Here, the work of animal welfare scientists is likely to be crucial. An obvious starting point would be to say that any practices that led to the infliction of anything but a minor amount of pain on animals would be prohibited under my principle.

GLF: The problem, of course, is that your approach still leaves us with an idiosyncratic normative assessment of what constitutes "a minor amount of pain" that would justify not using animals. There are others who, like you, embrace the protectionist approach but who would not come to the same conclusions that you do because they disagree as to what constitutes an acceptable level of suffering.

●●●

GLF: You claim that no one can claim that progress has not been made by the new welfarists. That's not true. I do not think that progress has been made. Indeed, I think we have gone backward. The movement, as represented by the large, corporate organizations, has actually succeeded in legitimizing animal use by making "humane" treatment the only issue on the table.

RG: Our disagreement here crystallizes our respective positions. A great deal depends, of course, on how "progress" is defined and what time-scale is chosen. To finish on a note of consensus, we can both agree that animals endure unacceptable levels of suffering, that this suffering ought to be eliminated, and that encouraging a debate about the best means of achieving this goal is a priority.

GLF: Agreed.

Index of Proper Names and Organizations

This book constitutes a discursive exploration of one topic: the debate between the abolition and the regulation of animal exploitation. Therefore, the authors decided not to present a subject index and offer this index of names of individuals and animal organizations mentioned in text for ease of reference.